GALATIANS

NCCS | New Covenant Commentary Series

The New Covenant Commentary Series (NCCS) is designed for ministers and students who require a commentary that interacts with the text and context of each New Testament book and pays specific attention to the impact of the text upon the faith and praxis of contemporary faith communities.

The NCCS has a number of distinguishing features. First, the contributors come from a diverse array of backgrounds in regards to their Christian denominations and countries of origin. Unlike many commentary series that tout themselves as international the NCCS can truly boast of a genuinely international cast of contributors with authors drawn from every continent of the world (except Antarctica) including countries such as the United States, Australia, the United Kingdom, Kenya, India, Singapore, and Korea. We intend the NCCS to engage in the task of biblical interpretation and theological reflection from the perspective of the global church. Second, the volumes in this series are not verse-by-verse commentaries, but they focus on larger units of text in order to explicate and interpret the story in the text as opposed to some often atomistic approaches. Third, a further aim of these volumes is to provide an occasion for authors to reflect on how the New Testament impacts the life, faith, ministry, and witness of the New Covenant Community today. This occurs periodically under the heading of "Fusing the Horizons and Forming the Community." Here authors provide windows into community formation (how the text shapes the mission and character of the believing community) and ministerial formation (how the text shapes the ministry of Christian leaders).

It is our hope that these volumes will represent serious engagements with the New Testament writings, done in the context of faith, in service of the church, and for the glorification of God.

Series Editors:
Michael F. Bird (Ridley College, Melbourne, Australia)
Craig Keener (Asbury Theological Seminary, Wilmore, KY, USA)

Titles in this series:
Romans Craig Keener
Ephesians Lynn Cohick
Colossians and Philemon Michael F. Bird
Revelation Gordon Fee
John Jey Kanagaraj
1 Timothy Aída Besançon Spencer
2 Timothy and Titus Aída Besançon Spencer
Mark Kim Huat Tan
2 Peter and Jude Andrew Mbuvi
1 Corinthians B. J. Oropeza
Luke Diane G. Chen

1–2 Thessalonians Nijay K. Gupta
1–3 John Sam Ngewa
Acts Youngmo Cho and Hyung Dae Park

Forthcoming titles:
James Ruth Anne Reese
Matthew Jason Hood
1 Peter Eric Greaux
Philippians Linda Belleville
Hebrews Cynthia Westfall
2 Corinthians Ayodeji Adewuya

GALATIANS

Jarvis J. Williams

CASCADE *Books* · Eugene, Oregon

GALATIANS

New Covenant Commentary Series

Cascade Books
An Imprint of Wipf and Stock Publishers
199 W. 8th Ave., Suite 3
Eugene, OR 97401

www.wipfandstock.com

PAPERBACK ISBN: 978-1-62564-284-4
HARDCOVER ISBN: 978-1-4982-8880-4
EBOOK ISBN: 978-1-5326-6494-6

Cataloging-in-Publication data:

Names: Williams, Jarvis J., author.

Title: Galatians / by Jarvis J. Williams.

Description: Eugene, OR : Cascade Books, 2020 | New Covenant Commentary Series | Includes bibliographical references and indexes.

Identifiers: ISBN 978-1-62564-284-4 (paperback) | ISBN 978-1-4982-8880-4 (hardcover) | ISBN 978-1-5326-6494-6 (ebook)

Subjects: LCSH: Bible. Galatians—Commentaries.

Classification: LCC BS2685.3 W55 2020

Manufactured in the U.S.A.   03/11/20

For "Auntie," "Uncle" Wendell, Aunt Lorena, Uncle Kenneth, Keisha, and mom, who taught me much about love

Contents

Outline of Galatians ix

Preface xi

Abbreviations xv

Introduction   1

Galatians 1   12

Galatians 2   38
  *Fusing the Horizons: Ethnic and Racial Division
  in the Church is Anti-Gospel* 61

Galatians 3   82
  *Fusing the Horizons: The Importance of the Cross
  and the Spirit in the Christian Life* 111

  *Fusing the Horizons: Honoring Women and Hating Misogyny
  in the Church Honor the Gospel* 131

Galatians 4   134

Galatians 5   150
  Fusing the Horizons: The Christian and Sin 165

Galatians 6   167

Select Bibliography 179

Ancient Document Index 187

Author Index 211

Outline of Galatians[1]

1. **Defense of the Divine Origin of Paul's Gospel (1:1—2:21)**
   a. Salutation (1:1–5)
   b. A Shocking Turn to another Gospel (1:6–9)
   c. Genuine Persuasion and Paul's Gospel (1:10—2:10)
   d. A Misunderstanding of the Gospel at Antioch (2:11–21)

   Fusing the Horizons: Ethnic and Racial Division in the Church is Anti-Gospel

2. **A Defense of Paul's Gospel from Scripture and Spiritual Experience (3:1—5:1)**
   a. Argument from Experience: Reception of the Spirit by Faith apart from Works of the Law (3:1–5)
   b. Argument from Scripture: The Blessing of Abraham (3:6–14)
      i. Abrahamic Offspring by Faith (3:6–9)
      ii. The Cross, the Curse, and the Spirit (3:10–14)

      Fusing the Horizons: The Importance of the Cross and the Spirit in the Christian Life

   c. The Superiority of the Promise over the Law (3:15—4:11)
      i. Temporary Nature of the Law (3:15–18)
      ii. The Law's Purpose (3:19–25)
      iii. Sons of God and Abraham's Offspring (3:26–29)

      Fusing the Horizons: Honoring Women and Hating Misogyny in the Church Honor the Gospel

      iv. Out of Slavery to Adoption in Christ (4:1–7)

---

1. The outlines of Schreiner 2010: 58–59 and Moo 2013: vii influenced my outline of the letter. Yet, my outline of the letter also differs from theirs.

v. Turning to the Law Leads the Galatians to Idolatry (4:8–11)

d. Argument from Hospitality and Friendship (4:12–20)

e. Argument from Scripture and an Exhortation (4:21—5:1)

3. **A Warning, an Anathema, and Exhortations to Walk in the Spirit (5:2—6:10)**

a. Avoid Circumcision or Perish and Await the Hope of Righteousness by Faith and Live (5:2–6)

b. Circumcision Leads to an Anathema (5:7–12)

c. Walk in Step with the Spirit by Loving One Another (5:13—6:10)

i. Love for Fellow Christians Fulfills the Whole Law (5:13–15)

ii. Walk in the Spirit (5:16–26)

Fusing the Horizons: The Christian and Sin

iii. Bear the Burdens of One Another (6:1–5)

iv. Do Good by Sowing in the Spirit (6:6–10)

4. **A Final Shocking Appeal to the Galatians, A Final Attack of the Opponents, and A Final Defense of Paul's Gospel (6:11–18)**

Preface

As I write these words, I cannot express the satisfaction (and trepidation!) I feel to have finally finished writing my first commentary on one of Paul's most important New Testament epistles. I feel a special sense of joy as I have completed the writing of this commentary the week of my fortieth birthday. I accepted the invitation to write it in my early thirties. Now, approximately five years later, I pen these words as the conclusion of the writing process of this commentary. Before I begin my exposition, I must make a few prefatory remarks.

Readers of this commentary should know that I have written a commentary of Galatians and not a commentary on commentaries of Galatians. Many scholars have influenced my understanding of this important letter, which will be apparent throughout the commentary. But I relied heavily upon and cited the commentaries of A. Andrew Das and Thomas R. Schreiner more than any others throughout the commentary. Das's commentary influenced this commentary the most, pointing me to many Greco-Roman and Second Temple Jewish texts and helping me see the various exegetical options for a variety of difficult texts in the letter. Schreiner's commentary was particularly helpful on introductory matters and on selected exegetical matters in the letter. Though space constraints have limited the amount of scholars I have cited and with whom I have interacted, I have made every effort to document throughout the commentary places where I have directly and knowingly borrowed, quoted, or paraphrased the ideas and comments from these and other commentators.

I readily admit that I am indebted to many interpreters of Galatians who have gone before me. There is nothing new or fresh in this commentary. Someone has said before (and likely better!) what I have written in these pages. My aim has not been novelty or freshness here, but rather to engage in a sensible grammatical-historical exegesis of the letter without overwhelming the reader with detailed footnotes about the scholarship on Galatians. I have read much (so much but not nearly enough!) on Galatians in the five years I worked on this commentary. Yet, this commentary marks the beginning of a (hopefully) life-long academic journey with Galatians, not the end of one. The mountain of scholarship on this letter is too high (at least for me!) to climb in total. One would need a lifetime to master the literature on Galatians in English-speaking scholarship, not to mention the scholarship written in other languages. My commentary endeavors to immerse readers into the ancient social setting of the text by critically engaging the text and selections of Greco-Roman and Second Temple Jewish literature that shine rays of light onto Paul's message and arguments in the letter.

In keeping with the expectations of the New Covenant Commentary Series, I have also included four sections on practical application along the way, in short sections called Fusing the Horizons, to help readers think intentionally about ways in which to apply some important texts and concepts in the letter. Readers interested in the many scholarly and critical details of this letter not mentioned in this commentary should consult the many critical commentaries, monographs, and articles written throughout the years. I have unapologetically written this commentary for the non-specialist. Though I hope scholars and specialists would read this commentary with interest and attentiveness and benefit from my work, this commentary primarily endeavors to serve students, bible teachers, and pastors.

Many thanks are in order to many people for the completion and publication of this commentary. I'm thankful to my good friend and colleague at The Southern Baptist Theological Seminary (Southern Seminary), Brian J. Vickers, for recommending me to the editors of this series, Mike Bird and Craig Keener. Many thanks to Mike and Craig for accepting Brian's recommendation to include me within the series. Many thanks to Mike, Craig, and the Wipf and Stock team for graciously giving me extension after extension to ensure a better final product. I'm thankful to my *Doctorvater* and colleague at Southern Seminary, Thomas R. Schreiner (Tom), for reading the entire commentary and giving me helpful feedback before I submitted it to the editors. As always, Tom's careful eyes, his exegetical precision, and his love for the text pointed out helpful suggestions and corrections. Any deficiencies in this commentary are the fault of my own.

I'm very thankful to the board of trustees at Southern Seminary for granting me a sabbatical leave for the 2017 spring academic semester. This leave allowed me to finish the vast majority of the commentary. Many thanks to my Greek exegesis students at Southern Seminary. I'm fortunate to teach a yearly Greek exegesis class on Galatians to graduate students, as well as PhD seminars related to my interest in Pauline soteriology in Romans and Galatians in its Second Temple Jewish context. Our campus is filled with many gifted and intelligent students who are zealous for the biblical languages, who are astute students of Paul and Pauline theology, and who love the Greek NT. Though there are too many students to mention by name, many have contributed to the completion of this commentary and have taught me so much.

I'm especially thankful to my PhD student and teaching assistant Trey Moss for formatting the commentary, conforming the style to the series format, and for completing the abbreviations page. Many thanks to the many churches and conferences where I either preached through or taught Galatians the past five years. Many, many thanks to my wife Ana and my son Jaden for creating a loving and joyful environment at home as I worked hard (but often failed) to balance scholarship and family fun during the writing of this commentary. I'm very grateful Ana and Jaden know the difference between fun and scholarship and that they are especially good at the former. I'm especially thankful they always remind me there's more to life than writing books.

Finally, I dedicate this commentary to "Auntie," "Uncle" Wendell, Aunt Lorena, Uncle Kenneth, Keisha, and mom, who taught me much about love.

Jarvis J. Williams
Louisville, Kentucky
May 2018

Abbreviations

BDAG   Danker, Fredrick W., Walker Bauer, William F.
        Arndt, and F. Wilber Gingrich. *Greek-English
        Leixcon of the New Testament and Other
        Early Christian Literature.* 3rd. ed. Chicago:
        University of Chicago Press, 2000

IG   *Inscriptiones Graecae. Editio Minor. Berlin: de
        Gruyter,* 1924-

NPNF[1] *Nicene and Post-Nicene Fathers,* Series 1

Ancient Sources

Jewish Sources

Apocrypha

Add Esth	Additions to Esther
Bar	Baruch
Bel	Bel and the Dragon
1 Esd	1 Esdras
Jdt	Judith
1–4 Macc	1–4 Maccabees
Pr Azar	Prayer of Azariah
Pr Man	Prayer of Manasseh
Sir	Sirach
Tob	Tobit
Wis	Wisdom of Solomon

Dead Sea Scrolls

CD	Cario Genizah copy of the *Damascus Document*
1QH	*Thanksgiving Hymns*
1QM	*War Scroll*
1QpHab	*Pesher Habakkuk*
1QS	Rule of the Community
1QSa	Rule of the Community (Appendix)
4QFlor	Florilegium, Midrash on Eschatology[a]
4Q158	*Reworked Pentateuch*[a]
4QpNah	Pesher Naham
4Q164	Pesher Isaiah[a]
4Q171	Pesher Psalms[a]
4Q174	*Eschatalogicla Midrash*[a]
4Q215	Testament of Naphtali
4Q246	Apocryphon of Daniel
4Q394	4QMMT[a]
4Q395	MMT[b]
4Q398	papMMT[e]
4Q399	MMTf
4Q403	*Songs of the Sabbath Sacrifice*[d]
4Q416	*Instruction*[b]
4Q417	*Instruction*[c]
4Q418	*Instruction*[d]
4Q436	*Bless, Oh my Soul*[c]
4Q504	*Words of the Luminaries*
4QMMT	*Some Precepts of the Law*
11QT[a]	Temple Scroll[a]

Josephus

Ag. Ap.	*Against Apion*
Ant.	*Jewish Antiquities*
J.W.	*Jewish War*
Life	*The Life*

Philo of Alexandria

Abr.	On the Life of Abraham
Congr.	On the Preliminary Studies
Flacc.	Against Flaccus
Ios.	On the Life of Joseph
Leg.	Allegorical Interpretation
Mig.	On the Migration of Abraham
Mos.	On the Life of Moses
Rewards	On Rewards and Punishments
Somn.	On Dreams
Spec.	On the Special Laws
QG	Questions and Answers on Genesis

Pseudepigrapha

As. Mos.	*Assumption of Moses*
2 Bar.	*2 Baruch (Syriac Apocalypse)*
3 Bar.	*3 Baruch (Greek Apocalypse)*
1 En.	*1 Enoch (Ethiopic Apocalypse)*
2 En.	*2 Enoch (Slavonic Apocalypse)*
4 Ezra	*4 Ezra*
Jos. Asen.	*Joseph and Aseneth*
Jub.	*Jubilees*

LAB	*Liber antiquitatum biblicarum (Pseudo-Philo)*
Let. Aris.	*Letter of Aristeas*
Odes Sol.	*Odes of Solomon*
Pss. Sol.	*Psalms of Solomon*
Sib. Or.	*Sibylline Oracles*
T. Ab.	*Testament of Abraham*
T. Ash.	*Testament of Asher*
T. Benj.	*Testament of Benjamin*
T. Dan	*Testament of Dan*
T. Jos.	*Testament of Joseph*
T. Jud.	*Testament of Judah*
T. Levi	*Testament of Levi*
T. Mos.	*Testament of Moses*
T. Naph.	*Testament of Naphtali*

Rabbinic Literature

m.	*Midrash*
Mek.	*Mekilta*
Qidd.	*Qiddushin*
Tanh.	*Tanhuma*
Tg. Ps.-J.	*Targum Pseudo-Jonathan*

Early Christian Sources

Justin Martyr

Dial.	*Dialogue with Trypho*

Origen

Cels.	*Against Celsus*

Chrysostom

Hom. Gal.   *Homilae in epistulam ad Galatas commentarius*

Jerome

Comm. Gal.   *Commentariorum in Epistulam ad Galatas libri III*

Papyri

P.Oxy   *Oxyrhynchus papyri*

P.Lond   *London papyri*

Other Greco-Roman Sources

Aristotle

Rhet.   *Rhetoric*

Cicero

Inv.   *De inventione rhetorica*

Dio Chrysostom

Alex.   *To the People of Alexandria*

Epictetus

Diss   *Dissertationes*

Heraclitus of Alexandria

All.   *Allegoriae*

Herodotus

Hist.   *Histories*

Horace

Sat.   *Satires*

Juvenal

Sat.   *Satires*

Lucian

Tox.   *Toxaris*

Quintillian

Inst.   *Institutio oratoria*

Plato

Resp.   *Republic*

Pliny

Nat.   *Natural History*

Plutarch

Cic.   *Cicero*
Demetr.   *Demetrius*
Mor.   *Moralia*
Quaest. Conv.   *Quaestionum convivialum libri IX*

Seneca

Ot. Sap.	*De otio sapientis*
Lucil.	*Ad Lucilium*

Strabo (47)

Geogr.	*Geography*

Seutonius

Dom.	*Domitianus*

Trypho of Alexandria

Trop.	*On Tropes*

Xenophon

Anab.	*Anabasis*

Introduction

Paul's epistle to the Galatians is arguably his most urgent and most rhetorically charged letter in the NT.[1] He immediately establishes his apostolic authority (1:1), grounding it in the resurrection of Jesus Christ and stating its origin is Jesus Christ and God, the Father, who raised Jesus from the dead (1:1). He invokes witnesses of his apostolic authority to establish further the divine origins of his gospel (1:2). He frontloads the letter with grace (1:3), the resurrection (1:1), and the cross (1:4). He offers no thanksgiving, as he often does in his other letters (cf. Rom 1:8; 1 Cor 1:4; Phil 1:3; Col 1:3; 1 Thess 1:2; 2 Thess 1:3). He attacks those who teach another gospel in the Galatian assemblies (1:6–7). He attacks the Galatians for listening to them (1:6), and he warns both groups (the Galatians and the trouble making teachers) of the certainty of God's judgment if they preach (or accept) another gospel besides the one he and his colleagues preached to them (1:8–9). He further makes shocking statements about the law. He distances God from the law by saying it came through angels to Moses and then to the people in order to argue that the law is inferior to God's original promises to Abraham (3:15–19). He identifies the law with an inferior mode of mediation (3:19–20). He associates the law with the present evil age (1:4), a curse (3:13), slavery (3:23—4:25), sin (3:22), and the *ta stoichea tou cosmou* (4:3, 9). He states circumcision does not matter (6:15), which is contrary to Gen 17 and Lev 12:3.

Paul also makes some startling statements about those who preach another gospel. He calls them troublemakers (1:6). He prays they (and anyone else who preaches another gospel) would be accursed (1:8–9). He offers sharp (no pun intended!) rhetoric about the trouble-makers' efforts to circumcise the Galatians' flesh, wishing they would go all the way and cut off their own penises (5:12)! He accuses them of preaching circumcision because they are afraid to be persecuted because of the cross of Christ (6:12). He asserts they do not keep the law they preach

---

1 Unless otherwise indicated, all translations of New Testament texts in this commentary are mine.

(6:13). He suggests instead they preach circumcision in order to boast in the Galatians' circumcised flesh (6:13).

Paul also attacks the Galatians. He accuses them of turning away from his gospel to a distorted gospel (1:6–7). He threatens them with God's eschatological judgment (1:8–9; 5:21; 6:8–9). He calls them foolish (3:1). And he expresses despondency over them (4:11, 20), expressing fear that perhaps he has labored over them in vain (4:11).[2]

The Message of Galatians and the Situation in Galatia[3]

As John Barclay says in his important essay on mirror-reading, readers of ancient texts are faced with the difficulty of trying to reconstruct the ancient social settings. Ancient letters present limitations to us in our efforts in historical reconstruction, because they record only one side of the ancient conversation. Paul's letter to the Galatians gives us the most reliable information to which we have access about the Galatian situation. However, as Barclay has pointed out in his important essay on mirror reading, interpreters of Galatians must be very careful when trying to reconstruct either the situation in Galatia or Paul's opponents in Galatia from his remarks in the letter.[4] Galatians is a rhetorically charged letter in which Paul fiercely seeks to attack his audience and his opponents for the purpose of winning over his audience to his view against his opponents. Thus, one cannot always easily discern whether Paul's remarks about the opponents are descriptions of their character and motives or rhetorical hyperboles to dissuade the Galatians from listening to their "other" gospel.

Additionally, as many scholars have pointed out, no one can read Galatians in a neutral way as though the last 500 years of post-Reformational readings of Galatians "never happened."[5] Like it or not, current readers of Galatians are forced to read the letter in light of and along side of the various interpreters that preceded them.[6] I, therefore, admit from the outset

2 Schreiner 2010: 31.

3 Schreiner (2010: 21–59) influenced my organization of the introductory material.

4 Barclay 1987: 73–93; 2002: 366–82.

5 For this precise point, see Schreiner 2010: 21. As Schreiner points out, Fee (2007: 1) seems to think one can read Galatians as though the Reformation "never happened." The very suggestion reinforces that when we read Galatians, we are aware the Reformation happened.

6 For a history of interpretation of Galatians, see Riches 2013.

of this commentary that I stand in a long line of interpreters, influenced by a specific social and theological setting, trying to understand the message of this letter. I am both consciously and subconsciously influenced by my own social location, by the different streams of interpretive traditions, and by my own presuppositions. The most influential theological tradition on me is by far the Protestant Reformation and a certain stream of soteriological Calvinism. But let the reader of this commentary hear loudly and clearly: Paul's problem with the Galatians was not the same problem Martin Luther had with Rome, and it was not the same problem many Christians face today in their Western American churches. Still, his problem with the Galatians was, nevertheless, soteriological, just as Luther's problem with Rome was soteriological.

The social settings and ecclesiological contexts of Paul and Luther forced them to address two different social and soteriological problems. Paul addresses the divine origin of his gospel and argues that Gentiles should not turn away from his gospel and embrace the law to become part of the Abrahamic family.[7] However, for Paul, the soteriological problem was also an ethnic problem: namely, can Gentiles become part of the people of God as Gentiles?[8] Luther dealt with the question of how does the individual sinner become right with God in a context where the Roman Catholic church emphasized human works as the means by which one gained right standing before God. Paul's primary concern is the authority of his gospel and an urgent appeal to the Galatians not to turn away from it, lest they fall short of inheriting the kingdom of God. Luther's primary concern was justification by faith and an urgent appeal to reject the Roman Catholic dogma of meritorious salvation.[9]

In Galatians, justification by faith serves Paul's major argument about the divine origins of his gospel and serves to show why Gentiles are not required to do Jewish works of the law to be justified and to become the offspring of Abraham: namely, because God justifies Jews and Gentiles by faith in Jesus Christ and not by works of the Jewish law (2:16). This letter is about the gospel, which deals with both ethnic/social

7 The above differs from Cosgrove 1988, who argues Paul's thesis is clearly stated in Gal 3: namely, the Spirit provides everything the Galatians need to live a life pleasing to God.

8 Scholars have recognized this is an important question Paul seeks to answer in the letter.

9 For a helpful discussion of the differences between Paul and Luther, see Stendahl's important 1963 article. See also Westerholm 2004.

issues and soteriology. Ethnic and sociological issues (i.e., Jewish and Gentile relations) intersect with soteriology, and the two (ethnic identity and soteriology) are inseparable in the letter and from the gospel (e.g., 2:11—5:1).

To be sure, Paul does critique effort and says a thing or two about anthropology (2:16—3:12), but his critique of effort and comments on anthropology do not take the same shape in Galatians as in Romans. There are no contradictions between the two letters, but they have two entirely different social situations and theological contexts to which he wrote both letters. He responds to a severe problem in Galatians related to a misunderstanding of his gospel and to convince the Galatians not to turn away from his gospel. In Romans, he writes to introduce his gospel to them so that they would help him on his journey to Spain (cf. Rom 1:8–17; 15:22–28) and possibly so that he would resolve some Jewish and Gentile tension in the Roman congregations (cf. Rom 14:1—15:12). His remarks about effort and anthropology in Galatians are connected to his larger exposition of the gospel regarding how Gentiles become part of the people of God and how they relate to the Abrahamic promises along with fellow Christ-believing Jews. This commentary seeks to highlight that what Paul says about ethnicity, cosmology, and anthropology in Galatians is soteriological in nature.

The Soteriological Significance of the Cross and the Spirit in Galatians

The cross of Jesus Christ and the Spirit are crucial to Paul's argument in Galatians and vital for the Christian life. In fact, the cross and the Spirit are both marks of Christian identity and symbols that God has invaded the present evil age to inaugurate a new age in Christ apart from the law. Paul begins the letter with an implicit reference to the cross in 1:1 when he refers to the resurrection. He explicitly refers to the cross in 1:4 when he asserts Jesus died for our sins to deliver us from the present evil age.

By my count, there are at least 14 references to the cross when one considers Paul's remarks about the death of Christ (1:4; 2:20–21; 4:5), the cross of Christ/crucifixion (2:19; 3:1, 13; 5:11, 24; 6:12, 14), or the marks of Jesus (6:17). In Galatians, the cross changes everything. It turns the ages (1:4; 6:15), provides deliverance from the present evil age (1:4), and provides redemption from the curse of the law (3:13; 4:5). The cross (and the resurrection) inaugurates new creation (6:15) and brings the old age to its fulfillment (cf. Gal 5:13–14) and to its end (6:15–16). The cross is the means by which the Spirit is universally distributed to the cosmos and begins to dwell in the heart of Jews and Gentiles redeemed from the curse of the law (3:13–14; 4:5–6).

The cross of Jesus Christ makes the law no longer necessary for Jews or Gentiles aspiring to be part of the people of God and the family of Abraham (3:10–13). This does not mean, however, that Jews neither can nor should any longer practice a Jewish way of life in Galatians (5:6; 6:15). Instead, the cross and the Spirit make the practicing of the law irrelevant as a marker of the people of God and as a marker of those who are welcomed into the Christ-following assemblies (1:4; 3:1–14; 4:5–6).

Jewish Christ-followers can still practice circumcision and do works of law if they choose in keeping with their Jewish heritage and way of life, as long as they do not impose these things onto Gentile Christians. Paul accentuates throughout the letter that Jews (or Gentile sympathizers to Judaism) should not require a Jewish way of life marked by circumcision and law-observance for Gentiles before granting them entrance as full members within the family of Abraham and within Christ-following communities (cf. 5:2—6:18).[10] In Paul's view, neither circumcision nor un-circumcision is an identity marker of God's people now that the true descendant of Abraham, Jesus Christ, died on the cross for our sins to deliver us from the present evil age and to inaugurate the new age, or now that the Spirit has been universally distributed to Christ-following Jews and Gentiles by faith via the cross and resurrection of Jesus Christ (1:4; 2:19–21; 3:1–29; 4:5–6, 21–31; 5:1–5; 6:14–16). The arguments against circumcision and against the law in Galatians are primarily addressed to Gentiles against the teachers (who likely identify as Christ-following Jews).

Christ-following Jews are implicated too if they use their Jewish identity as a barrier of division between Christ-following Gentiles (2:11–14), because their Jewish identity must now be transformed and reevaluated in light of Christ and by Christ (cf. 3:13–14; 3:28; 6:15). Jewish identity is not eradicated, replaced, or superseded in Christ, but reevaluated and transformed in Christ. The turning of the ages via the Christ's cross and the distribution of the Spirit require Jews to place faith in Jesus as the Jewish Messiah and to accept Gentile Christ-followers as full members of the Messianic community without requiring them to

---

10 For a discussion of four patterns of Jewish universalism, one of which is Gentile sympathizers, see Donaldson: 2007.

receive any Jewish marks of distinction, not even the covenantal mark of circumcision (5:2–6; 6:11–18; cf. Gen 17).

Paul strongly argues justification comes by faith in Christ and not by doing works of the Jewish law in the central sections of the letter (2:16, 21; 3:6, 8, 11, 21; 5:4–6). Paul's remarks about justification by faith in Galatians serve his primary argument regarding the divine origins of his gospel: namely, his gospel comes from God and the crucified and resurrected Christ (1:1). Paul uses his apostolic authority and the divine origins of his gospel as the foundational parts of his appeal to the Galatians that they must not turn away from his divinely given gospel lest they suffer eschatological judgment.

That is, Paul wrote the letter to dissuade the Galatians from turning away from his authoritative and God-given gospel about the crucified and resurrected Christ (cf. 1:1, 4, 6–7), a gospel that justifies Jews and Gentiles by faith in Christ and distributes to both groups an equal portion of the Abrahamic promise of the Spirit (2:16—3:14; 4:6). He strongly warns them if they turn away from his gospel, they will not inherit eschatological life (cf. 3:10–14; 5:2–5), because Jews and Gentiles are justified by exclusive faith in Jesus Christ apart from Jewish works of law (2:16). If one counts the Greek relative pronouns and adjectives, Gal 1–2 contains at least 15 references to the gospel (1:6–9, 11, 16; 2:2, 5, 7, 14). This gospel includes justification by faith (2:16; 3:10–12; 5:4–5) and more (e.g., the cross [1:4; 3:13], the resurrection [1:1], Jewish and Gentile unity [Gal 2:11–14], etc.).

Jewish and Gentile Christians are the seed of Abraham by virtue of their identification with Jesus Christ, Abraham's seed (3:16–29). The chief evidence of this is the indwelling presence of the Spirit in both groups (3:1–14; 4:5–6), which they receive precisely because Christ died to redeem them from the curse of the law (3:1–14; 4:5–6). Only Jewish and Gentile Christians on this side of the cross are children of the promise in accordance with Isaac (4:28–31), neither Torah-observant Jews who reject Jesus as the Jewish Messiah nor Gentiles who think Jesus is the Messiah but then add works of the Jewish law to their faith (4:21–27; cf. 5:2–6). Those under the law without faith in Christ are still subject to and slaves of the present evil age and all of its powers (cf. 1:4; 4:8–11), including the law (3:15—4:31). Christ delivered Jews and Gentiles from the present evil age by dying for their sins (1:4), by redeeming them from the curse of the law (3:13), and by becoming a curse for them (3:13). His death for Jews and Gentiles enslaved to the present evil age

(1:4; 4:21–25), under a curse (3:10), under the law (3:23; 4:5), under sin (3:22), and under the *ta stoicheia tou cosmou* (4:3, 9) distribute the blessing of Abraham to Jews and Gentiles (3:14a), namely the Spirit, by means of their faith (3:14b).

Paul argues in 3:1—5:1 that God in Christ set free the Galatians via the cross and granted to them the Spirit by faith. The Spirit comes to Jews and Gentiles via the cross, not by means of law-observance (3:13–14). The Spirit frees the Galatians from the slavery of the law (5:1). Paul urges the Galatians to live in step with that freedom instead of using their freedom as an occasion for the flesh (5:1—6:10). He further urges them to reject what his opponents are saying with respect to circumcision and the law because it is the opposite of his gospel (1:6–9; 5:2–4; 6:11–16), which came from God (1:1; 1:10—2:10).

Destination of Galatians: North or South?

The destination of Galatians is one of many contested issues in NT scholarship. The debate has focused on whether Paul wrote to northern Galatia or southern Galatia. Not every scholar has agreed with Stephen Mitchell's bold claim "there is virtually nothing to be said for the northern Galatian theory."[11]

As Thomas R. Schreiner discusses in his commentary on Galatians, the destination of Galatians determines how one relates the material in Galatians to Acts.[12] Is Gal 2:11–14 historically prior to the Apostolic Council in Acts 15 (many southern Galatian theorists) or after it (northern Galatian theorists).[13] In 25 BC, "Galatia became a Roman province."[14] The Celts (Galatians) were one of the many diverse ethnic groups in the province.[15] These groups migrated to Asia minor in 278 BC.[16] The northern Galatian thesis argues Paul sent the letter to the northern part of Galatia to these ethnic (or tribal) Galatians who migrated to the northern part of the province.[17] Northern Galatia includes the cities of Ancyra,

11 Mitchell 1993: 3.
12 Schreiner 2010: 22.
13 Schreiner 2010: 22.
14 Schreiner 2010: 23.
15 Schreiner 2010: 23.
16 Schreiner 2010: 23.
17 Schreiner 2010: 23.

Pessinus, and Tavium.[18] The southern Galatian thesis argues Paul wrote the letter to the cities he visited on his first missionary journey in Acts 13–14.[19] These cities were Pisidian Antioch, Lystra, Iconium, and Derbe.[20] The goal of this commentary is not to overwhelm readers with the detailed arguments for or against the two options. Readers should consult the critical commentaries on Galatians for detailed argumentation and documentation. A choice between the two options mainly affects Pauline chronology, not how one views the basic message of the letter. My commentary accepts the southern Galatian hypothesis.[21]

Date

The north versus south Galatian theory impacts at some level one's reading of certain texts in Galatians (e.g. Gal 2:1–10).[22] However, the discussion mainly impacts Pauline chronology and one's dating of the letter. South Galatian theorists generally agree Paul wrote the letter before the Apostolic Council in Acts 15:1–35. This may explain why Paul does not explicitly refer to it in Galatians 2. If Paul wrote the letter prior to the Apostolic Council, then he may have written the letter approximately CE 48, which would make Galatians Paul's first letter and one of the earliest (if not the earliest) witnesses to early Christianity in the NT era. On the other hand, those who hold to the southern Galatia theory may likewise affirm Gal 2:1–10 refers to the Apostolic Council in Acts 15:1–35. If this is correct, then these scholars would approximately date the letter around CE 50. Scholars who advocate a northern Galatian theory date the letter around the time of CE 50–57.[23]

---

18 Mitchell 1993: 3.

19 See Schreiner 2010: 23–30, and sources cited in notes 7–8.

20 Schreiner 2010: 23–30.

21 For advocates of the Northern versus Southern Galatian hypotheses and their arguments, see discussion in Longenecker 1990: lxii–ixxii; Schreiner 2010: 23–30; Moo 2013: 2–8; Das 2014: 20–30. For a detailed discussion of and defense of the Southern Galatia theory, see the excursus in Keener 2012.

22 So Schreiner 2010: 22.

23 Schreiner 2010: 22–31.

Paul's Opponents

John M. G. Barclay's essay on mirror-reading Galatians (referred to above) offers helpful criteria by which to discern the situation in Galatia and those whom we identify as his opponents.[24] One of many dangers Barclay points out is "over-interpretation" of the data. Barclay states "in a polemic letter like this we are inclined to imagine that every statement by Paul is a rebuttal of an equally vigorous counter-statement by his opponents."[25] Barclay argues one need not assume this.[26] For example, Paul's so-called opponents likely did not view themselves as his opponents. Perhaps they did not share Paul's perspective. Likewise, his remarks in 5:11 about not preaching circumcision are not necessarily a response to an accusation made against him by his so-called opponents.[27] Since Paul seems to identify the agitators in Galatia as opponents, I refer to them as such throughout the commentary. But who were these agitating opponents in Galatia?

A Modified Traditional View

With modifications, I hold the traditional view of Paul's opponents in Galatia.[28] In my view, Paul's opponents in Galatia appear to be Jewish Christ-followers seeking to persuade the Galatians (Gentiles) to live a Jewish way of life in addition to faith in Christ. Paul's opponents were not teaching so-called legalism as traditionally defined as legalistic works-righteousness. Rather, they were compelling these Galatians to live a Jewish way of life and requiring this as a prerequisite for them to inherit the blessing of Abraham. This Jewish way of life included receiving the mark of circumcision (2:6; 5:2–5; 6:12–13) and possibly a select few additional Jewish laws in Torah (cf. table-fellowship in 2:11–14; "works of law" in 2:16; "days," "months," "seasons," and "years" in 4:10). Below I summarize additional views.

24 Barclay 2002: 372–73.
25 Barclay 2002: 373.
26 The rest of the paragraph summarizes Barclay's point in Barclay 2002: 372–73.
27 Barclay 2002: 372–73.
28 Barclay 2002: 372–73.

Two-Front Theory

In 1919, Wilhelm Lütgert argued against the traditional view suggesting that the trouble-makers preaching another gospel in Galatia were two factions of both Jewish legalists and antinomians.[29] In a 1945 article, Frederic R. Crownfield argued the trouble-makers in Galatia preaching another gospel were a syncretistic group that incorporated ideas from Judaism with pneumatic experiences.[30]

Gnostic View

In a 1972 monograph on Paul, Walter Schmithals argued the trouble-making preachers of another gospel in Galatia were "Jewish Christian gnostics." According to Schmithals, the opponents in Galatia created a crisis that related to antinomianism, not to Judaism.[31]

Radical Jewish Zealot

In a 2002 essay on the identity of Paul's opponents in Galatia, Robert Jewett argues they were "Jewish zealots" and were the source of much violence in Palestine. According to Jewett, this group of zealots directed revolutionary action against Jewish Christians because they mingled with the Gentiles. Jewett concludes that this violent hostility from Jewish zealots motivated the opponents, whom Paul said preached another gospel in Galatia, to visit the churches of Galatia and "compel" the Galatian Christians to be circumcised.[32]

Gentile Proselytes

Mark D. Nanos argues Paul's "influencers" were probably "proselytes." They represented the Jewish synagogue. They disagreed with Paul's gospel in that they required Gentiles to live a Jewish way of life in order to gain full acceptance within the people of God. Paul opposes "influencers"

---

29 Lütgert 1919. Cited in Schreiner 2010: 40

30 Crownfield 1945: 491–500. Summary in Schreiner 2010: 40.

31 Schmithals 1972: 13–64. Above discussion paraphrased from Schreiner 2010: 41.

32 Schreiner 2010: 39–41 influenced my summary of the identity of the opponents in Galatia. See also Longenecker 1990: lxxxviii–xcvi; Jewett 2002: 334–47.

in Galatia who interpret Jewish traditions. These influencers are not from the apostolic community. According to Nanos, the "influencers" in Galatia are not even Christians. Instead, they are loyal to the interests of the Jewish community in Galatia, but not to the interests of the Christ-followers in Galatia—the group of which Paul's Galatian audience is part.[33]

Structure[34]

As Schreiner, and numerous scholars, have observed, scholars have used ancient rhetoric as a tool for studying Galatians. There are three basic types of rhetoric: judicial, deliberative, and epideictic. Judicial rhetoric refers to the language of the court of law. The language of "defense and accusation" are prominent in this form of rhetoric as the orator considers "guilt and innocence." Deliberative rhetoric appeals to humans to "consider the future" as the orator seeks to "persuade or dissuade" them "from a specific course of action." Epideictic rhetoric celebrates "common values or aspirations, or indicting something that is blameworthy."[35]

As Schreiner summarizes in his commentary, scholars have identified at least four parts to ancient rhetorical speeches: "*exordium* (introduction)." The latter is an introduction with the intent of creating empathy from the reader for the discussion following the introduction.[36] The "*narratio* (narration)" contains the thesis and gives important "background information" to support the main argument.[37] "The *probatio*" states evidence to support the primary thesis.[38] "The *peroratio*" gives a summation of the material and concludes the argument to convince the audience of the arguments presented.[39] Many commentators have noted the most famous rhetorical analysis of Galatians is Hans D. Betz's commentary on Galatians.[40] More than one scholar has responded to Betz's thesis.[41]

33 Nanos 2002a: 396–407

34 Entire summary comes from Schreiner 2010: 52–53. For further discussion of a rhetorical reading of Galatians and to see the method in practice, see Betz 1979; Witherington 1998.

35 Schreiner 2010: 53.

36 Schreiner 2010: 53.

37 Schreiner 2010: 53.

38 Schreiner 2010: 53.

39 Schreiner 2010: 53.

40 Betz 1979.

41 E.g., Hansen 1989; Davies 1962. For further introductory matters, see

Galatians 1

Introduction: Defense of the Divine Origin of Paul's Gospel
(1:1—2:10)

From the outset of the letter in Gal 1, Paul gets straight to the point rather quickly. He begins by emphasizing the authority of his gospel over and against the authority of the other gospel preached by his opponents. He flaunts both his apostolic authority and the divine origin of his gospel to prove the authority of his gospel insisting his gospel comes from God, the Father, and the Lord Jesus Christ (Gal 1:1). He appeals to other missionaries as witnesses to the authority of his gospel (Gal 1:2). He wishes that God and Jesus would grant the Galatians grace and peace (Gal 1:3). He reminds the Galatians Jesus gave himself for the sins of Jews and Gentiles ("our sins") so that he would deliver "us" from this present evil age (Gal 1:4). He expresses shock about their turn from his gospel to another gospel (Gal 1:6–10). He asserts with a short autobiographical section that he instead turned from Judaism to the gospel of Jesus Christ when God revealed this gospel to him by divine revelation (Gal 1:11–24).

Paul continues to discuss the divine origin of his gospel in 2:1–10 when he comments on his trip to Jerusalem to meet the pillars of the Jerusalem church 14 years after he began preaching the gospel. At this private meeting with the pillars of the church, the apostles affirmed his ministry, acknowledged God graciously appointed him as an apostle to the Gentiles, and gave him the right hand of fellowship (2:9). They only asked him to remember the poor (2:10), which he was eager to do (2:10).

Salutation (1:1–5)

Interpreters may be tempted too quickly to gloss over the introductory remarks in Paul's letters as though they are irrelevant to the letter's body. However, similar to Romans—but with a stronger polemical tone—Paul's

Longenecker 1990: lxii–ixxii; and Schreiner 2010: 55–59.

salutational comments in Galatians come with great rhetorical and theological pop! He identifies himself in 1:1 as "Paul" and with the qualifying noun "apostle" (*apostolos*) to enforce the authority of his gospel to the Galatians and to dissuade them from embracing his opponents' gospel.

Paul refers to himself often in his letters as an apostle.[1] He uses the noun *apostolos* to refer to a special "messenger," "envoy," or "ambassador" of the crucified, resurrected, and exalted Christ.[2] He accentuates in 1:1 his gospel came from God and Jesus and in 1:11–12 that he received his gospel via a "revelation of Jesus Christ." The latter statement at least means God revealed to him the message of the gospel about Jesus by means of a divine revelation of/from/about Jesus. Paul confirms this interpretation in 1:15–16 when he states God desired to reveal to/in him his Son, while he was within his mother's womb, so that he would proclaim him as good news amongst the Gentiles. Acts 9 likewise confirms this supernatural apocalypse of God in Christ to Paul while he was on his way to Damascus. As Paul states in 1 Cor 15:8–9, his apostolic calling was an untimely birth into apostolic ministry by means of a fresh vision of the crucified and resurrected Christ.

Paul intentionally appeals to his apostolic authority in order to dissuade the Galatians from turning to his opponents' "other gospel" (cf. 1:7). The rest of Paul's remarks in 1:1 discuss the divine origin of his apostleship. He asserts his apostleship comes from Jesus Christ and God, the Father, who raised him from the dead (1:1b). This first line in the salutation sets up the argument in the rest of the letter. The Galatians should not turn away from Paul's gospel to embrace his opponents' gospel, because he received his apostolic gospel from Jesus and God, whereas his opponents' gospel comes from man. Paul's gospel centers on the crucified, resurrected, and exalted Jesus, whom God raised from the dead. But the opponents' gospel emphasized circumcision (cf. 2:3; 5:2–3, 11; 6:12–13). God and Jesus approve the validity of Paul's gospel (1:1–2:10). The opponents, however, boast in their own gospel (cf. 6:12–13).

In verse 2, Paul mentions other brothers with him as co-senders of the letter to the churches of Galatia.[3] He perhaps mentions these brothers especially for rhetorical reasons in light of verse 1: namely, to associate

---

1 Rom 1:1; 11:13; 1 Cor 1:1; 9:1–2; 15:9; 2 Cor 1:1; Gal 1:1; Eph 1:1; Col 1:1; 1 Tim 1:1; 2:7; 2 Tim 1:1, 11; Tit 1:1.

2 See Das's helpful discussion of the meaning of apostle. Das 2014: 73–75.

3 Co-senders attest to Paul's apostolic authority. For the role of co-senders in first century letters, see Richards 2004.

other gospel missionaries with his gospel to support its divine origin.[4] Gospel missionary companions could attest to the veracity of the divine origins of Paul's gospel (cf. Acts 9:10–19, 26–30). Missionary attestations of his apostolic gospel may be a reason he says later in the autobiographical section he did not visit the other apostles until years after his calling-conversion to preach the gospel of Jesus Christ. This visit affirmed his apostolic ministry, but did not create it (Gal 1:16—2:10). The plural form (assemblies) clarifies that Galatians was likely a circular letter sent to multiple churches throughout Galatia. The biggest historical question in verse 2, of course, pertains to the destination of Galatia (north or south).[5]

In verses 3–4, Paul mentions three, essential parts of his gospel: grace, peace, and the death of Jesus for sins. Expressions of well-being occur in Greco-Roman salutations,[6] but Paul uses "grace" and "peace" here in a fresh way.[7] Grace and peace occur in context of his defense of the divine origin of his apostolic gospel and in context of his apostolic curse upon those who preach a gospel contrary to his gospel (1:8–9). God called Paul by his grace to preach Jesus as the good news to the Gentiles (1:15–16). The apostolic pillars of the church (Peter, James, and John) gave to him and Barnabas the right hand of fellowship to preach the gospel because they saw the grace that was given to Paul (2:9).

In 2:21, Paul asserts he will not nullify the grace of God by preaching a message of righteousness/justification by means of works of law. Likewise, in 6:16, Paul pairs peace with mercy and applies the phrase to the Israel of God. The latter phrase in all likelihood refers to Jews and Gentiles who express faith in Paul's apostolic gospel since Paul argues for the unity of Jews and Gentiles in Christ as sons of Abraham in 2:11—3:29. In 6:18, Paul prays the "grace of our Lord Jesus Christ" would be with the Galatians.[8]

---

4 Paul mentions co-senders in other letters apart from rhetorically charged contexts. E.g., 1 Cor 1:1; 2 Cor 1:1.

5 For my discussion, see the introduction to the commentary.

6 Richards 2004.

7 For recent work on grace as divine gift in Paul, see Barclay 2015.

8 In 1:3, Paul prays the gospel's blessings of grace and peace would be added to the Galatians. This is exactly the prayer the Galatians needed because they were beginning to turn and at the very least seriously contemplating a turn from Paul's gospel to another gospel (1:6). This turn and this serious contemplation resulted in the Galatians' fall from the saving grace of Paul's gospel (5:4).

In verses 1 and 3, Paul makes two high Christological statements.[9] In verse 1, he says his apostleship comes through both Jesus Christ and God, the Father. In verse 3, he states grace and peace come from God, our Father, and the Lord Jesus Christ. The terms Christ and Lord, and Paul's statement that God, the Father, and Jesus are the ones from whom both his apostolic gospel and grace and peace come, support that Paul esteems Jesus with the same divine authority as the Father. He distinguishes between God, the Father, and the Lord Jesus Christ, but he speaks of Jesus as sharing God's identity and authority.[10]

In verse 4, Paul adds a descriptive statement to the phrase Lord Jesus Christ with the words "who gave himself for our sins so that he would deliver us from this present evil age according to the will of our God and Father" (cf. 4 Ezra 6:9; CD VI.10).[11] The Lord Jesus Christ "gave himself for our sins." This statement is a reference to Jesus' substitutionary death for the sins of others. Paul uses the exact phrase in 1 Cor 15:3. The phrase "for our sins" does not by itself speak to substitution since Paul asserts the purpose of Jesus' death "for our sins" was to "deliver us from the present evil age."[12] Unlike Gal 3:13 and Rom 5:8–9, Gal 1:4 asserts Jesus' death delivers from the "present evil age" without reference to deliverance from God's wrath (Rom 5:8–9) or a curse (Gal 3:13). But substitution is still present in Gal 1:4.

Paul's remarks about the death of Jesus in 1:4 are striking. He says Jesus delivers us "from the present evil age." He does not say from our sins or from God's wrath. The present evil age in Galatians is the antithesis of "new creation" (Gal 6:15). The present evil age is the age dominated by sin (3:22), the law (3:10, 3:19—4:7), a curse (3:10), spiritual slavery (3:19—4:7), and *ta stoicheia tou kosmou* (4:5–11).

Commenting on Gal 3:28, Hans Betz says, "Being rescued from the present evil age and being changed to a new creation implies these radical social and political changes. The Christian's relationship to the social and political structures of this world follows the rule set forth in 6:14: through whom [=Christ] the world is crucified to me and I to the world.

---

9 By high Christological, I mean Paul describes God, the Father, and Jesus, his Son, as co-distributors of Paul's gospel and of grace. For a similar point with respect to Gal 1:1, see Das 2014: 76.

10 For Christology and divine identity, see Bauckham 1998 and 2008.

11 Jewish sources mentioned in Das 2014: 84.

12 For recent work on substitution in Paul's theology, see Williams 2012; Gathercole 2015.

The Christian is now dead to the social, religious, and cultural distinctions characteristic of the old world-order (cf. Gal 2:19)."[13]

Christ's deliverance of "us" from the present evil age is an already-not-yet experience for Christ-followers. Jesus died to deliver "us" from the judgment that is to come to those who live under the authority of the present evil age instead of under the authority of Christ (cf. Gal 3:10–13). And the Christian's Spirit-empowered walk is evidence that such deliverance has already come via the cross (3:13–14; 4–6; 5:16). But the deliverance of the "us" from the present evil age will be fully realized when the "us" inherit the kingdom of God (5:21) and new creation (6:15) at the end of this present age. Yet, the present certainty of this deliverance has already been experienced now by those for whom Jesus died as they are justified by faith in Christ, receive the Abrahamic blessing of the Spirit, and walk in the Spirit (2:16—5:1, 5, 16–26).[14]

The present evil age in Galatians represents the current world's domination by sin and all of the forces of evil (3:19—4:12). The weak and poor elements of the world are part of this present evil age (4:3, 9). The "present evil age" is currently enslaved to the power of sin due in part to the pedagogue of the law (3:19—4:7; 4:31—5:1). Jesus' death, therefore, delivers Jews and Gentiles from this present evil age through his invasion of the current cosmos. The current cosmos is enslaved to sin and the demonic forces of evil, from which Jesus delivers us by removing us from one lordship to another, from the lordship of sin, evil, and the law to the lordship of the Lord Jesus Christ and the Spirit (cf. 3:10—5:1). This deliverance was God's will (1:4). Thus, Paul concludes verse 5 by praising God.

There are at least five truths related to the origin of Paul's gospel in 1:1–5 that Paul wants to ring loudly in the Galatians ears. First, God and Jesus gave him his apostolic gospel (1:1). Second, God raised Jesus from the dead (1:1). Third, grace and peace come from God and Jesus (1:3). Fourth, Jesus voluntarily died for the sins of Jews and Gentiles to deliver them from this present evil age (1:4). Fifth, to reject Paul's gospel about the crucified and resurrected Messiah would be to reject God's provision of deliverance from this present evil age (1:4).

---

13 Betz 1979: 190.

14 So Das 2014: 84–85.

A Shocking Turn to Another Gospel (1:6–9)

In the letter's body, Paul abruptly moves from his brief salutation in 1:1–5 to his expression of shock in 1:6–9. This entire section—and indeed the entire letter—is emphatic and urgent! The absence of a typical Pauline thanksgiving formula in the body, the tautologies of cognate forms of the Greek noun gospel and the verb preach the gospel (1:6–9), his expression of shock (1:6), his use of the two adverbs *arti* ("now") and *palin* ("again") (1:9), and his twofold apostolic curse pronouncement upon anyone—angelic or human—who preaches another gospel to the Galatians besides the one that he preached to them make this section unusually urgent, because the Galatians are seriously contemplating a turn from Paul's gospel. As one scholar states, from 1:5 to 1:8–9, Paul moves from "Amen to anathema!"[15] These things and the absence of a thanksgiving formula reveal Paul's shocking and urgent tone in this letter.

Paul begins the body of the letter by expressing shock that the Galatians are "so quickly" turning from his gospel to another gospel (1:6). The verb *thaumazō*, which I have translated as "to shock," refers to astonishment in the NT (e.g., Matt 27:4; Mark 15:5; John 5:28; 7:21; Acts 3:12; 1 John 3:13). According to A. Andrew Das, ancient authors commonly began their letters with an expression of amazement "in order to shame" their audiences into embracing a new path of life.[16] He points out that Cicero (106–43 BCE), a famous Roman philosopher, lawyer, politician, and orator, commented that "expressions of amazement" or shock served as a rhetorical means of "appealing to audiences" threatened with opposition (Cicero, *Inv.* 1.17.25).[17] In other NT contexts, the verb communicates shocking disbelief (Luke 2:33; 24:12, 41). The latter seems to be Paul's intent in 1:6 because he is astonished due to the Galatians' turn from his gospel, which saves, to another, which brings a curse (cf. 1:6–9; 3:10).

Paul uses the present tense verb (*metatithesthe*, "you are turning") to express the reason for his shocking disbelief. In 2 Maccabees, the verb refers to "abandoning allegiance to God" and Torah as a result of compulsion from Antiochus Epiphanes IV (2 Macc 7:24).[18] In LXX Deut 27:17, the verb is associated with a curse (cf. with Gal 1:6, 8–9 and 3:10).

---

15 Thought from Das 2014: 99.

16 Paraphrased from Das 2014: 99.

17 Das 2014: 99.

18 Das 2014: 100–101.

In Gal 1:6, the verb is in the present tense, but it could be timeless.[19] The shock in 1:6 is understandable, though, if at least some of the Galatians had already begun to turn from Paul's gospel after having originally received it before he left their presence. He does say, after all, the Galatians were turning "so quickly." This could mean "so quickly" after hearing the opponents' teaching, "so quickly" after Paul left, or "so quickly" after their conversion.[20] Perhaps each of the preceding is intended with the phrase "so quickly."

In Gal 3:2–6, he asserts the Galatians received the Spirit by faith apart from works of the law (3:2), that they entered into the faith by the Spirit apart from works of the law (3:3–4), and that God gave to them the Spirit by faith apart from works of the law (3:5), just as Abraham believed God and it was reckoned to him as righteousness (3:6). Christ redeemed both Paul and the Galatians from Torah's curse by faith. Jesus' redemption of Jews and Gentiles imparted to them the blessing of Abraham by faith (3:13–14). He identifies the Galatians as brothers (1:11; 3:15; 5:13; 6:1, 18).

In 5:2–5, he suggests if the Galatians subscribe to the Mosaic law, then they have fallen from grace (aorist verb). In 5:10, he expresses absolute confidence the Galatians will not turn away from his gospel. He asserts the Galatians were called (aorist verb) to freedom in Christ (5:13). Perhaps some of the Galatians had already begun to turn away from Paul's gospel (hence, 1:6). However, Paul makes positive statements about the Galatians as the people of God throughout the letter (cf. 3:15; 4:12, 28–29, 31; 5:1, 10, 13; 6:1). Many of them may only have been seriously contemplating a turn away from his gospel to the opponents' message (cf. 5:7).

The Galatians' contemplative turn was a contemplation to abandon Paul's gospel for another (1:7). Interpreters should not minimize Paul's warning here. He is concerned the Galatians will become apostates.[21] His expression of shock that they are "turning from the one who called them by the grace of [Christ] to another gospel" supports this interpretation (1:6).

Paul was shocked the Galatians were "turning from the one who called you." *Kaleō* in Paul often refers to effectual calling: i.e., to the

19 This seems to be the case also with the present tense verbs in Gal 1:10 and in 2:16.

20 For different options and scholars who defend them, see Moo 2013: 76.

21 Similarly Das 2014: 100–101.

calling that creates spiritual life/conversion (cf. Rom 4:17; 1 Cor 1:9; 7:18, 20, 24; Gal 5:13). The agent of the call is not clear in 1:6. Does God call or Paul? The question of whether *Christou* was original or a scribal addition makes the referent ambiguous. The participle (*kalesantos*) likely has God as its subject since God is the one who called Paul "through his grace" in 1:15–16 (cf. 1:6).[22] In Paul's letters, God is the one who effectually calls (cf. Rom 4:17; 8:30; 9:24; 1 Cor 1:9; 7:15; 1 Thess 2:12; 4:7; 5:24).[23]

In Gal 1:15–16, Paul uses the verb to refer to God's calling-conversion of him to preach Jesus as good news amongst the Gentiles. In 5:13, Paul says the Galatians' calling resulted in freedom. This freedom refers to God's deliverance of those under the law from its power when they embraced Christ by faith (1:4; 2:16–21; 3:10—4:8; 4:21—5:1). Paul associates the Galatians' calling with grace. Grace is a gospel category in Galatians because Paul uniquely attaches grace to his gospel (1:3, 6–9, 15–16; 2:9, 21; 5:4; 6:18). Thus, Paul is shocked with disbelief that the Galatians were contemplating a turn away from his gospel because such a turn would mean an outright abandonment of the God of grace who called-converted them by delivering them from the present evil age (1:4). They would be turning from life in order to embrace another gospel that inevitably leads to a curse (1:8–9; 2:11; 3:10–11).

In 1:7, Paul clarifies what he means by "another gospel" in 1:6. Scholars have argued the other gospel in 1:7 is not different in "content" from 1:6, but a different "form" of the same gospel in 1:6.[24] Others have suggested *allos* ("another") could be "another of the same kind" and *heteros* ("different") is "another of a different kind."[25] Paul identifies the opponents' gospel as "an-other" gospel in 1:7. The switch to *allo* ("other") in 1:7 from *heteron* ("other") in 1:6 is stylistic without any exegetical or theological significance. Paul seems to use these two words as synonyms in his letters (cf. 1 Cor 12:10; 15:39–41; 2 Cor 11:4).[26]

Paul uses *heteron* three times in Galatians (1:7, 19; 6:4), and he uses *allo* only twice (1:7; 5:10). In 5:10, he uses *allo* when he urges the Galatians not to yield to his opponents' gospel. Paul may have unintentionally confused the Galatians if he would have chosen to use the same adjective

22 Against Oakes 2015: 43–44.

23 So Das 2014: 101. So also Schreiner 2010: 85–86.

24 Schröter 2006: 133–53.

25 So Robertson 1937: 747. Above sentence paraphrased from Das 2014: 103.

26 Das 2014: 103. See also the NT texts cited in Moo 2013: 86–87.

in 1:6–7 to describe his opponents' rival gospel. Using the same word could have suggested to the Galatians they were turning to a *heteron euaggelion* ("another gospel") (1:6), which is not a *heteron* ("another") gospel (1:7). The Galatians could have responded by saying "What? I thought the trouble-makers' gospel was a *heteron* gospel since that is what you said, Paul, in the previous verse?"

To avoid confusion, Paul says they were turning to a *heteron euaggelion* ("another gospel") (1:6), which is not an *allo* ("another") gospel since there is only one gospel (1:7).[27] The reason for 1:7 is to defend there is only one gospel. This one gospel is the gospel Paul received from God and Jesus (1:1, 11–12), the gospel he preached to the Galatians (1:11), the gospel the Galatians received from him (1:9), and which is contrary to the opponents' gospel (1:6–7; 5:2–6). Paul presented his gospel to the pillars of the church. He did not yield to an-other gospel when his gospel was threatened so that the truth of the gospel would remain with the Gentiles. Paul's apostleship to the Gentiles and Peter's to the Jews were not two different apostolic ministries with two opposing gospels (one for Gentiles and one for Jews). Their gospel was the same gospel focusing on different ethnic contexts (2:2–7). As a result, Peter, James, and John gave Paul and Barnabas the right hand of fellowship when they saw that he had been entrusted with the same gospel for the un-circumcision as Peter had been entrusted with the gospel for the circumcision (2:7–9).

In 1:7, Paul further clarifies the opponents' gospel is not a gospel when he pronounces "but" some were troubling the Galatians and desired to distort the gospel of Christ. The participles ("troubling" and "wishing") might communicate the opponents were troubling the Galatians while Paul wrote the letter.[28] The rival teachers preached a message different from Paul's message. Yet, their message was close enough to Paul's so that it was persuading some (and maybe even many) of the Galatians. Paul says the opponents were trouble-makers and distorters of the gospel because they proclaimed the necessity of obeying Torah and trusting in Christ to Gentiles instead of proclaiming Christ alone.

The verb (*metastrephō*) that Paul uses for distort occurs in 1 Esd 3:20. In the latter text, the verb refers to wine's ability to turn one's desires toward feasting, cheerfulness, and to help one forget his grief and debt. In 4 Macc 15:11, the verb refers to the resilience of a Jewish mother who

27 A similar point in Das 2014: 97.

28 Das 2014: 104.

refused to pervert her religious reason by her unwillingness to embrace a Gentile manner of life. She resisted the Gentile tyrant's threats while watching her seven sons tortured because of their zeal for the law. In Acts 2:20, the verb apocalyptically refers to the cosmos' transformation during the great and dreadful Day of the Lord. Paul uses the verb in Gal 1:7 to identify his opponents' rival gospel as a distortion of the gospel "of Christ." The opponents preached Christ and law, not law instead of Christ. This emphasis on Christ and law for Gentile Christ-followers distorted Paul's divinely appointed gospel to the Gentiles (cf. 1:15–16).

The phrase "gospel of Christ" translates the phrase *euaggelion tou Christou*. The genitive (*Christou*) here is ambiguous. A crucial word in 1:7 is the noun *euaggelion* ("gospel") and its verbal cognate *euaggelizō* ("I announce the gospel") in 1:8–9, 1:11, and in 1:16 (cf. also 1:8–9; 2:14). "Gospel" (*euaggelion*) and its verbal cognate *euaggelizō* refer to an announcement (cf. LXX Isa 40–66). In Galatians, the announcement is about God's redemptive work of delivering Jews and Gentiles from the present evil age through the cross and resurrection of Jesus Christ.[29] Isaiah provides a background behind Paul's use of the terms for gospel in Galatians (cf. LXX Isa 40–66).[30] Paul's gospel was from Christ and given by Christ (1:1, 11–12). His gospel was the good news about Christ (1:16). Paul's basic point is his opponents preached a different message about Christ in comparison to the one he received from God and Christ and then preached to the Galatians. Paul's gospel about the Christ comes from God (1:1; 1:10—2:10). However, the opponents' "other" gospel is a distortion. Instead, they turn/change/distort Paul's gospel, which comes from God, from Jesus, and about Jesus Christ. The opponents preach this rival gospel so that the Galatians would turn from the one who called-converted them to the gospel of Christ to a rival gospel. Ironically, the gospel of Christ blesses them, but the "other" gospel curses them (cf. 1:6, 8–9).

A Shocking Turn to Another Gospel Continued (1:8–9)

In 1:8–9, Paul now discusses the superiority of his gospel against his opponents' gospel by emphasizing the severe consequences of preaching another gospel besides his. The emphatic nature of 1:8–9 is apparent by

29 For a discussion of the gospel, see Silva 2014: 2.306–13.

30 Harmon 2010.

the adversative construction "but even" (*alla kai*) in 1:8, by Paul's appeal to other missionaries in 1:8, by his appeal to an angel in 1:8, by his use of the curse formula anathema in 1:8–9, and by his reiteration of 1:8 in 1:9. He asserts that even if he, other missionaries, or even an angel from heaven should announce as good news another good news besides the announcement of good news that he made, may that person be accursed.

The pronoun "we" in 1:8 includes Paul, other missionaries, or anyone who preaches a different gospel from Paul. Gal 1:2 mentions fellow missionaries, and 1:9 uses the indefinite pronoun "anyone" to prohibit anyone without exception from preaching another gospel. Paul's prohibition is intensified when he includes angels and anticipates his later remarks about the law being appointed through angels by a mediator (cf. Gal 3:19). In the Hebrew Bible (Ezek 8:2–3; Dan 10:5–6; Zech 2:7), in Second Temple Judaism (1 En. 1:2; 4 Ezra 2:44–45; 4:1–4; 2 Baruch),[31] and in early Christianity (Revelation), angels imparted divine revelation to humans (cf. Gal 3:19). Later in Galatians, Paul acknowledges this point when he argues for the superiority of the Abrahamic promise over the Mosaic law. The former came directly from God to Abraham, while the latter came through angels to Moses, and then to the people (Gal 3:19–20).[32] Even if other so-called Christian missionaries or an angel from heaven preaches another gospel besides the one Paul originally preached to the Galatians, Paul prays they will be accursed by God.

In the OT, anathema is associated with judgment (LXX Judg 1:17). OT curses are plentiful (Gen 3:14; 12:3; Deut 27:15—28:19).[33] Ancients generally viewed curses could destroy a person from the inside out.[34] The Hebrew Bible describes curses as "penetrating the body" (Num 5:27).[35] Paul supports the physical nature of the curse when he anathematizes his opponents by wishing they would cut off their penises (Gal 5:12). In Paul's writings, along with its function in the OT, the anathema refers especially to being set apart for divine judgment/destruction (cf. LXX Deut 7:26; Jos 6:17–18; Zech 14:11).[36] The thing devoted to destruction

31 Das 2014: 106. Dunn 1993: 45.

32 Cf. also LXX Exod 20:19, 21, 22; Lev 26:46; Deut 5:4, 5, 22, 23, 27, 31; 33:2; NT Acts 7:38, 53; Heb 2:2; 9:15.

33 Das 2014: 107n45 pointed me to the above texts. For the presence of scripture in Gal 1 and 2, see Ciampa 1998.

34 Moreland 1995: 158. Das 2014: 107n46 pointed me to this reference.

35 Das 2014: 107n46.

36 Moreland 1995: 158; Das 2014: 107n46; DeSilva 2018: 127; Keener 2018: 43–44.

is set apart as a sacrifice of worship to the one and true living God (cf. LXX Deut 13:1–18).[37] But if the thing devoted to destruction should remain within the community, God pledged to visit the community with his wrath (Jos 7:1, 11–13; 22:20; 1 Chr 2:7).[38]

Paul says he would wish himself to be anathema from Christ for the sake of the salvation of the Jewish people if it were possible (Rom 9:3). He prays that all who do not love the Lord Jesus Christ would be anathema (1 Cor 16:22). In Gal 1:8–9, anathema is an apostolic curse pronouncement of God's judgment placed upon those who reject Paul's apostolic gospel. Paul wishes those who preach a gospel contrary to his to be set apart for God's eschatological destruction (cf. Gal 2:11; 5:5, 16–21).[39]

In Gal 1:9, Paul repeats his statement from 1:8, reminding the Galatians they received the gospel from him. With the words "as we have said beforehand, also now again I say to you,"[40] Paul likely recalls his previous mission in Galatia where he labored to help them understand the truth of his gospel (cf. Gal 4:11; Acts 13–14).[41] Paul received his gospel from Jesus Christ and God, the Father, not from men (1:1, 11–12). The Galatians received their gospel from Paul (1:9; 4:12–19), who received it from God and Jesus (1:1, 15–16). He warns them if they turn to a false gospel, then they, along with the opponents who preach this other gospel, will be devoted to God's destruction (cf. Deut 13:1–18 with Gal 3:10). This curse results in the failure to inherit the kingdom of God (5:21) and to participate in new creation (6:15). The only acceptable gospel is a gospel received from God and Jesus and proclaimed as good news without distortion to men, not a distorted gospel about Christ, received from men, and proclaimed to the assemblies of Galatia as a gospel from God. The Galatians had already received the one true gospel that comes from God when Paul publicly portrayed Christ as crucified to them (cf. 1 Cor 11:23; 15:1, 3; Gal 1:12; 3:1; Phil 4:9; Col 2:6; 1 Thess 2:13; 4:1; 2 Thess 3:6).[42]

37 Summary from Das 2014: 107.

38 Das 2014: 107–8. Moo 2013: 80. For ancient curse rituals, see McLean 1996; Davis 2002.

39 Above discussion influenced by Schreiner 2010: 87. For the idea of excommunication, see Dunn 1993: 46–47.

40 For primary texts, see Das 2014: 110n62.

41 So also Das 2014: 109; Schreiner 2010: 88.

42 Similarly Das 2014: 110.

Genuine Persuasion and Paul's Gospel (1:10–24)

In Gal 1:10—2:10, Paul provides a concise autobiography. This section describes his activity of persecuting the assembly of God before his faith in Christ and his missionary activity after he encountered Christ and received his conversion-call from him on the Damascus Road. In 1:10–13, Paul supports his remarks in 1:6–9 with several clauses that begin with the word "for" (*gar*). In 1:10, he asks "for am I seeking to persuade men or God or am I seeking to please men? If I were still pleasing men, then I would not be a slave of Christ." In 1:11, he says, "for I make known to you, brothers, that the gospel, which was preached by me, is not in accordance with man." In 1:12, he says, "for I neither received it from man nor was I taught it." In 1:13, he says, "for you heard about my former manner of life in Judaism." The *gar* in 1:10 is likely inferential.[43] The rest of the *gar*-clauses work together to provide support for 1:10. Paul's argument in these verses can be summarized as follows:

> I cannot believe you are turning from my gospel to the opponents' gospel, which is not a gospel but a distortion (1:6–7).
> Indeed (but?), even if an angel from heaven or another missionary preaches a gospel different from the one I originally preached to you, may that person experience God's wrath (1:8–9).
> Therefore, I please God, not men (1:10)
> Because my gospel is from God and not men (1:11)
> Because I received my gospel from God and not man (1:12)
> Because you heard that I formerly persecuted the church but I was called-converted by God [and not by man] to announce Jesus as good news amongst the Gentiles (1:13–17) (brackets mine)

Paul poses two related questions in 1:10. The first question asks whether he persuades men or God and the second whether he pleases men or God. The single response in 1:10c answers both questions. Commentators have connected Paul's curse pronouncements in 1:8–9 with the concepts of "persuasion" and "flattery" in 1:10. By this, they suggest Paul is both seeking to persuade God to bring a curse upon those who reject his gospel and seeking to persuade the Galatians to reject the opponents'

---

43 Schreiner 2010: 88–89.

gospel.[44] Josephus provides lexical evidence for this interpretation.[45] He connects a form of the verb persuade (*peithō*) with an appeal to God to fulfill a curse pronouncement against the enemies of God's people (Jos. *Ant.* 4.6.5).[46]

In 1:10, however, Paul uses the language of persuasion/flattery and pleasing synonymously to assert he pleases God with his gospel message instead of men.[47] Flattery with the intent of persuasion was used both positively and negatively in antiquity (cf. 1 Cor 2:4; Gal 5:7–11).[48] Jewish literature describes the flatterers/people-pleasures as wicked people in the midst of the pious (cf. Pss. Sol. 4). Thus, by persuading God and not men in 1:10a, Paul refers to God as the object of the pleasure instead of men. The second question and the answer in 1:10b explicitly address the issue of pleasing God. His primary point in 1:10 seems to be his gospel pleases God, not men.[49] The chief example of this in Galatians is Paul's confrontation of Peter in Antioch because he did not walk in a straight forward manner in the truth of the gospel (Gal 2:11–14).

Paul's remarks in 1:11–24 are emphatic, supported by the numerous negative particles that occur in the verses.[50] Paul has 8 negative statements in these verses.[51] As a result, J. Louis Martyn called these verses a "negative travelogue."[52] This emphatic construction confirms the divine origins of and the superiority of his gospel over his opponents' message.

In 1:11–12, Paul restates 1:10 and echoes 1:1 without asking "am I pleasing God." He asserts the gospel preached by him is not in accordance with man (1:11). The phrase "in accordance with man" means the same thing as the phrases "from men" (1:1), "through man" (1:1), and "from man" (1:12). Paul has already established the divine origin of his gospel in 1:1 and in the harsh indictment of 1:6–9. He asserts it again in 1:11 ("I make known to you, brothers") and reiterates it in 1:12 ("For I neither received it from man nor was I taught it."). Paul neither denies he

---

44 Das 2014: 112–13.

45 Das 2014: 112.

46 Das 2014: 112.

47 Against Das 2014: 112. In agreement with Moo 2013: 84.

48 Das 2014: 113.

49 Rightly Moo 2013: 84.

50 Rightly Das 2014: 118.

51 See negative particles in Gal 1:11–12, 16–17, 19–20.

52 Martyn 1997: 178. So also Das 2014: 1117–18, 118n62.

learned some things from the apostles nor from other disciples of Jesus. His remarks in 1:11–24 connect with his comments about the gospel in 1:6–9.[53] Yet, his gospel neither originated from the apostles nor from any human being. To the contrary, he received his gospel from God by means of a "revelation of Jesus Christ" (1:12).

The phrase "revelation of Jesus Christ" refers to a divine revelation, because Paul asserts in 1:15–16 that God separated him from his mother's womb to reveal his Son in him. The introductory formula ("I make known to you") in 1:11, the reference to his "revelation of Jesus Christ," the emphasis on "the gospel preached by me" (1:11), and on the gospel "I received" (1:12) accentuate both the importance of and the divine nature of his gospel.[54] Paul contrasts his divinely received gospel from God with the human gospel of his opponents. Both the noun "revelation" (*apocalypsis*) in 1:12 and the verb "to reveal" (*apocalyptō*) in 1:16 are applied to Christ (1:12) or to God and Christ (1:12, 16). These words suggest God gave Paul a divine revelation (cf. LXX 2 Sam 7:27; Eph 1:17; 3:3). As a Pharisee, Paul would have taken great pride in receiving traditions handed down from his teachers (i.e., "the ancestral traditions" [Gal 1:14]).[55] But as a follower of Jesus Christ, he boasts in receiving his gospel by direct revelation from God without the revelation being transmitted through human teachers.[56]

The specific revelation to which Paul refers is likely his Damascus Road encounter with the resurrected and exalted Christ (cf. Acts 9:1–9). The revelation of/about/from Christ, then, affirms Jesus is the resurrected and exalted Lord. This, therefore, is at the very heart of Paul's gospel: the invasion of God in Christ via his incarnation, crucifixion, and exalted resurrection over the entire cosmos with a particular emphasis on a Gentile mission and Jewish and Gentile inclusion within the Abrahamic family (cf. Acts 9:1–19; 22:6–11; 26:12–18; 1 Cor 15:1–8; Gal 1:6–16; and 3:1—5:1).[57] The genitive modifier "of Christ" (*Christou*) supports

---

53 Similarly Das 2014: 117.

54 For examples of a connection between knowledge and divine revelation, see Dan 2:23, 28–30, 45; 5:7–8, 15, 17; 1QpHab VII. 4–5; 1QH XII [=IV]. 27–28. Primary texts listed in Das 2014: 119.

55 Das 2014: 121.

56 Das 2014: 121.

57 Das (2014: 121–22) points out that Paul's revelation of Christ was an encounter with "the *living* Crucified One." He cites the above texts from Acts to support this statement.

this interpretation. God gave Paul a revelation about Jesus on the Damascus Road, a revelation that literally changed Paul's entire course of action (Acts 9). This revelation about Christ emphasized Jesus' exaltation as Lord (cf. 1:3). God had planned this encounter before Paul was born by setting him apart from his mother's womb to announce Jesus as good news amongst the Gentiles (1:15–16).

Paul continues discussing the divine origin of his gospel and its superiority over the opponents' message in 1:13. He provides his own transformation as proof of the divine origin of his gospel.[58] Paul encourages the Galatians to imitate his faithful obedience to the gospel that he received from God (cf. Gal 4:12). As to the authority of his gospel, Paul appeals to his former, violent life of Judaism about which they have heard (Gal 1:13–14).[59]

Paul did not operate as an apostle to the Gentiles within Judaism.[60] Rather, he appeals to his conduct in Judaism as a "former" conduct (1:13). After his calling-conversion, he lived out his Jewish identity as a Christ-follower in a fresh way (cf. 1:13—2:10).[61] He even reminds Peter "we are Jews by nature and not sinners by association with the Gentiles" (Gal 2:15).[62]

"Zeal was associated with Torah-observance" (Acts 22:3).[63] With the word "zealous," Paul links his previous manner of Jewish living with a violent form of Jewish identity (cf. 1 Macc 2).[64] This violent form of Jewish living received its inspiration in part from Phinehas, whose burning zeal for God's law moved him to execute an Israelite man and Gentile

58 For examples of ancient authors putting forth individuals as examples to be followed, see Quintilian, *Inst.* 3.8.36, 66; Aristotle, *Rhet.* 3.17.12. So also Das 2014: 122–23.

59 They probably heard about Paul's previous life from him (cf. Acts 13–14; Gal 1:9; 4:12–20). The assertion "you have heard" suggests a "shared common knowledge of information (cf. Matt 5:21, 27, 33, 38, 43; 26:65; Luke 7:22; John 8:38; Eph 3:2; 4:21; Phil 2:26; 4:9; Col 1:6, 23; Jas 5:11; 1 John 2:7, 18, 24; 3:11; 2 John 1:6)." So Das 2014: 123n34; Cummins 2001: 121.

60 Rightly Schreiner 2010: 98. Against Nanos and Zetterholm 2015.

61 For a work arguing that Paul was a former Jew in Christ, see Sechrest 2009.

62 For work on ethnicity, race, and identity in Paul, see Kimber Buell 2005; Hodge: 2007; Sechrest 2009. For work that discusses race in the classical period, see Snowden 1991, and the response of Isaac 2004.

63 Das 2014: 127.

64 On the zealot movement, see Hengel 1997.

woman.[65] Paul mentions his previous zeal to present his gospel as coming from God and to present it as superior to his opponents' gospel. Saul, the Pharisee, was more zealous for Torah than his opponents in Galatia. Yet, he tells the Galatians in 1:15–24 that God revealed to him a better way than Torah: namely, Christ. In Christ, Paul was no longer "*in Ioudaïsmos.*" But he was still a *Ioudaios* (cf. Rom 11:1; Gal 2:13).[66]

The term "Judaism" (*Ioudaïsmos*) in 1:13–14 refers to Paul's "former" Jewish way of life as a strict devotee of Torah (cf. Acts 22:3; 23:6; 26:5; Phil 3:4–6).[67] The term occurs only here in the NT.[68] The double use of *Ioudaïsmos* emphasizes his former manner of living Jewishly (cf. with Gal 2:14).[69] The first and earliest place *Ioudaïsmos* occurs in extant Greek literature outside of Galatians is in the apocryphal books of 2 Macc 2:21 (pre-dates Galatians) and in 4 Macc 4:26 (post-dates Galatians). In both 2 and 4 Maccabees, *Ioudaïsmos* refers to a Jewish way of life distinct from "Hellenism" in the context of Gentile persecution of Jews. In 2 Macc 2:21, *Ioudaïsmos* is the philosophy of God's people in contrast to "Hellenism," which was the philosophy of Greeks (cf. 2 Macc 4:13). 2 Macc 2:21 links the word *Ioudaïsmos* with zealous, Torah-observant Jews who fought to ensure that Jews could continue to live in a Jewish manner corresponding to Torah (2 Macc 4:2—8:36).

1 Maccabees expresses Jewish zeal to fight for Torah against the Greeks even more strongly than 2 and 4 Maccabees, but without using *Ioudaïsmos.* Similar to the zeal of Phinehas in Num 25—whose zeal for

---

65 Cf. LXX Num 25:1–13 with Jud 9:2–4; Jub. 30:5–20; Sir 45:23–24; 1 Macc 2:54; 4 Macc 18:12.

66 Contra Sechrest 2009.

67 Sources cited in Betz 1979: 68n123.

68 I generally agree with those commentators who hesitate to transliterate *Ioudaïsmos* as "Judaism" because of how Christians and non-Christians alike have pejoratively referred to, treated, and identified the Jewish people in a post-biblical, pre-holocaust, and post-holocaust world. *Ioudaïsmos* in its ancient context was the anti-thesis to *Hellenismos* ("Hellenism"). When the term first occurred in Jewish literature in 2 Macc 2:21, there was no contemporary Christianity that functioned as its opposite. Though I recognize the anachronistic problems and pejorative evocations that the translation "Judaism" might evoke in the minds of the readers of this commentary, I have, nevertheless, chosen to transliterate *Ioudaïsmos* as "Judaism." But by "Judaism," I mean a "Jewish way of life." I do not mean a so-called legalistic religion that was radically opposed to and at odds with grace-driven Christianity.

69 So also Das 2014: 123–24. Josephus and other ancients would have very much considered *Ioudaïsmos* to be a philosophy (e.g., 4 Macc 1:1; 7:9; Jos. *Ant.* 1.18) or a sect (e.g., Jos. *Ant.* 13.171).

the law compelled him to kill one of his fellow Jews for mingling with a Gentile woman (cf. 1 Macc 2:26, 54; 4 Macc 18:12)—Torah-observant Jews fought to preserve the integrity of YHWH's name by stamping out any Gentile threats against them and his law. The concepts of violent persecution (Gal 1:13–14), fathers' traditions (=at least the law) (Gal 1:14), and zeal (Gal 1:14) link Paul with the traditions about Phinehas (Num 25:1–11 and 4 Macc 18:12) and the Hasmonean dynasty (1 and 2 Maccabees).

Saul the Pharisee violently persecuted Christians not because of legalism, but because they likely seemed to be a genuine threat to the preservation of Jewish identity (cf. with 1 Maccabees). The proclamation of the early Christ-followers emphasized Jesus as YHWH and was Gentile inclusive (Acts 1:8; 8:1–40). Paul uses some harsh words in the imperfect tense perhaps to emphasize the continuous aspect of his violent pursuit of the assembly of God: "was persecuting the assembly of God" (Gal 1:13), "was attempting to destroy it" (Gal 1:13), and "was advancing in a Jewish way of life" (Gal 1:14). The verb "to persecute" (*diōkō*) refers to the pursuit and destruction of apostate Jews in Second Temple literature (1 Macc 2:47; 3:5).

Josephus uses the verb "to destroy" (*portheō*) to refer to the destruction of cities and towns (Jos. *J. W.* 4.534).[70] Mattathias, Judas Maccabeus' father, urged all Jews who were zealous for God's law to join him in battle against Gentile invaders who wanted to pervert their Jewish way of life, because he burned with zeal for the law (1 Macc 2:15–28).[71] Writing in the same general cultural context as Paul, Philo asserted there were zealots for the laws who were willing to stone to death a criminal who violated such laws (*Spec.* 2.253).[72]

Along the lines of Phinehas, the Torah-observant Jews after him, and far beyond his Jewish contemporaries (cf. Gal 1:13–14 with Phil 3:5–6), Saul, the Pharisee, relentlessly and zealously worked to preserve the name of YHWH and Jewish particularity by fighting against and participating in the extermination of Christ-followers (cf. Gal 1:13–14 with Acts 9:1–3, 21).[73] But, in Christ, Paul made "a decisive social and religious break"

70 Das 2014: 124n42.

71 Paraphrased from Das 2014: 126. For other texts about zeal for Torah, see 1 Macc 2:23–28, 42–48, 50; 2 Macc 4:2.

72 Das (2014: 126) pointed me to this text in Philo.

73 Cf. Acts 7:58–8:3; cf. also 2 Cor 11:23–26.

with Judaism,[74] although he was still Jewish (cf. Rom 11:1). However, he was a transformed Jew.

Paul's Gospel Comes from God, not Man, cont. (1:15–24)

Paul's autobiography dramatically changes in 1:15–16. The change occurs with a dramatic "but when," which signals the turn of the ages for Paul (cf. 1:4; 4:5).[75] In Judaism, Paul violently persecuted the church, sought to destroy it, and progressed in his status within Judaism because he was more zealous for his fathers' ancestral traditions than his contemporaries (1:13–14). What happened to effect this dramatic change? Paul's answer is his encounter with Jesus Christ or more specifically "but God" (1:15–16).

The Greek syntax of 1:15–17 is difficult. The main thought of the verses occurs in 1:16c–17. Gal 1:15–16b provides grammatically subordinating information to the main verbal ideas in 1:16c–17. Paul's thought is outlined in summary form as follows:

> But I neither immediately consulted with flesh and blood (1:15a–16c)
> Nor did I go to Jerusalem to those who were apostles before I became one (1:17a)
> But I went away to Arabia and I returned again to Damascus (1:17b)
> When [God], who separated me from my mother's womb and who called me through his grace so that I might announce him [=Jesus] as good news among the Gentiles, was pleased to reveal his Son in me (1:15a–16)

The summary above demonstrates the main verbal clauses in 1:16c–17 focus on Paul's missionary activity prior to his encounter with any of the other apostles. The subordinating clauses provide the theological reason why he did not consult with any other apostle: namely, God revealed his Son in Paul (1:15–16). Paul mentions 1:15–17 in order to emphasize his gospel comes from God and Jesus, not from any man—not even from any apostles. With the above summary in mind, I now explain each individual verse, beginning with 1:15.

Paul's remarks in 1:15–17 provide a strong contrast with his previous remarks in 1:13–14. He formerly persecuted the church of God and

---

74 Das 2014: 124.

75 So Das 2014: 129. Schreiner 2010: 100.

advanced in Judaism by attempting to destroy it. In 1:15–16, he introduces the Galatians to the reason why he no longer advances in Judaism. His previous life in Judaism changed when God, who separated him from his mother's womb and called him through his grace, desired to reveal his Son in him to announce him (=Jesus) as good news to the Gentiles.

Paul describes his radical transformation from a persecutor of the church to one called to preach Jesus as good news to Gentiles. He describes his calling similar to Isaiah (49:1) and Jeremiah (1:5). Isaiah says the Lord called him from the womb and called him by name from the belly of his mother (Isa 49:1). In Jer 1:5, the Lord says to Jeremiah he knew him before he formed him in his mother's womb and before he was born that he set Jeremiah apart as a prophet to the nations.[76] God had planned to appoint Paul as a prophet-preacher of Jesus to the Gentiles before his birth. Paul's language here might also suggest he understood himself to be a personification of Isaiah's Suffering Servant who takes the gospel to the Gentiles (cf. Acts 13:36–37).[77] Paul suffers as he takes the gospel to the Gentiles (Gal 4:12–20; 6:17), just as the Servant suffers as he bears the sins of the many (Isa 42:6; 52:12—53:13).

The above interpretation is supported by the verb "he desired it to be good" (*eudokēsen*) in 1:15. *Eudokeō* ("to desire to be good") occurs as an aorist first singular verb in the NT to refer to God's good pleasure in his beloved Son (Matt 3:17; 17:5; Mark 1:11; Luke 3:22; 2 Pet 1:17) and as an aorist third singular to refer to God's good desire to do something for his purposes (Matt 12:18; Luke 12:32; 1 Cor 1:21; 10:5; Col 1:19). The verb occurs in different tenses to refer to God's lack of good favor toward the one who turns away from faith in Jesus (Heb 10:38). Thus, in accordance with God's desire for Paul prior to his birth, God decided to set apart Paul for the purpose of gospel ministry to the Gentiles.

Paul describes God's setting apart of him as a calling through grace. This is the second time Paul refers to calling in chapter 1. In 1:6, he expresses shock the Galatians turn from the one who called (*kalesantos*) them by the grace of Christ to another gospel. Now, he asserts God separated him from his mother's womb and called him through grace (*kalesas*). Both the Galatians and the apostles received a divine calling from God. This calling in 1:15 is an effectual calling that created life in Paul.

---

76 For a defense of a Jer 1:5 echo, see Sandnes 1991: 61, 63–64. Das (2014: 130n67) pointed me to Sandnes.

77 Similarly Das 2014: 131. For Paul as the personification of Israel's universal mission to the Gentiles, see Windsor 2014. Windsor primarily focuses on Romans.

The Galatians were called in the realm of God's saving grace through Christ (1:6). Paul was called into the realm of God's saving grace through Christ for the purpose of prophetically announcing good news amongst the Gentiles (i.e., non-Jews).

For years, scholars have argued the tired thesis that Paul did not convert to a new religion but God called him to a new purpose.[78] In my view, Paul was called-converted. That is, he was prophetically called to announce the good news about Jesus amongst the Gentiles. And this calling made him part of a new predominately Jewish movement (at least when God called-converted him) known as Christ-follower. Thus, he was called-converted.

This point seems highly probable based on the way Paul contrasts his previous life in Judaism in 1:13–14 with his calling to preach/announce Christ as the good news amongst the Gentiles in 1:15–16. He would not have made this announcement prior to the Damascus Road vision. In fact, if one takes seriously Acts as a reliable historical source, Luke seems to present Paul's calling to the Gentiles as a conversion to a new way of life because, prior to Damascus, he persecuted the assembly of God and, after Damascus, he preached Jesus as the Christ (cf. Acts 7:58—8:3; 9:1–22). Furthermore, Paul states the God who separated and called him from his mother's womb did so because he desired to "reveal his Son in me so that I would announce him as good news amongst the Gentiles." Like Jeremiah, Paul was called to be a prophetic witness amongst the Gentiles. Unlike Jeremiah, Paul was converted to Jesus to announce him as the good news of salvation to the Gentiles.

Paul identifies Jesus as God's Son in Gal 1:16. More than one Jewish source uses the phrase Son of God as a titular reference to the Messiah (4QFlor I.10–13 on 2 Sam 7:14; 1QSa II.11–12; 4Q246; 4 Ezra 7:28–29; 13:32; 14:9).[79] "Son" also appears in 2:20, 4:4, and 4:6. Paul has already identified Jesus as Lord and Christ (Gal 1:2; cf. Paul's use of Christ in 1:22; 2:16, 21; 3:13; 6:12), who dies "for our sins to deliver us from the present evil age" (1:4). In 3:13–14, he asserts Christ died to "redeem us from the curse of the law" so that we would receive the Spirit. 4 Ezra explicitly states the Messiah will die before the final day of judgment (4

78 For a representative of this view, see Dunn 1993: 65–67. However, Dunn uses the language of conversion when he refers to the account of Paul's "conversion" in Acts and when he discusses Paul's transformed "perception" of Christ. For a helpful discussion in defense of conversion, see DeSilva 2018: 145–47.

79 Summary comes from Das 2014: 133. See also Longenecker 1990: 31.

Ezra 7:29). 4 Ezra calls the redeemer-figure God's Son (7:28–29; 13:32, 37, 52; 14:9). Paul conflates the identities of God's Son and the Messiah into one human identity and associates Jesus' messianic status as God's Son with a redeeming death for Jews and Gentiles on a Roman cross (Gal 1:4; 2:20; 3:13; 4:4–5; 6:12).[80]

God's revelation of his Son in Paul was given for the purpose of commissioning Paul to announce Jesus Christ (God's Son and the seed of Abraham) as God's good news to Gentiles to bring about their inclusion within Abraham's offspring (Gal 3:1–29). God's revelation of Jesus in Paul and his calling/conversion/commission to the Gentiles was the moment when he realized God's universal promise of blessing to Abraham is fulfilled in Jesus (cf. Gen 12:1–3; Gal 3:8, 14, 16, 28–29).[81] Paul's emphasis is on God's "activity and movement" in his life.[82]

Paul received his gospel from God by means of a revelation from God (1:12). In 1:16, he describes that revelation as a revelation of the Son "in me" (*en emoi*). By "in me," Paul likely means God's revelation about Christ did something in him. Namely, this revelation transformed him so that he would preach God's Son as the good news to the Gentiles (cf. 1:11–14).[83] In 2:20, Paul says Christ lives in him with the same phrase as in 1:16.[84] As a result of Christ living in Paul, he lives by faith in the Son of God (2:20).[85] In 4:6, Paul also says God sent his Spirit into "our hearts."[86] God's revelation of Jesus in Paul was an apocalypse that inwardly both transformed him and set him apart to announce the good news to the Gentiles (Gal 2:19–20; cf. 2 Cor 4:6).[87]

The moment when God revealed his Son in Paul as the good news for the Gentiles, Paul "died to the law through the law so that he would live to God" (Gal 2:19a). He also became "crucified with Christ" as Christ

80 Das 2014: 133. However, contrary to Das, my explanation emphasizes that Paul conflates Jesus' identity as the Christ and God's Son in Galatians into a singular statement about the redeeming death for Jews and Gentiles on a Roman cross in light of 1:4 and 3:13.

81 Against De Boer 2011: 91. He emphasizes Paul's conversion, not calling.

82 De Boer 2011: 91.

83 De Boer 2011: 91.

84 Longenecker 1990: 32.

85 Longenecker 1990: 32

86 Longenecker 1990: 32.

87 Similarly Dunn 1993: 64; Jervis 1999: 45; Eastman 2007: 35n28; Das 2014: 132–33. Contra Martyn 1997: 158.

began to live "in" him (*en emoi*) (2:20). God's revelation of Christ in Paul concurrently happened when God "poured out the Spirit of his Son into our hearts" (4:6; cf. Jer 31:31–33; Ezek 36–37).[88] God's work "in" Paul to the Gentiles through God's revelation of Jesus Christ was a reason the churches in Judea glorified God "in" Paul (*en emoi*) (1:24).

In 1:16, Paul uses a cognate verbal form (*apocalyptō*) of the noun revelation (*apocalypsis*) in 1:12. When the verb takes God as its subject, it speaks to heavenly mysteries being unveiled by God to those upon the earth (LXX Dan 2:22). This appears to be the meaning in Gal 1:16a. Along with the verb *euaggelizōmai* in 1:16b, *apocalypsai* in 1:16a speaks to God's invasion of the current cosmos from heaven by means of a revelation of his exalted Son in Paul. This invasion of the Son into the cosmos resulted in Paul's announcement of Jesus as the good news of salvation to the Gentiles. Paul directly identifies Jesus as the good news by making "him" (*auton*) the direct object of the verb *euaggelizōmai* ("I preach/announce good news," cf. Rom 1:1–2; 15:18–20). Paul's remarks here shed light both on the "gospel of Christ" in 1:7 and on the reason he is so puzzled the Galatians contemplate a serious turn from it: namely, God revealed in Paul from heaven Jesus as the good news for the Gentiles (1:15–16; cf. 1:1). The implication is God did not reveal from heaven to Paul the Torah as the good news to the Gentiles.

In 1:16b, Paul states he did not consult with flesh and blood after he received God's vision of his Son. Of course, Paul consulted with flesh and blood in general after God revealed himself in Paul. Ananias baptized him; he preached the gospel in Damascus, and disciples of Jesus helped him escape the city when Jewish opposition to the gospel arose there (Acts 9:10–25). Rather, he means his gospel did not originate with man. He did not even consult the pillars who were apostles before him (Gal 1:17 ["apostles before me"]). Paul did not have a well thought out set of criteria for what qualified a person to be an apostle at this point in his ministry. But he seems to suggest here that because he saw the risen Lord and followed him, he was an apostle with the same authority as those who preceded him (cf. 1 Cor 9:1–7; 15:5, 7, 9).

God's revelation of Jesus Christ "in" Paul led him to announce the good news amongst the Gentiles, not to consult with "flesh and blood" (i.e., the pillars) (Gal 1:16). Paul confirms this point in 1:17 by adding that he did not go up to Jerusalem to consult with any of the original

88 For a similar point, see Das 2014: 132–33.

apostles. Instead, he went to Arabia and again returned to Damascus. Arabia refers to the Nabatean Kingdom.[89] This kingdom extended from "Damascus to the Gulf of Aqaba" (Jos. *J. W.* 5.159).[90] King Aretas IV ruled this kingdom (cf. 2 Cor 11:32).

After Paul's trip to Arabia, he returned to Damascus, a city within the Nabatean Kingdom (Gal 1:17). He made both trips before he went to Jerusalem three years after his trips to Arabia and Damascus. He mentions these journeys because he wants the Galatians to understand his gospel comes from God. This autobiography both highlights his gospel is equally superior with the pillars' gospel, although he did not receive it from them, and provides a testimony about God's activity in his life.[91] His emphasis in 1:13–2:10 is he neither received his gospel, his call, nor conversion as an apostle from any man, but from God. Since Paul participated in missionary activity before he went to visit the pillars (cf. Acts 9), he likely went to Arabia to preach the gospel there.

Paul visited Cephas (=Peter's Aramaic name [cf. John 1:42; 1 Cor 1:12; 15:5]) for a period of fifteen days in Jerusalem so that he would become acquainted with him. This visit likely included many important theological conversations about the gospel and about Jesus (Gal 2:7–10). But the visit added nothing to Paul's apostolic calling or gospel. Paul went up to Jerusalem three years after his initial encounter with Christ and after his trips to Arabia and Damascus (1:18).[92] While he was there, he did not see any of the apostles, "except James, the Lord's brother" (1:19). The most interesting statement in this verse is Paul's designation of James, the Lord's brother, as an apostle.

Of course, one could read 1:19 to say Paul neither saw another apostle but he saw James, who was not an apostle.[93] Paul could also mean he saw none of the other apostles with the exception of seeing James, the Lord's brother, who was also an apostle.[94] The latter is the most likely interpretation.[95] Just as the resurrected and exalted Jesus Christ appeared to

89 Das 2014: 136.

90 De Boer 2011: 95–96.

91 On the latter point above, so De Boer 2011: 91; Barclay 2002: 139.

92 A few commentators have argued that ancient witnesses support that Cephas and Peter were different people. For the discussion of the Cephas-Peter debate, see sources in Das 2014: 139n112. But rightly Das on this issue.

93 Das 2014: 141–42.

94 Das 2014: 141–42.

95 Das 2014: 142.

Paul after the resurrection, so also James saw him after the resurrection.[96] Both were, therefore, qualified to be apostles as a result of their encounter with the risen Christ (cf. 1 Cor 15:7). James' post-resurrection encounter with Jesus uniquely qualified him as an apostle along with the original apostles, who followed Jesus before the resurrection.[97]

To validate his autobiography, Paul takes an oath and calls God as his witness (1:20). As Das points out, the Hebrew Bible permits oaths in the name of the Lord to support the truthfulness of a statement (Deut 6:13; 10:20).[98] He continues oaths also rhetorically functioned in the Greco-Roman world "outside of the courtroom" but in legal contexts to warn someone that one would "stand trial" to defend the veracity of his claims (Quintilian, *Inst.* 5.6.1–2; 9.2.28).[99]

Paul continues his autobiography in the following verses. He mentions his trips to the districts of Syria and Cilicia (1:21). He continued to advance the gospel he received from God independently of the Jerusalem apostles. Paul confirms this in 1:22 with his acknowledgment that the assemblies in Christ in Judea did not know him. They did not know Paul in Judea because he spent no time there after he received his gospel from God and Jesus. Instead, the assemblies in Christ in Judea only heard Saul of Tarsus, the former persecutor of the church, "now is announcing as good news the faith that he was formerly attempting to destroy" (1:23). As a result, the assemblies in Christ in Judea glorified God in Paul.

Paul's statement here might initially seem problematic, for his persecuting activity included Jerusalem, which was in Judea (Acts 7:58—8:3; 9:1–3). Paul was not entirely unknown to the churches in Judea. Rather, he was unknown by sight ("I was ignorant to the face with respect to the churches in Judea.") (Gal 1:22). These churches had never personally become acquainted with Paul face to face as he had personally become acquainted with Peter face to face during his fifteen day visit to Jerusalem after his three year preaching ministry (Gal 1:18). Yet, the churches in Judea knew of Paul's previous reputation as a persecutor of the church and his proclamation of the same faith he formerly persecuted (1:23). They praised God because of the work he had done in him (cf. 1:13–14 with 1:22–24). The pillars affirmed Paul's gospel fourteen years after he

96 Das 2014: 142.

97 See also deSilva's (2018: 161–65) discussion of James.

98 Das 2014: 142.

99 Summary from Das 2014: 142.

began preaching it (2:1–7). Likewise, the churches of Galatia, predominately Gentile congregations that personally knew Paul, should praise God, embrace his message, and resist the message of the trouble-makers in Galatia.

Paul's gospel is attached to the Gentile mission. His gospel and his Gentile mission came from God. This good news about Jesus and the announcement that Paul made would certainly include the universal blessings that his cross and resurrection distribute to all the families of the earth (1:1, 4; 2:15 — 5:1). Paul's argument is a sharp rhetorical move to set his opponents against his gospel and his gospel against his opponents in order to dissuade the Galatians from turning away from his gospel. Paul's insistence that his apostleship and gospel come from God instead of from man (1:1, 10–14), his amazement that they were in danger of turning away from his gospel (1:6), and his attack of the opponents' gospel as a perversion of the gospel of Christ (1:7) work together with 1:15–21 to emphasize the authority of his gospel over the opponents' perverted message.

Galatians 2

Defense of the Divine Origin of Paul's Gospel, cont. (1:1—2:10)

Paul's Gospel Comes from God, not Man, cont. (2:1–10)

Paul continues his brief autobiographical discussion to highlight his gospel comes from God and not man and to evoke a response of faith from the Galatians (2:1–10). This extended autobiographical discussion serves his rhetorical argument against the opponents. They preach a perverted message (1:7), which focuses on circumcision, distinct from Paul and the pillars of the church. After discussing the events that took place after he encountered Christ (1:13–22), Paul now discusses the events that took place "after" fourteen years. Some interpreters occupy themselves with what Paul means by fourteen years. Is it fourteen years after his encounter with Christ, fourteen years after his fifteen day visit with Peter three years after his encounter with Christ, or do the fourteen years generally refer to the time frame from his encounter with Christ until the second visit to Jerusalem for a private visit with the pillars of the assembly.[1]

Nevertheless, Paul asserts again his gospel comes from God, not man, and that his encounter with Christ and his gospel ministry amongst the Gentiles preceded all of his meetings in Jerusalem with those who were apostles before him. The Jerusalem pillars received his gospel when he presented it before them during his second Jerusalem visit without imposing circumcision on his missionary colleague Titus, although he was Greek. As Paul says, "But not even Titus . . . was compelled to be circumcised although he is Greek" (Gal 2:3)!

To the contrary, Paul argues sneaky, "false" brothers were the only ones who imposed a message of circumcision upon Titus and upon Paul's gospel (Gal 2:1–4). From Paul's perspective, the "false brothers"

---

1 Of course, nailing down a specific time frame is important for Pauline chronology. But, in this commentary, my focus is on the meaning of these verses in the argument in which they occur in the text. For a detailed Pauline chronology, see Riesner 1997. For a discussion of the different perspectives of time, see Das 2014: 161–63.

identified with the Christian community ("brothers"), but they were not truly part of the in-Christ community ("false"). Rather, they were "false brothers."[2] Paul's remarks in 2:1–10 serve to persuade the Galatians to see his gospel is from God; the opponents' gospel is not. The Galatians, therefore, should turn away from their gospel and return to his gospel that he received from God, preached to them, and that they originally received by faith. By calling them "false brothers," "spies," and by accusing them of wanting to enslave those who were free in Christ from the law, Paul rhetorically disparages those who enforced circumcision on Titus to set his opponents in Galatia against his gospel and to align them with the "false brothers." Just as the "false brothers" in Jerusalem advocated a false gospel with respect to the circumcision of Titus, Paul's opponents preached a distorted and false gospel with respect to the circumcision of the Gentile Christians in the assemblies of Galatia (cf. 1:6–7).

Paul and the other apostles preached a message they received from God and Jesus. Their gospel focused on non-Torah-observance for Gentile Christ-followers. Paul's gospel is superior to the opponents' distorted and false message precisely because he received it from God and Jesus. As a result, the Jerusalem pillars did not impose circumcision upon his gospel to the Gentiles. The proof of this is Titus, converted through Paul's ministry (Titus 1:4), a partner with him in the gospel (2 Cor 2:13; 7:6, 13–14; 8:6, 16, 23; 2 Tim 4:10), and present with him in Jerusalem when he presented his gospel to the pillars of the church in Jerusalem (Gal 2:1–3).[3]

Paul conveniently mentions he took Titus (an uncircumcised Greek) up to Jerusalem with him to meet the pillars when he presented before them his gospel (2:1–3). But, although Titus was an uncircumcised Greek,[4] the pillars of the Jerusalem in-Christ assembly did not compel him to be circumcised (Gal 2:3). Rather, "false brothers" compelled him to be circumcised (2:4). However, neither Paul, Barnabas, or Titus nor the pillars yielded to the "false brothers" ("not even for an hour") (2:5).[5] The "false brothers" persistently compelled Titus to be circumcised. But

2 Against Nanos 2002b: 61–68.

3 Das 2014: 163; Schreiner 2010: 122–24.

4 Das asserts Paul uses the term "Greek" here to refer to "the entire civilized world" (cf. Rom 1:14, 16; 2:9–10; 3:9; 10:12; 1 Cor 1:22, 24; 10:32; 12:13; Gal 2:3; 3:28; Col 3:11). Das 2014: 169.

5 See Das 2014: 157–58 for a discussion of the textual variant that would offer an alternative reading. Rightly, however, Das 2014: 157–58. See also Moo 2013: 139.

Paul resisted their pressure, so that gospel truth would remain "with you" (2:5). The phrase *pros humas* could be translated as "for you" or "with you." Every other occurrence of this phrase in Galatians refers to association and should be translated as "with you" (4:18, 20; cf. also 1:17–18; 2:14).[6]

Private Jewish compulsion of Gentile-circumcision was not widespread in Second Temple Judaism. Terence Donaldson discusses numerous Jewish texts suggesting Gentile sympathizers to the Jewish way of life neither needed to receive the mark of circumcision nor should become proselytes in order to participate in the age to come.[7] But there are also examples where Jews did compel Gentiles to be circumcised and that Gentiles yielded to this private compulsion.

Eleazar, a Jew, compelled Izates, a Gentile king, to receive the mark of circumcision after he embraced a Jewish way of life (Jos. *Ant.* 20.33–45). Eleazar's compulsion of this Gentile king served to correct Ananias, a Jew, who told Izates that he could be devoted to the Jewish way of life without receiving the mark of circumcision since to do the latter would hurt him politically in his Gentile kingdom (Jos. *Ant.* 20.33–42). Izates (a Gentile) thought he could not be fully devoted to a Jewish way of life without the mark of circumcision, but Ananias urged Izates that he could if he worshiped the true God of the Jews since worship of the true God was "a greater lordship than being circumcised" (Jos. *Ant.* 20.41). Eleazar (a Jew) privately compelled Izates to be circumcised when he saw him reading the law of Moses. He accused Izates of failing to practice the law of Moses in the proper way since he did not receive the mark of circumcision (Jos. *Ant.* 20.44). He suggested failure to be circumcised was "ungodliness" (Jos. *Ant.* 20.45). When Izates heard this, he immediately

---

6 The preposition possibly means "with" or "for" in 2:14 when Paul rebukes Peter, Barnabas, and the other Christ-following Jews for their failure to walk in a straightforward manner with the truth of the gospel when Peter compelled Gentile Christ-followers to live a Jewish manner of life. Similarly, 2:5 likely means Paul and Barnabas and the pillars stood firmly against the "false brothers" so that all Gentile Christ-followers, like the Galatians, would not lose the gospel truth by taking on Torah-works. Paul even asks in 5:7 "who hindered you not to be persuaded by the truth." The interpretation offered here fits with Paul's earlier remarks that God revealed his Son in him to preach Jesus as good news amongst the Gentiles (1:16). The above interpretation fits well with the reason Paul went up to Jerusalem with Barnabas and Titus: namely, to present to them his gospel that he preached to the Gentiles (2:2). Paul's gospel had nothing to do with compelling Gentiles privately to be circumcised.

7 For primary sources, see Donaldson 2007 and Bird 2010.

went to a private room, summoned a physician, and received the mark of circumcision (Jos. *Ant.* 20.46).[8]

As scholars have pointed out, interpreters of Galatians should remember that in the ancient world, circumcision was neither only a religious rite nor were Jews the only ones who practiced it (Jos. *Ant.* 1:214; 8:262; Philo, *QG* 3.48).[9] Still, circumcision was an important mark of Jewish identity and the Abrahamic covenant (Gen 17).[10] Circumcision eventually became part of the Mosaic covenant (Lev 12:3). The mark of circumcision would have been visual in the Greco-Roman world if one bathed in public or participated in the athletic games (cf. Jason the high priest, who persuaded Antiochus IV to permit him to build a gymnasium in Jerusalem [1 Macc 1:11–15; 2 Macc 4:7–15]).[11] Some Jews even tried to undue their circumcision with *epispasm* to avoid public ridicule (cf. 1 Macc 1:15; T. Mos. 8:1–3; Suetonius, *Dom.* 12.2).[12] Athletes today compete in uniforms, but they competed in the nude in the Greco-Roman world (cf. Jub. 3:30–31; 1QS 7:14–16; Philo, *Flacc.* 36–40).[13] Jewish circumcised flesh (as well as Gentile un-circumcised flesh) would have been exposed before all to see during the baths and athletic games.[14]

Receiving the mark of circumcision in the Greco-Roman world brought shame and honor upon some who received it. According to Das, Strabo (first century BCE), the famous Greek historian and geographer, asserted that circumcision was a "superstitious" perversion of the "Jewish faith."[15] Other notable Greco-Roman authors criticized the Jewish rite of circumcision (Horace, *Sat.* 1.9.68–74; Petronius, *Satyrica* 68.8; 102.14; Martial, *Epigrams* 7.30, 55, 82; 11.94; Juvenal, *Sat.* 14.99).[16] Even Philo (a Jewish philosopher) records some non-Jewish groups ridiculed Jews for

---

8 Josephus (*Life* 113) also speaks of Jews compelling Gentiles by force to be circumcised. Bernat (2010: 473) pointed me to this reference in Josephus. The story of Joseph and Aseneth shows a Gentile can live a Jewish way of life without circumcision in the case of Aseneth (a Gentile woman). See also Das 2014: 172.

9 Bernat 2010: 471–74.

10 For primary texts, see Cohen 1999: 39–49; Barclay 1996: 438–39.

11 Kerkeslager 2010: 402–3; esp. 403; Eliav 2010: 432–34.

12 E.g., see Das 2014: 6n23 and 7n26.

13 Primary sources cited in Das 2014: 6.

14 Das 2014: 6.

15 Strabo, *Geogr.* 16.2.37; 16.4.9. Das 2014: 6n24.

16 Paraphrased from Das 2014: 6n23.

receiving the mark of circumcision (Philo, *Spec.* 1.1).[17] According to Das, citing Troy Martin,[18] this ridicule appears to have come in part because certain non-Jewish observers of the circumcised Jewish males thought the rite made them appear to be perpetually aroused sexually (cf. Martial, *Epigr.* 7.30.5; 11.94; Tacitus, *Hist.* 5.2).[19] As David A. Bernat points out, the Testament of Moses hints at the persecution of Jews because of circumcision and their attempt to erase the mark of circumcision by *epispasm* (T. Mos. 8:1–3; cf. 1 Cor 7:18).[20]

As Bernat points out in his article on circumcision, many Jews fought valiantly to continue to practice the right of circumcision (1 Macc 2:46). Jewish literature tells of many Gentiles receiving the mark of circumcision because of their fear of the Jewish God (LXX Est 8:17). Appropriating Gen 17, Jub. 15:25–34 asserts males not circumcised on the eighth day are outside of God's covenant with Abraham and would be destroyed from the earth. Jubilees says even angels were circumcised from the day of their creation (Jub. 15:27).[21]

Bernat further discusses there are also statements about the importance of circumcision in the Qumran literature. Citing Jubilees, the composer of CD 16:6 asserts "Abraham circumcised himself." The *Hodayot* suggests the uncircumcised man would not pass upon "God's holy path" (1QH 14:20). Pseudo-Philo possibly suggests Moses had the mark of circumcision when asserting Pharaoh's daughter looked upon the covenant of Moses' flesh (LAB 9:13–15). In retelling the narrative of Josiah's reform, 2 Baruch states the king had "every Israelite" circumcised (2 Bar. 66:5). In the Odes of Solomon, the Holy Spirit circumcises the Psalmist (Odes Sol. 11:2).[22] Bernat also suggests other Jewish texts highlight failure to be circumcised would result in eternal judgment (Jub. 15:33–34).[23]

Bernat points out 1 Maccabees (second century BCE) is the earliest place where the terms "covenant" and "circumcision" are synonymously used.[24] A reason the Hasmoneans, led by Mattathias and his son

---

17 Das 2014: 7n26.

18 Martin 1999: 87–89.

19 Paraphrased from Das 2014: 7n24.

20 Paragraph influenced by Bernat 2010: 472–73.

21 Bernat 2010: 472.

22 Bernat 2010: 472–73.

23 Bernat 2010: 472.

24 Bernat 2010: 472.

Judas Maccabeus, revolted against Antiochus Epiphanes IV is because he prohibited Torah's prescription of circumcision (1 Macc 1:48, 60–63; cf. 2 Macc 6:10; 4 Macc 4:25; Jos. *Ant.* 12.253–56; *J.W.* 1.34).[25] 1 Maccabees also sharply criticizes renegade Jews who forsook the laws of Torah and refused the mark of circumcision (1 Macc 1:13–15).[26] The Hasmoneans, who represented a violent form of Judaism similar to Paul's (cf. 1 Macc 1–2 with Gal 1:13–14), even forced uncircumcised males to take the mark of circumcision (1 Macc 2:46).[27]

Yet, Paul has a very different view of circumcision. In Christ, it no longer matters (cf. 5:6; 615). In fact, according to Paul, to receive the mark of circumcision is an "anathema" (1:8–9). As a result, the Jewish and circumcised, Christ-following pillars of the assembly of God did not compel "even" Titus, an uncircumcised Greek, to be circumcised as a prerequisite for his inclusion within the people of God when he accompanied Paul to present his gospel to them (Gal 2:3).

Instead, because Paul's gospel was from God, centered on the cross and resurrection of Jesus Christ, and shared the same content as the pillars' gospel (Gal 1:1—2:10), they added nothing to but affirmed Paul's non-Torah-observant gospel to the Gentiles when he went up to Jerusalem fourteen years after his conversion and after his first missionary journeys (2:9). Paul does not appear to have a problem in Galatians with circumcised Christ-following Jews, who would have already been circumcised prior to their faith in Christ. Rather, he forcefully contends that circumcision is absolutely unnecessary for Gentiles as a mark of covenant inclusion within the family of Abraham or as a necessary mark for those who have been redeemed by the Christ and who have received all of the soteriological privileges of that redemption (Acts 15:1–11; 21:25; Rom 2:25—5:5; 1 Cor 7:17–20; Gal 1:4; 3:13–14; 5:1–15; 6:11–18; Eph 2:11–22; Phil 3). Paul likewise argued that in Christ, circumcision is no longer the covenantal mark for Christ-following Jews (5:6; 6:15). Jews and Gentiles experience justification before God and receive the Spirit by faith in the crucified and resurrected Christ (Gal 2:16—5:1; cf. Rom 2:1—4:25).

Bernat notes that while affirming Paul's understanding of circumcision, Christian literature post-dating the NT developed an anti-Jewish

---

25 Bernat 2010: 472–73.

26 Bernat 2010: 472.

27 Bernat 2010: 472.

polemical tone against circumcision to emphasize its irrelevance for the people of God. The *Epistle of Barnabas* (second century CE) contends circumcision is "evil and false" (*Barn.* 9:3–4).[28] According to Bernat, in his *Dialogue with Trypho*, Justin Martyr suggests circumcision is a mark of both God's rejection of the Jews and the Jews' rejection of God. He also says circumcision serves as evidence that the Jews rightly suffer under Roman domination (*Dialogue with Trypho* 16; 19).[29]

Without an anti-Semitic polemic, Paul still sharply criticizes circumcision, stating in Christ Jesus, neither circumcision nor un-circumcision is anything (Gal 3:28; 5:6; 6:15). His gospel de-emphasizes circumcision as a necessary mark of the people of God and proclaimed the mark is altogether unnecessary for Gentiles to be included within Abraham's family. The strongest evidence of this in Gal 2 is the statement "but not even Titus was compelled to be circumcised although he is Greek" (2:3)! As discussed above, Josephus tells us Izates was compelled to be circumcised (Jos. *Ant.* 20.33–42). 1 Maccabees tells us the Hasmoneans compelled Jewish boys to be circumcised (1 Macc 2:46). But the Jewish pillars of the church did not "even" compel the Greek Titus to be circumcised when Paul presented him before the pillars along with his Gentile-inclusive gospel (Gal 2:3).[30]

The reasons Paul likely took Barnabas with him to speak to the pillars of the church were prudent. He was Paul's strongest supporter, a trusted co-worker, and a partner in the gospel (Acts 13:1—14:28). Barnabas, after all, convinced the disciples of Paul's sincere devotion to the risen Lord (Acts 9:26–27).

But why does Paul mention he took Titus, a Greek, to consult with the Jewish pillars of the church? This was an important rhetorical move on Paul's part to win the Galatians to his gospel. He states he took an uncircumcised Gentile follower of Christ with him to show that the Jerusalem church associates with his non-Torah observant gospel. Paul wants to dissuade the Galatians from turning away from his gospel and from embracing his opponents' gospel, which emphasizes circumcision, by accentuating no one compelled Titus to be circumcised—not even any of the Jewish pillars of the Jerusalem church—when Paul took him up

28 Bernat 2010: 473.

29 Bernat 2010: 473.

30 For a recent monograph on a biblical theology of circumcision, see Deenick 2018.

with him on his trip to speak with the important parts of the Jerusalem assembly of God.

But there is another reason Paul took Barnabas and Titus with him: namely, "according to a revelation" (2:2). He states earlier he received his gospel through a revelation of Jesus Christ (1:12). He declares God desired to reveal his Son in him (1:16). Now, he states he went up to Jerusalem "because of a revelation" (*kata apokalypsin*) (2:2). He does not explain the nature of the revelation (whether directly from God or from God through a human agent).

Paul could refer here to the prophecy of Agabus (Acts 11:27–30). Barnabas and Paul were together when Agabus gave the prophecy about a famine in Jerusalem. The elders of the church in Antioch sent Paul and Barnabas to Jerusalem with some financial assistance for the saints who would suffer poverty and hunger due to the famine (cf. Gal 2:10). Paul could be referring to the revelation of some Jewish Christ-followers in Judea who came from James and upset the Gentile brothers by saying they needed to be circumcised and keep the law of Moses in order to be saved (Acts 15:1–2).

Regardless of the agent or the means of Paul's "revelation," based on the way Paul uses revelatory words in Galatians, we can assume the "revelation" was a divine "revelation" from God (Gal 1:12, 1:16). Paul used the noun revelation or its cognate infinitive form ("to reveal") in the previous verses (Gal 1:12, 16). Paul could be referring to a revelation that Luke does not mention in Acts. This revelation could have revealed to Paul the need to go to Jerusalem, just as he received multiple revelations from Jesus about his safety (Acts 18:9–10) or about his mission (Acts 22:21). The Lord often revealed to Paul unusual visionary experiences (2 Cor 12:3). Paul's point is God told him to go up to Jerusalem.

Once Paul arrived in Jerusalem, the pillars of the church did not instruct him regarding the gospel. Instead, he privately presented to them the gospel he preached to the Gentiles (2:2), so that he would not be accused of running in vain. Paul did not receive his gospel from man or from any of the pillars of the Jerusalem church. Yet, he had to identify with the pillars at some point in his ministry since he could be falsely accused of preaching a contradictory and competing message from the one preached by Jesus' very first followers.

Paul uses the phrase "in vain" (*eis kenon*) elsewhere in his letters (2 Cor 6:1; Phil 2:16; 1 Thess 3:5). In Phil 2:16, he uses the phrase along with the same verb (*edramon*) as he uses it in Gal 2:2. As in Gal 2:2, Phil

2:16 emphasizes the authenticity of Paul's gospel. If Paul's ministry was in vain, he would have been an opponent of the ministry of the Jerusalem pillars.

But, because he received his gospel from God and Jesus instead of from man, he was a fellow co-worker with them. His participation in the gospel with them and his mission to the Gentiles with this same gospel are two reasons he needed to go up to Jerusalem to present his gospel to them. The pillars affirmed his gospel, but the sneaky, "false brothers" crashed the meeting with false pretense and "compelled" Titus to be circumcised (Gal 2:3). The verb "compelled" (*anagkazō*) is always used negatively in Galatians to refer to Jewish pressure to impose circumcision onto non-Jewish Christ-followers (Gal 2:3, 14; 6:12). In some Jewish sources, this verb refers to Gentile pressure to compel Jews to forsake a Jewish way of life and to embrace a comprehensive form of Hellenism (cf. 2 Macc 6:1; 7:1; 4 Macc 5:2, 27). And, in every occurrence in Galatians, an external group is putting pressure on someone to do something against one's volition (Gal 2:3, 14; 6:12).

Contrary to some early interpreters,[31] Titus remained uncircumcised and none of the pillars of the assembly in Jerusalem put pressure on him to receive the mark. Paul's point is not that Titus willingly received circumcision without being compelled to do so. This interpretation smacks in the face of Paul's criticism of the sneaky, false brothers who seem to have hijacked Paul's private meeting with the pillars with the intent to compel Titus (and all Gentiles) to be circumcised.

Moreover, interpreters who assert Titus was circumcised cannot adequately explain Paul's statement about the pillars not adding anything to his gospel or Paul's denigration of the status of the Jerusalem pillars in the face of the impartiality of God and his gospel ("I don't care what they formerly were; God does not receive the face of man" [Gal 2:1–6; esp. 2:6]).[32] They likewise ignore the force of the verb compelled in the rest of the letter (cf. 2:14; 6:12). If Titus was circumcised without being compelled, why should the Galatians resist circumcision when the opponents compel them? The pillars stood with Paul and his colleagues against the "false brothers" (2:7–9), giving to them the "right hand of fellowship." This latter phrase was an idiomatic pledge of friendship (Jos.

31 Robinson 1964: 24–42; Nock 1938: 118.

32 For texts about God's impartiality, see Gen 19:21; 32:21; Lev 19:15; Deut 1:17; 10:17; Sir 35:12–14; Jub. 5:16. Also in the NT Rom 1:18—3:20; Jas 2:1–7; 1 Pet 1:17. For additional primary texts, see Das 2014: 180n143. He pointed me to these texts.

Wars 6.318–20, 345, 356, 378).[33] They only requested he would help the poor (2:10), and Paul said he was eager to do this. If Paul would have yielded and compelled Titus to receive circumcision, his gospel would have been compromised and his law-free mission to the Gentiles would have been over.

Interpreters occupy themselves with whether Paul's visit preceded Acts 15, was the visit recorded in Acts 15, or a separate visit from the one recorded in Acts 15. Certainty on this issue is impossible. Six things are evident from 2:3–10. First, the fourteen-year visit was a private visit (2:2). Second, Paul visited the pillars "privately" so that he would not run in vain (2:2). Third, once Paul and his co-workers arrived in Jerusalem, the pillars did not compel Titus to be circumcised although he was an uncircumcised Greek (2:3). Fourth, false brothers sneaked into this meeting to spy out the liberty of the gospel in order to enslave Christ-followers (2:4). Fifth, the apostles added nothing to Paul's gospel but gave to him and Barnabas the right hand of fellowship once they observed the grace given to him as an apostle to the Gentiles (2:5–9). Sixth, the pillars "only" requested that Paul would help poor people, which he gladly consented to do (2:10; cf. 2 Cor 8:1–15).

The Divine Origin of Paul's Gospel, cont. (2:11–21)

A Misunderstanding of the Gospel at Antioch (2:11–14)

Paul continues to emphasize the divine origin of his gospel in 2:11–21. He rebuked Peter when he erected the dividing wall of Torah between Jewish and Gentile Christ-followers in that he withdrew from table-fellowship with them and in that he compelled them to become Jewish. In 2:15–21, Paul provides a reason why Peter should not compel Gentile Christians to become Jewish: namely, because Jews and Gentiles are justified by faith in Jesus Christ apart from works of the law.

Paul records the incident at Antioch to aid his argument against his opponents' Torah-observant and distorted message. This is supported by the following. First, Paul states Peter was condemned when he came to Antioch because he withdrew from table fellowship with Gentiles (2:11–12). Second, Paul mentions Peter's actions were hypocritical in that they

---

33 Longenecker 1990: 58. The idea of giving one's hand to signal accord occurs in the LXX to imply the submission of an inferior to the superior (LXX 1 Chr 29:24; 2 Chr 30:8; Ezek 17:18; Lam 5:6). For this material, see Longenecker 1990: 58.

were not in compliance with the gospel (2:13–14). Third, Paul arduously argues Jews and Gentiles are justified by faith in Jesus Christ apart from works of the law (2:15–16).

Paul opposed Peter to his face when he went down to Antioch because Peter stood condemned (2:11). Acts mentions two cities named Antioch: Pisidian Antioch and Syrian Antioch. Paul ministered in both places. Paul and Barnabas ministered in Antioch in Syria (Acts 11:27; 13:1), the capital city of Syria. Das, and others, observe that Antioch had approximately "250,000 people" and was "the third largest city" in the Roman Empire, following only Rome and Alexandria.[34] Das continues, because of its nearness to Jerusalem, there was a large population of Jews in the city.[35] Some have estimated "20,000 to 50,000" Jews lived in Antioch in the NT era.[36] Josephus confirms the Jewish nation was scattered throughout the entire world and it was very much "mixed together" with Syria in Antioch because it was "great and because of the greatness of the city" (Jos. *J. W.* 7.43, 45).[37]

Acts 11:19–26 states Jewish Christians scattered from Jerusalem because of Stephen's stoning. As they scattered, they preached the gospel to both Jews and Hellenists (i.e., Greeks). As a result, many Jews and Greeks believed the gospel and became part of the church at Antioch of Syria (Acts 11:21), where both Barnabas and Saul ministered prior to their first missionary journey (13:1).

The multi-ethnic nature of the community of Christ-followers in Antioch is likely one reason they first received the title of *Christianoi* in Antioch (Acts 11:26). The names listed in Acts 13:1 demonstrate the Christ-following community in Antioch of Syria was a mixed Jewish and Gentile community. Niger (=black), Lucius of Cyrene, which was the capital city of Libya (cf. Acts 2:10),[38] Manaen (possibly a Jewish man), and Barnabas and Saul (=Jews). Thus, some of the leadership within the Christ-following community in Antioch of Syria was a mixed Jewish and Gentile community and presumably possessing differing shades of skin

---

34 Das 2014: 200.

35 Das 2014: 200.

36 Hengel and Schwemer 1997: 189.

37 Also Hengel 1974; Barclay 1996. For additional sources, see Das 2014: 200n32.

38 Africa has a strong presence in the NT and in the development of early Christianity. Unfortunately, modern interpreters of Galatians often ignore this presence. For a commentary that prioritizes the presence of Africa in the NT, see Blount, Felder, Martin, and Powery 2007. For Christianity in Roman Africa, see Burns and Jenson 2014.

color. Paul confirms the ethnic diversity of the Christian community in Antioch in Gal 2:13 when he states Cephas (a Jew) led the rest of the Jews in Antioch of Syria into hypocrisy by withdrawing from table-fellowship with Gentiles. Paul further illustrates this ethnic diversity in Antioch by contrasting his natural Jewish identity with natural Gentile identity (2:14–15).[39]

Paul "opposed" Peter to his face when he came down to Antioch because he was condemned (2:11).[40] This opposition was a direct face to face confrontation between Paul and Peter. God does not care about the face of man (i.e., he is impartial) (2:6), and neither did Paul. This encounter must be understood within the honor and shame context in the Greco-Roman Mediterranean world of the first century.[41] Honor and shame were statuses given based on the perceptions of those within society about groups. Peter was reputed to be a pillar (2:2, 6) and likely had the status of honor from many within the Jewish Christ-following community because he witnessed the ministry and the resurrection of Jesus (cf. 2:3, 6; 1 Cor 15:1–8). This interpretation seems plausible since Barnabas and the other Christ-following Jews were led astray by Peter's hypocrisy when he stopped having table-fellowship with Gentiles (Gal 2:12–13).[42]

Yet, Paul says Peter stood condemned. Who condemned Peter: God, Paul, or both? Yes! Paul and God. The verbal statement "he was condemned" translates from the Greek verb *kataginōskō*. This verb occurs in the LXX (Deut 25:1), in Jewish literature (Sir 14:2; 19:5), and in the NT (1 John 3:20–21) to refer to the condemnation of someone. Additionally, Paul's remarks about Peter's condemnation in Gal 2:11 are embedded between two curse pronouncements of judgment. In 1:8–9, Paul pronounces an apostolic curse upon anyone (an angel or an apostle) who preaches another gospel different from the one he preached and received from God. In 3:10, he remarks cursed is the one who relies upon works of the law. Thus, Peter stood condemned by Paul and by God in Antioch because he advocated another gospel different from the one he and Paul

---

39 For an ancient example of hypocrisy, see Epictetus Diss. 2.920. Cited in Betz 1979: 110n474.

40 Cf. Deut 19:15.

41 For work on the honor and shame context of the NT, see deSilva 2000.

42 For a discussion of the honor and shame context of Paul's confrontation of Peter, see Esler 1998: 127–29, 132; Witherington 1998: 130. I do not agree with every element of the exegesis of Esler or Witherington.

received from God and because he was placing himself and the Gentiles under the curse of the law. Paul, however, asserts in 1:4 Jesus "gave himself for our sins to deliver us from this present evil age." He states further in 3:13 "Christ redeemed us from the curse of the law by becoming a curse for us." When Peter withdrew from table-fellowship with the Gentiles, he was erecting the wall of Torah between Jewish Christians and Gentile Christians. Consequently, he was placing himself and them under the law, which only leads to a curse (3:10), not to life (3:21).

Paul describes Peter's hypocritical actions in 2:12. Before "some from James came," he ate with the Gentiles. But, "when they came," he stopped because he feared "those from the circumcision." Jewish and Gentile Christ-followers were meeting together for worship and sharing meals together.[43] They did not have separate "ethnic" specific services in which these two groups were separated into their own homogenous group.[44] They were living as "one in Christ" (3:28).

This verse raises at least six exegetical and historical issues. First, why was Jewish and Gentile table-fellowship such a big deal? Second, was Peter eating with Gentiles in general or with Gentile Christians in particular? Third, who is the group from James? Fourth, who is the group from the circumcision? Fifth, why was Peter afraid of the circumcision group? Sixth, how did Peter compel the Gentiles to become Jewish: by his actions or by preaching another gospel? I answer each question in consecutive order below.

Jewish and Gentile relations in the Second Temple period were complex. The OT outlines strict food laws for Jews (Lev 11:1–47). Eating a meal with Gentiles represents associating with Gentiles. There were many Jewish and Gentile associations in the Second Temple period (e.g., Joseph and Aseneth). Certain associations with Gentiles were forbidden in certain Second Temple Jewish texts (e.g., Jub. 22:16–22; Let. Aris. 142). Sharing a meal with someone in antiquity had social implications for the participants (e.g., Philo, *Abr.* 107–14). For Jews, to share table-fellowship with Gentiles would have symbolized an acceptance of a Gentile way of life, whose way of life included idolatry (Jos. Asen. 8:5; 21:14–15; 4 Macc 5:2; LXX Dan 1:3–20; Jdt 10–12; esp. 12:1–4, 19; LXX Add Esth 14:17; 3 Macc 3:4–7; Jub. 22:16).[45] In Acts 10:28, Peter believed that it

---

43 So Das 2014: 206.

44 Similarly Das 2014: 206.

45 Das 2014: 224–25 points to these texts.

was forbidden for a Jewish man to associate with a non-Jew. Jesus showed him otherwise by telling him to eat unclean animals that are now clean in Christ, and when God poured out his Spirit on the Gentiles (Acts 10–11).[46]

One of the things that distinguished Jews from Gentiles was Torah/Mosaic law.[47] A Jew identified himself as a worshipper of Israel's one and true God by identifying with and obeying God's law given to his people after the Exodus (see Exod 20:2—Deut 33:29). Torah/the Mosaic law and Jewish appropriations of Torah in the Second Temple period suggest Jews and Gentiles should not mingle (cf. Jub. 22:16; Jos. As. 7:1). For example, observe the following statements, from the OT and from the Second Temple period, that forbade the Jews from eating or associating with Gentiles. I italicize the words that refer to Gentiles for emphasis in the texts below.

> When the LORD your God brings you into the land that you are entering to take possession of it, and clears away many *nations* before you, the *Hittites*, the *Girgashites*, the *Amorites*, the *Canaanites*, the *Perizzites*, the *Hivites*, and the *Jebusites*, seven *nations* more numerous and mightier than you, and when the LORD your God gives *them* over to you, and you defeat *them*, then you must devote *them* to complete destruction. You shall make no covenant with *them* and show no mercy to *them*. You shall not intermarry with *them*, giving your daughters to *their* sons or taking *their* daughters for your sons, for *they* would turn away your sons from following me, to serve other gods. Then the anger of the LORD would be kindled against you, and he would destroy you quickly. But thus shall you deal with *them*: you shall break down *their* altars and dash in pieces *their* pillars and chop down *their* Asherim and burn *their* carved images with fire. For you are a people holy to the LORD your God. The LORD your God has chosen you to be a people for his treasured possession, out of all the peoples who are on the face of the earth (ESV Deut 7:1–6).

> You shall surely destroy all the places where the *nations* whom you shall dispossess served their gods, on the high mountains and on the hills and under every green tree. You shall tear down *their* altars and dash in pieces their pillars and burn *their*

---

46 For an analysis of 2:15–21 within an apocalyptic and covenantal framework, see Bird 2016: 134–69.

47 This is one of the points I make in Williams 2012.

Asherim with fire. You shall chop down the carved images of *their* gods and destroy *their* name out of that place. You shall not worship the LORD your God in that way (ESV Deut 12:2–4).

After these things had been done, the officials approached me and said, The people of Israel and the priests and the Levites have not separated themselves from the *peoples* of the lands with their abominations, from the Canaanites, the Hittites, the Perizzites, the Jebusites, the Ammonites, the Moabites, the Egyptians, and the Amorites. For they have taken some of *their* daughters to be wives for themselves and for *their* sons, so that the holy race has *mixed* itself with the *peoples* of the lands. And in this faithlessness the hand of the officials and chief men has been foremost (ESV Ezra 9:1–2).

In his wisdom, the legislator, in a comprehensive survey of each particular part, and being endowed by God for the knowledge of universal truths, surrounded us with unbroken palisades and iron walls to prevent our *mixing* with any of the *other peoples* in any matter, being thus kept pure in body and soul, preserved from false beliefs, and worshipping the only God omnipotent over all creation (Let. Aris. 139). . . . So, to prevent our being perverted by contact with *others* by *mixing* with bad influences, he hedges us in on all sides with strict observances connected with meat and drink and touch and hearing and sight, after the manner of the Law (Let. Aris. 142).

Separate yourselves from the *gentiles*, and do not eat *with them*, and do not perform deeds like *theirs*, and do not become *associates* of *theirs*. Because all of *their* deeds are defiled, and all of *their* ways are contaminated, and despicable, and abominable. *They* slaughter *their* sacrifices to the dead, and to the demons *they* bow down. And *they* eat in tombs. And all *their* deeds are worthless and vain. And *they* have no heart to perceive, and *they* have no eyes to see what *their* deeds are, and where *they* wander astray, saying to the tree you are my god, and to a stone you are my lord, and you are my savior, and they no heart. But (as for) you, my son, Jacob, may God Most High help you, and the God of heaven bless you. And may he turn you from *their* defilement and from all *their* errors (Jub. 22:16–19).[48]

As the above texts highlight, Jewish and Gentile associations were complicated, because God uniquely chose Israel to be his people and separated them as his people with the dividing wall of Torah (cf. Eph

48 See also Tacitus *Histories* 5.5.1–2.

2:14–15).[49] Some Jews may have had more reservations than others about certain associations with Gentiles (Acts 10:11–20, 28–29).[50] However, it is interesting, though, that even in Acts, God must convince Peter (after Pentecost!) through a vision about clean and unclean foods that Jews and Gentiles can mingle in Christ (Acts 10–11).

However, an important clarification of the above is necessary. It is historically inaccurate to suggest Jews never associated with Gentiles in everyday life. There are numerous examples in Second Temple (Jewish and Christian) literature that positively mention Jew and Gentile relations within marital contexts (Joseph and Aseneth), within governmental contexts (Letter of Aristeas), and within shared religious/philosophical contexts (Acts 14:1–2). In Jewish sources, there are examples of both friendly Jewish and Gentile relations and strict separation.[51] Based on the complexities within Judaism, the hypocrisy of Jewish Christ-followers in Antioch did not represent what all Jews thought about Jewish and Gentile associations. Rather, they represented at least the view of those who came from James. The reason for which they came is not clear in Gal 2.

The issue at stake in Antioch was the very gospel itself (Gal 2:14), because Peter decided to abstain from associating with Gentile Christ-followers. Paul's response shows Peter that the gospel unifies. Paul esteemed the gospel big enough to permit "important cultural distinctions between Jews and Gentiles, in so far as those distinctions posed no threat to the fellowship of Jews and Gentiles."[52]

Paul states nothing specific about the kind of food they were eating. Peter could have been eating kosher Jewish food to maintain his witness in non-Christ following Jewish communities or in Christ-following Jewish communities continuing to wrestle with how to relate to Christ-following Gentiles. Appropriate food, however, at this particular meal is likely too if many of the Christ-following Gentiles in Antioch were God-fearers prior to becoming followers of Christ.[53] The issue might not have been the meal but the Jewish and Gentile participants at the meal. Perhaps this is why Paul rebukes Peter and accuses him of not walking in a straightforward manner in the truth of the gospel (2:14). Namely,

49 For more primary texts, see Barclay 1996 and Donaldson 2007.

50 Similarly Das 2014: 226.

51 For a discussion and primary texts, see Das 2014: 227–30. These pages in Das influenced my thoughts in the entire paragraph.

52 Braxton 2007: 336.

53 So also Hays 2000: 232.

Peter broke table-fellowship with Gentile Christ-followers and compelled them to live a Jewish way of life out of fear because they were Gentiles, not because of the meal served. As one scholar famously says the issue was not the "menu but the venue,"[54] and another says "not the cuisine but the company."[55] Besides, Paul says nothing specifically about the food.[56]

The specifics of the crisis in Antioch are hard to pin point because of the paucity of verses and information about the situation. Yet, the imperfect verbs in 2:12 *hupestellen* ("he was beginning to withdraw"), *aphōrizen* ("he was beginning to separate himself"),[57] and the present tense verb *anagkazeis* ("you are compelling") could suggest Peter's withdrawal from table-fellowship with and compulsion of the Gentiles was ongoing. His actions stressed the need for Gentiles in Antioch to receive the marks of Jewish identity because "he feared the circumcision party" before he would continue in table-fellowship with Gentile Christ-followers (2:12). Because of fear for the circumcision party, a fear created by the report of those from James, Peter urged Jewish Christians to disassociate from Gentiles unless they embraced Torah. The report led to fear and fear led to hypocrisy (2:13).

Gentiles in general seem to be the group from which Peter and the rest of the Jews disassociated. Paul does not specify where Peter was eating with the Gentiles. This encounter could have happened in the assembly of God, which would make these Gentiles Christian Gentiles. Or this separation could refer to general social interaction with Gentiles. Since Paul wrote the letter to the "assemblies of Galatia" (1:2), perhaps the crisis in Antioch happened in the context of the Christian assembly. Regardless, Peter withdrew from Gentiles because of his fear of the "circumcision party" (2:12).

Paul asked Peter when he separated from the Gentiles "why are you compelling the Gentiles to live a Jewish way of life" (Gal 2:14)? In the apocryphal texts of 2 Maccabees and in 4 Maccabees, the verb "to compel" (*anagkazeis*) refers to Antiochus Epiphanes IV's compulsion of the Jews to adopt a Greek way of life (2 Macc 6:18–31, esp. 6:1, 4; 4 Macc 5:2, 27).[58] Antiochus pressured the Jews with verbal threats and physical per-

54 I heard this phrase from Tom Wright.

55 I heard this phrase from Michael Bird.

56 For a detailed discussion of the different options and for detailed support for the same position I argue here, see Das 2014: 216–32.

57 Cf. LXX Mal 2:2–7.

58 For an additional example of the verb referring to intense pressure, see also 2

secution if they refused to assimilate fully within Hellenism. 1 Esdras 3:24 uses the verb to refer to wine's ability to pressure/compel sensible people to act and speak in foolish ways. In Ptolemy, History of King Herod, the verb refers to conquered and subjugated Gentiles who were "compelled" (*anagkasthentes*) to be circumcised and counted amongst the Jewish nation.[59] The context of these statements suggests these particular Gentiles were "compelled" by force.

Although compulsion by force to be circumcised is nowhere in this text, Paul's use of the verb *anagkazeis* ("to compel") likewise refers to intense pressure to live a Jewish way of life. In Gal 2:3, Paul states the pillars of the church did not compel Titus to be circumcised, "although he was a Greek." In Gal 6:12, he asserts his opponents were compelling the Galatians to be circumcised because of bad motives. The means by which the opponents compelled and/or pressured the Galatians to embrace circumcision and to live in a Jewish manner of life was by proclaiming the necessity of the circumcision of the Gentiles (e.g., 1:7–9; cf. 5:2–5). Paul emphatically states a gospel about circumcision is not a gospel (1:1—2:10). He no longer preached circumcision as gospel (5:11). If he preached the latter, he would not be a servant of Christ (5:11), but a servant of Torah (cf. 3:10–13; 4:21–31; 5:2–5) and a servant of a violent form of Judaism (1:13–14). Thus, in Galatians, the verb is associated with pressure to live a Jewish manner of life via circumcision, a pressure that comes by means of a proclamation that emphasizes the circumcision of the Gentiles. Peter was beginning to pressure/compel Gentiles with the same kind of proclamation as Paul's opponents. Both Peter's and their proclamation distracted from God's cosmological and salvation-historical work of fulfilling the promise of Abraham through his seed, Jesus Christ (cf. 1:4; 3:13–14, 16; 4:4–6).

Just as the opponents preached circumcision because they were afraid to be persecuted by the cross of Christ (6:12), so also Peter was afraid to be persecuted because of the cross of Christ.[60] The cross of Christ destroys the dividing wall of the law between Jews and Gentiles by ending the division between both groups (1:4; 2:18; 3:13). Peter wanted to erect that wall between Jews and Gentiles because he was afraid (cf. 2:18). In essence, he suggested Gentile faith in Jesus Christ was insufficient for

---

Macc 11:11.

59 Donaldson (2007: 373–74) pointed me to this reference.

60 Fear of the Jews was common in the gospel of John (7:13; 9:22; 19:38; 20:19). Texts cited in Betz 1979: 109n466.

inclusion within the people of God along with Jewish Christians. Instead, Peter, along with the opponents, those from James, the circumcision party, and the other Jewish Christ-followers in Antioch, suggested, at least indirectly, the Gentiles had to embrace the Mosaic law along with their faith in Jesus to be included as Abraham's offspring (contra 3:29).

Several statements in Galatians support this interpretation. First, Peter's actions led astray other Jews into hypocrisy—not Gentile Christians—in Antioch. The actions of Peter and the Christ-following Jews who followed them were hypocritical because they were contrary to what Peter believed to be true about Gentile Christ-followers and contrary to how he and the other Jewish Christians lived amongst Gentiles prior to those from James coming down to Antioch (1:18; 2:2–3, 5–10; cf. Acts 10–11). Peter knew one is justified only by faith in Christ (2:16), and he was living like a Gentile (2:14). But he was still "compelling" the Gentiles to live a Jewish way of life, while he was living a Gentile manner of life in Antioch (Gal 2:14). Jewish sources often "negatively use the word group" for hypocrisy to refer to deception (Let. Aris. 219, 267; Sir 32:15; 33:2; Pss. Sol. 4:20, 22; 2 Macc 6:21, 24; 4 Macc 6:15, 17).[61]

Second, Peter was not walking in a straightforward manner in the truth of the gospel. The truth of the gospel refers to the one gospel Paul received from God (Gal 1:1, 11–12). This is the gospel about Christ (1:7), the gospel that the opponents distorted (1:7), the gospel that God revealed to him (1:15–16), the gospel that he preached to the Galatians (1:8–9) and elsewhere (1:17, 21), and the gospel that Paul presented to the pillars of the church in Jerusalem (2:2) and with which they agreed (2:1–10).

Third, Peter's actions were hypocritical because he lived as a Gentile, although he was a Jew, while compelling the Gentiles to live as Jews (2:14). Peter "had the same theological convictions as Paul, but he did not dare to express them."[62] Fourth, Jews are Jewish by birth and not sinners by means of the Gentiles (2:15). Fifth, Jews and Gentiles are justified by faith in Jesus Christ apart from the works of the law (2:16). Sixth, the opponents preached a gospel of circumcision as the necessary mark for Gentiles to enter the community of faith (5:2–6; 6:12–13). As a result, the opponents' rival message downplayed the cross of Jesus (1:4; 2:21; 3:13), severed the Galatians away from God's saving grace in Christ (5:4),

---

61 Cf. Epictetus's remarks about a Gentile acting in a hypocritical manner because he was trying to be like a Jew. So Donaldson 2007: 390; Das 2014: 210.

62 So Betz 1979: 108. Against Schlier 1989: 84.

made them slaves under an apostolic curse (1:8–9), under the curse of the law (3:10–12; 4:21–31), under the present evil age (1:4), and under the demonic forces of evil (4:3–9).

When Peter was eating with the Gentiles, was he eating with Gentiles in general or with Gentile Christ-followers in particular? Of course, an answer to this question is neither obvious from Gal 2:12 nor can it be proven with any historical certainty. However, a case can be made that Peter was both eating and associating with non-Christ-following Gentiles in general outside of the assembly of God and with Christ-following Gentiles in particular within the assembly of God.

Paul uses the term *ethnē* most of the time in Galatians to refer to non-Jewish people (i.e., Gentiles) (2:8–9).[63] The term also refers to all people without ethnic distinction (i.e., Jews and Gentiles) (3:8, 14).[64] Paul uses this noun in the context of discussing the superiority of his gospel (1:11—2:10). The verb "he was eating" (*sunesthien*) could suggest in context that Peter regularly associated with and ate with all types of Gentiles.[65] Peter likely encountered non-Christ-following Gentiles as he lived in multi-ethnic Antioch. Based on the impact of Peter's actions on Jewish Christians, he probably associated with both Gentile Christians and non-Christian Gentiles on a regular basis both within the context of the church and without the context of the church. This table-fellowship could have happened within house-churches or over ordinary meals in the homes of non-Christian Gentiles.[66]

A reason why his associations with Gentiles are so troubling to those from James and a reason why his Gentile associations provoke fear within him is because he had altogether discarded Torah as a dividing wall between Jews and Gentiles by sharing table-fellowship with them (Acts 2, 10). He embraced Christian Gentiles as social equals without requiring them to live a Jewish way of life prior to the James group's arrival

63 For a discussion of ethnos, ethnicity, and race in Paul and early Christianity, see Byron 2002; Kimber Buell 2005, Hodge 2007; Sechrest 2009.

64 For a discussion of ethnos in Paul, see Scott 1995.

65 In Joseph and Aseneth, Joseph did not eat with (*sunesthien*) the Egyptians (i.e., Gentiles) (Jos. Asen. 7:1).

66 The above conjecture seems plausible based on Paul's associations with Gentiles in Acts (Acts 10). He met with the church in Antioch of Syria for an entire year and taught many people (Acts 11:26). Unless he participated in social functions with non-Christian Gentiles, he could not have reached them with the gospel. Acts suggests Paul's missionary endeavors were usually formal (Acts 13:5), but also casual (Acts 16:13–33; 17:17; 18:6–8). This is true for Peter as well (cf. Acts 2, 10–11).

in Antioch. Close social interaction between Jews and Gentiles would have been unacceptable with non-Christian Jewish resistant movements back in Judea,[67] or with Jewish Christians prior to the Jerusalem council (Acts 15).[68] Paul's gospel message required him to associate with Gentiles if he wanted to reach them with the gospel of Jesus Christ and to maintain association with them once they became part of the church. God, after all, revealed his Son in Paul "so that he might proclaim him as good news amongst the Gentiles" (Gal 1:15–16). Paul states Peter accepted the message of "some from James" and broke fellowship with the Gentiles "because he feared those from the circumcision" (2:12).

But who was the group from James; who was the group from the circumcision, and why was Peter afraid of the circumcision group? Each of these questions has different answers from an impressive list of scholars.[69] In my view, the group from James and those from the circumcision were not the same group.[70] The James group consisted of Jewish Christians. Those from the circumcision group consisted of non-Christian Jews back in Judea, from where (Judea) the James group came. Several arguments support this.

First, in Paul's autobiographical defense of his gospel in 1:11—2:10, he positively portrays James and those associated with him. Neither James nor the pillars enforced circumcision on Titus, but "the false brothers who sneaked in secretly to spy out the freedom" that the gospel provides for Jews and Gentile alike in Christ (2:2–4). But neither Paul nor the pillars yielded to the pressure of the false brothers (2:5). To the contrary, the pillars gave Paul and Barnabas the right hand of fellowship after they saw that God entrusted him with the truth of the gospel (2:6–9). Their only request of Paul was that he should continue to help the poor, which he was eager to do (2:10). Thus, James and the pillars are in direct opposition to the false brothers who opposed circumcision on Titus. This suggests at both the exegetical and historical levels that the false brothers in 2:4 are more closely aligned with "those from the circumcision" in 2:12 than James and the pillars since the latter groups gave Paul the right hand of fellowship.

67 On this point, see Jewett 1971: 198–212.

68 See Das 2014: 207–8.

69 For a discussion, see Das 2014: 206–7. See also De Boer 2011: 133.

70 So Schreiner 2010: 143–44. However, Das (2014: 207) points out that these groups could overlap with one another since Acts mentions a circumcision party within the Christian community in Judea (Acts 15:1, 5).

The designation "those from the circumcision" refers to non-Christian Jews (Rom 4:12), Jewish Christians (Acts 10:45; 11:2; Col 4:1), and to false teachers (Titus 1:10). In Gal 2:12, the phrase refers to non-Christian Jews who were likely aligned with a resistant form of non-Christian Judaism similarly to Paul's before his conversion.[71] If this is correct, then both Paul's and Peter's gospel would smack in the face of non-Christian Jewish perceptions of social interaction with the Gentiles since it focused on the unity of Jews and Gentiles in Christ apart from Torah-observance (2:7–9).

Prior to his calling-conversion, Paul aligned himself with a form of Judaism that was marked by violent zeal (1:13–14). Such zeal can be traced back to Phinehas (Num 25) and to the Hasmonean dynasty (1 Maccabees). A goal of Jewish resistant forms of Judaism was to maintain Jewish identity by strict observance of Torah, and by violence if necessary (cf. Acts 8–9; Gal 1:13–14). This in part meant resisting Jews sympathetic toward Gentiles (Acts 7:58—8:3; 9:1–2) or resisting Gentile movements that threatened Jewish particularity (1 Macc 1–2). Jerusalem eventually became a difficult place for the gospel to flourish due to the Gentile-inclusive nature of the gospel (cf. Acts 6, 8–9). Around the time that Stephen was stoned, Paul was violently persecuting the church and then converted (Acts 7–9; Gal 1:13–15).

Various Jewish resistant movements were contemporary with Paul's ministry and with his writing of Galatians.[72] These movements arose in response to the oppression of Jews both within and outside of Judea (cf. Jos. *Ant.* 20.97–117).[73] If the phrase "those from the circumcision" refers to a non-Christian resistant form of Judaism in Judea,[74] then Peter's fear

71 On the resistant movement as a zealot movement, see Jewett 1971: 198–212. Alternatively, see rightly Schreiner 2010: 144. He asserts the circumcision group was unbelieving Jews who persecuted Christians.

72 See Das 2014: 229–30.

73 Apart from identifying one of Jesus' disciples as a zealot (e.g., Simon, the zealot [Luke 6:15; Acts 1:13]), the NT is silent about this movement. Information about the zealot movement in first century Judea largely comes from the Jewish historian Josephus, a self-proclaimed Pharisee (37–100 CE). The violence of the zealot movement, along with additional resistant movements in Judea (e.g., the *sicarii* [Jos. *Ant.* 20.186]), reached a climax between the years 66–70 CE when the zealot movement took arms against fellow Jews, who did not fight with the zealots for liberty against the Romans (Jos. *Wars* 2.651; 4.160–579). The result of this conflict was the destruction of Jerusalem and its temple by the Romans in 70 CE.

74 Contra Hays 2000: 234.

could relate to his physical well-being and the well-being of other Jewish Christians. Peter does not appear to have a reason to fear fellow Jewish Christians from James since James, Peter, and John affirmed Paul's gospel by giving to him the right hand of fellowship and by adding nothing to his gospel (Gal 1:18—2:10). Thus, I cautiously maintain the following: (1) the group from James and the circumcision group were not the same. (2) The group from James consisted of Jewish Christians from the Jerusalem church. (3) The circumcision group was possibly a non-Christian, Jewish group concerned with living a Jewish way of life in compliance with Torah.

Once Paul saw Peter's actions were not walking in a straightforward manner in the truth of the gospel and that the rest of the Jewish Christians—even Barnabas—were being led away by their hypocrisy (i.e., going along with "someone else's agenda" to please them [cf. 1:10]) (2:13–14),[75] he rebuked Peter in the presence of all (i.e., in the presence of Jews and Gentiles). He reminded Peter that although he was a Jew, he had been living as a Gentile and not as a Jew. Peter was living a Gentile manner of life as a Jew (2:14). Paul informed Peter publicly and in the presence of both Jews and Gentiles that he was, therefore, wrong to compel the Gentiles to live like Jews.[76] Peter's actions suggested the Gentiles were not part of Abraham's family because they lacked Jewish identity (i.e., "works of law") (cf. Gal 2:15–16).

Peter's actions would have been correct prior to the incarnation, cross, and resurrection of Jesus Christ. But in Antioch, his behavior was wrong because it perverted the truth of the gospel and made vain Jesus' death, just as the opponents were doing by preaching works of law in the assemblies of Galatia (cf. Gal 1:4, 6–9; 3:13; 6:12). Peter's actions also contradicted Paul's gospel, which proclaimed that Jesus fulfills all of the promises of God to Abraham and his descendants (3:1—5:1). In Paul's view, Peter's actions represented "the effective preaching of anti-gospel in the midst of the Antioch church."[77]

For Paul, Jewish and Gentile unity in the gospel was not a peripheral social issue or secondary to the gospel. Just as Paul had to resist privately the false brothers' compulsion of Titus to be circumcised in Jerusalem because this was related to the truth of the gospel (2:5), so also Paul had

75 Similarly Hays 2000: 234.

76 For texts about compulsory circumcision, see LXX Est 8:17; Jos. *B.J.* 2.454, 463. Additional texts cited in Betz 1979: 112n497.

77 Hays 2000: 234 citing Martyn 1997: 235.

to resist publicly Peter's resistance of table-fellowship with Gentiles in Antioch because it was related to the truth of the gospel (2:14).[78] Jew-Gentile relations and Christian unity in Christ were important elements of his gospel. And, as we will see, Jew-Gentile relations and Christian unity are two reasons Paul introduces justification by faith in Gal 2:16 for the first time in the letter. Because of Peter's actions toward the Gentile Christians in Antioch, Paul reminded Peter of the impartiality of the gospel by rebuking him with a theological lecture on justification by faith (cf. 2:15–21).

Fusing the Horizons: Ethnic and Racial Division in the Church is Anti-Gospel

Since the birth of the Christian movement in first-century Judea, the church of Jesus Christ has struggled with ethnic unity. NT scholars disagree whether the term race is an accurate term to apply to the Jewish-Gentile division we see in the NT since the modern term race has a long and complicated history referring to a biological fiction of a racial hierarchy and to a superior or inferior ontology of one racial group over another.

Even though there is not a direct one to one correlation between Jewish-Gentile division and modern day problems of ethno-centrism, racism, nationalism, tribalism, and other forms of ethnic and racial discrimination, the gospel of Jesus Christ has much to say about the reconciliation of all Jews and Gentiles in Christ through the gospel. Any form of racism, ethno-centrism, and other examples of racial or ethnic discrimination are out of step with the gospel of Jesus Christ.

Peter was not acting out as a racist in Antioch in the modern sense of the term. Nevertheless, he was prioritizing his Jewish identity over Gentile identity, and he made Jewish identity a pre-requisite for Gentiles before admitting them into full table-fellowship with Jewish Christians. Peter behaved this way because he was afraid.

Paul's rebuke of Peter reminds every Christian the whole gospel must always be the unifying force between ethnically diverse Jews and Gentiles, and the gospel must always take priority over our fear of man. Ethnic division and racism are wrong and out of step with the gospel of Jesus Christ, even if we are complicit in these things out of fear.

78 Hays 2000: 235.

Unfortunately, too often these "isms" and various forms of discrimination have been front and center in so-called Christian churches. Too often certain Christians have historically espoused vague aspirations about so-called unity in the church. Too often many Christian organizations build their empires by perpetuating the very discrimination it claims to hate. In certain streams of American Christianity, ethnic and racial unity means ethnic or racial homogeneity, political uniformity, or cultural assimilation. In other streams of American Christianity, certain people in churches quickly abandon pursuits of Christian unity when such unity challenges or requires them to negotiate or leverage their racial or ethnic privileges and power for the sake of unifying diverse people in Christ.

Political identity, racial identity, ethnic identity, social identity, educational identity, national identity, or any other identity, as important as they are, should always be lived out in light of our identity as Christians. Jews and Gentiles are justified the same way: by faith in Jesus Christ. When one group of Christians imposes their political identity or their ethnic or racial identities or class identities onto another group of Christians and then require those Christians to assimilate within their man-made identities before they grant them full membership in the Christian community, in Christian churches, or in leadership positions at Christian institutions or organizations, then Paul would state loudly and clearly that those Christians have walked away from the gospel.

Certain Christians and churches especially need to hear this word since for too long many Americans have equated a certain American political identity with Christianity, as well as confusing so-called cultural Christianity with first-century Jewish and Gentile Christianity. And some American Christians have wrongly excluded other Christians with certain political persuasions and with different racial, ethnic, national, and economic postures from Christian table-fellowship from the Christian table or they have out right sold out certain groups of Christians from different racial, ethnic, national, economic, or political persuasions to preserve their own racial, ethnic, national, economic, or political identities.

The gospel focuses on the death and resurrection of the Jewish Messiah, who died to redeem Jews and Gentiles from the curse of the law and to renew the cosmos. This means in part that every race, ethnicity, gender, class, national identity, and political identity can be justified by faith in Christ and experience genuine Christian unity with each other in the churches and can experience genuine transformation by the Spirit. One of the problems in current American Christian culture is that certain churches have lost the gospel, some because they deny the historical Jesus of the gospels and others because they have created Jesus into a middle-class American.

Other Christians simply do not understand the gospel, focusing only on the vertical while flat out ignoring the horizontal elements of the gospel. Other churches have prioritized unbiblical identities, minimized Christian identity, and have created the idol of celebrity Christian culture so that many Christian churches have become one big fragmented group of people who claim to follow Jesus while remaining out of fellowship with fellow Christians from different ethnic, racial, economic, social, and political groups. Once more, other churches have become nothing more than social or political organizational factories with no clear gospel message about the cross and the resurrection of Jesus Christ, justification by faith, repentance, or the need for an individual conversion experience. Gospel-less social organizations that disguise themselves as gospel-believing churches provide no eternal theological substance that will create both vertical reconciliation with God, horizontal reconciliation with others, and cosmological renewal based on the cross and the resurrection of Jesus. Paul teaches us in the crisis at Antioch that when Christians make the unifying gospel of the crucified, resurrected, and exalted Christ secondary and endeavor to compel sisters and brothers in Christ into our own ethnic, racial, national, economic, or political identities and require this kind of compulsion as a prerequisite to Christian table-fellowship with diverse believers in the church, we destroy any hope for Christian unity and walk away from the gospel of Jesus Christ. May God, the Father, Jesus Christ, our Lord, and the Holy Spirit help Christian churches far and near to walk in a straight forward manner in the truth of the gospel.

Justification by Faith in Jesus Christ apart from Jewish Works of the Law (2:15–21)

Gal 2:15–21 is an important section in the argument of Gal 2:11–21. Paul continues his remarks to Peter in Antioch. Unlike the contextual clue in 3:1 ("O' foolish Galatians") and in 3:15 ("brothers"), there is no explicit textual clue suggesting a different addressee. But 2:15 continues Paul's rebuke of Peter without any contextual signal of a change in the audience. If this is correct, Paul now moves from rebuking Peter's behavior to providing Peter a theological reason why he should not compel Gentiles to be Jewish. This theological reason is justification by faith in Christ apart from works of law (Gal 2:16).

Paul reminds Peter Jews are Jews "by nature" (*physei*) (2:15), i.e., by birth, "not sinners from Gentiles." He asserts elsewhere Gentiles are Gentiles "by nature" too (cf. Rom 2:27). Some Second Temple Jewish texts affirm a Gentile could become a Jew (LXX Est 8:17; Bel 1:28; 2 Macc 9:1–17, esp. 9:17; Philo, *Spec.* 1:51; Jos. *J.W.* 7.44), while others agree with Paul that one is a Jew by birth or descent (3 Macc 1:3; 4 Macc 18:1; T. Levi 15:4; Pss. Sol. 9:9; 18:3; cf. with Rom 11:1; Phil 3:5).[79] As he says in Romans, the Jews have an advantage over the Gentiles because they received the oracles of God in Torah (cf. Rom 3:1–2). But Jews are not sinners by association with the Gentiles (Gal 2:15).

Citing numerous primary texts, Das rightly points out that Jewish texts identify a sinner as a Gentile who does not follow Torah (1 Sam 15:18–19; Tob 13:6; Jub. 22:16–22; 23:23–24; Pss. Sol. 2:1–2; 4 Ezra 3:28–36; 4:23).[80] Das continues the Jewish scriptures associate sinner(s) with lawless behavior (LXX Ps 54:4; 91:8; 100:8; 124:3; 128:3; 118:53).[81] He demonstrates "righteous Jews" identified "fellow Jews" as sinners if they disobeyed Torah (Ps 58:10; Sir 7:16; 9:11; 1 Macc 1:34; 2:44; 1 En. 5:4–7; 1QH X [=II].8–12; 1QpHab V.4–8; Pss. Sol. 4:8; 13:6–12).[82] Sinner(s) would be synonymous with the ungodly (LXX Ps 1:1, 5–6) and antonymous with the righteous (LXX Ps 1:5–6).[83]

Other Jewish texts identify Jews as "lawless ones" (*paranomoi*) when they compromised their national identity by forming a covenant with the Gentiles (1 Macc 1:11; 11:21). 3 Macc 2:17–18 identifies Gentiles as "lawless ones" (*paranomoi*) because they trampled down the "house of sanctification." A lawless one was a sinner (Tob 4:17; Wis 19:13; Pss. of Sol. 2). A Jew could become a "sinner" when he or she either violated or forsook Torah (1 Macc 1:34), while Gentiles were identified as sinners because they were not the recipients of Torah (2 Macc 2:44). "Jews commit sins when they transgress Torah,"[84] but "Gentiles are sinners as

---

79 For Jewish sources, see Donaldson 2007.

80 So Das 2014: 239.

81 Das 2014: 240.

82 Das 2014: 239–40.

83 Das 2014: 239–40.

84 Betz 1979: 115.

Gentiles."[85] Thus, Paul's statement in Gal 2:15 sharply contrasts with what we find in the OT (Lev 11:1–47; Deut 7; Ezra) and in many Jewish texts. A sinner by definition was a Gentile (Sir 41:5–11), an unfaithful Jew (=an apostate), or one who mingles with Gentiles.[86]

Gal 2:15 seems to agree with those Jewish texts that affirm sinners are non-Torah observant Jews ("we are Jews by nature"). Paul pushes against ideas in numerous Jewish texts that both affirm one can become a Jew and that assert association with Gentiles makes Jews sinners when he tells Peter he is a Jew by birth. Then, Gal 2:16 provides a theological reason why Peter's actions were wrong: justification by faith in Christ apart from works of the law!

Gal 2:16 is a difficult verse.[87] It is an exegetical landmine ready to explode as interpreters step on top of each word. Questions of justification by faith, the faithfulness of Christ, God's covenantal faithfulness, imputation of Christ's righteousness, the infusion of righteousness, and the meaning of works of law arise because of this one verse. In 2:16, Paul states "we (=Jewish Christ-followers) believed in Christ Jesus because we know that a man is not justified by works of law but by faith in Jesus Christ."[88] The major and minor premises of the verse are separated as follows:

> 2:16c: [And] even we ourselves believed in Christ Jesus
>
> 2:16d: so that we would be justified by faith in Christ and not by works of law
>
> 2:16e: because no flesh will be justified by works of law
>
> 2:16a: Because we know that no one is justified by works of law
>
> 2:16 b: but [one is justified] by faith in Christ

---

85 Betz 1979: 115.

86 Das (2014: 239–40) influenced my thinking in this paragraph. For examples from Jewish sources, see Let. Aris. 139, 142; Jub. 22:16–18; 30:7; Pss. Sol. 2:2; Sir 36:2; 1QS; 4Q394 conflated with 4Q395.

87 For examples, see the critical commentaries on this verse.

88 For a detailed analysis of the important Greek terms with different conclusions from me, see Ziesler: 1972. He argues the verb "to justify" is "relational and forensic" in Paul and the noun "righteousness" and the adjective "righteous" are "behavioral and lead to a transformed life in Christ." Thus, Ziesler suggests justification by faith (in the relational and forensic sense) and behavioral righteousness are not identical in Paul, but they are inseparable. See Ziesler 1972: 1. For the faith in/of Christ debate, see Bird and Sprinkle 2009.

The major thought of the verse is both Jews and Gentiles must be justified by faith in Christ apart from works of the law. Paul highlights this major premise with an appeal to LXX Ps 142:2 (MT Ps 143:2). Paul explicitly universalizes this verse to include Jews and Gentiles by substituting *anthropos* ("man") for *zōn* ("living one").

Paul mentions justification for the first time here in Galatians in a context of Jewish and Gentile table-fellowship.[89] If Galatians is Paul's first canonical letter, then the earliest place justification occurs in the Pauline corpus is in the context of the problem of broken Jewish and Gentile table-relations in Antioch. The preceding observation has caused some scholars to argue justification in Galatians should be defined as a declaration of whether Jews and Gentiles can eat together.[90]

Gal 2:16 is emphatic because it mentions justification three times, possibly faith two times, possibly the faith of Christ one time, and it contrasts justification by faith with justification by works two times. These tautologies could suggest 2:16 is the most important verse of the entire section of 2:11–21. In 2:16, Paul provides the central premise and reasoning of 2:11–21. This premise provides the theological foundation as to why Peter's actions were wrong and as to why he was not walking in a straightforward manner in the truth of the gospel.

Hays asserts the verb translated as "to justify" in 2:16 "points not merely to a forensic declaration of acquittal from guilt but also to God's ultimate action of powerfully setting right all that has gone wrong."[91] He says justification refers to being "declared in the right or placed in right relationship to God."[92] Hays agrees that the term has a forensic or law court origin.[93] However, he suggests in "Israel's prophetic literature" and in the Psalms the term has an "eschatological connotation."[94] In the midst of suffering, the prophets and the Psalms look to YHWH as the "source of future vindication."[95] God will justify his covenant people "by rescuing them and overthrowing their enemies and oppressors" (cf. Isa 50:7–8).[96]

---

89 A point observed by many interpreters.

90 Wright 1991; 2013; Dunn 1993.

91 Hays 2000: 237.

92 Hays 2000: 237.

93 Hays 2000: 237.

94 Hays 2000: 237.

95 Hays 2000: 237.

96 Hays 2000: 237.

According to Hays, "justification is the eschatological act of God."[97] He concludes Paul, thus, refers to "God's world-transforming eschatological verdict as it pertains to individual human beings."[98] In response to Hays, there are at least four things I want to highlight about justification in 2:16.

First, the verb *dikaioō*, translated as "to justify," communicates the idea of a forensic divine verdict in God's law-court (cf. Rom 3:20–22, 24).[99] The verb occurs in contexts where the judge condemns the guilty to be in the wrong and declares the innocent to be in the right (LXX Deut 25:1; 2 Sam 15:4; 1 Kgs 8:31–32; Prov 17:15; Isa 5:23).[100] Paul excludes works from the verdict of justification in 2:16. Instead, he bases the verdict exclusively on faith as the means by which Jews and Gentiles lay hold of salvation in Jesus. Support for a forensic declaration in God's law-court is strong in Paul's letters.[101] I support my interpretation from Galatians.

In Gal 3:6, Paul uses a cognate noun (*dikaiosynē*, "righteousness") to affirm that Abraham's faith in God was reckoned to him as righteousness (cf. Rom 3:21–4:25). The noun comes straight from LXX Gen 15:6. There God reiterates the promise to Abraham from Gen 12:1–3 that he would both bless Abraham and the nations through him. Abraham, old and barren and married to an old and barren wife, did not ultimately know how God would fulfill this promise. Yet, by faith he believed God's promise in the presence of God. Consequently, God reckoned Abraham's faith in his promise to him as righteousness in his presence. Even if the legal/forensic background is not exactly the same in Gen 15:6 as in Gal 2:16 (cf. 3:6, 8), the forensic/legal context of the verb is strong in Gal 2:16 since Paul states one is justified by faith apart from "works of law" (=Torah observance) and since Paul uses the same verb in 3:11 to deny that one is justified in God's presence by works of law. Abraham believed God, and God gave him a righteous status before him because of his faith. Similarly, Jews and Gentiles have faith in Christ and God grants them a status of righteous in his law-court because of their union with Christ by faith (cf. 2:16–17, 21 with 3:6, 11, 21, 24; 5:5).

97 Hays 2000: 237.

98 Hays 2000: 237.

99 For my discussion of justification and works of law in Romans and an interaction with scholars, see Williams 2012: 66–87.

100 Das 2014: 245. Cf. also Matt 12:36–37; Pss. Sol. 2:34–35; 13:11–12; 14:1–3, 9–10; 15:12–13. Das 2014: 245n61. Schreiner 2010: 155-56; Moo 2013: 48-62; 160-63.

101 E.g., Rom 3:20–24; 5:1, 9–10. For recent work on justification, see Schreiner 2015. See also Moo 2013: 48–62.

Second, Paul associates justification with believing in Christ instead of doing works of law (2:16, 21). God declares sinners to be in the right by faith in his presence instead of by Torah-works. For Paul, faith is not simply acknowledging the veracity of facts. Instead, faith in Galatians is closely associated with an obedient walk in the Spirit (Gal 3:1–29; 5:16–26). This appears to be one reason Paul emphasizes those who walk in the Spirit (i.e., those who have been justified by faith) will inherit the kingdom of God (5:16–21; esp. 5:21). In Galatians, faith refers to one's commitment to God's saving action in Christ, a commitment that places one in the Spirit-empowered age (3:2–5; 5:16–26). Faith enables the justified to yield to Jesus in faithful obedience until the end of one's life or until the end of this present evil age (cf. 5:16–24). Faith and obedience are not the same for Paul (cf. 2:16; 3:2–5 with 5:16–24), but they are both inseparable soteriological realities (cf. 2:16 with 3:1—5:24). Without obedience, faith is absent (cf. 5:16–21). And without faith, walking in the Spirit is impossible since Jesus died to deliver Jews and Gentiles from the present evil age (1:4) and to bestow upon them the Spirit (3:14), which is the blessing of Abraham (3:14a).

Third, justification in Galatians is a future verdict that has invaded this present evil age. In 2:16, Paul mentions justification with a present tense indicative verb (*dikaioutai*), with an aorist subjunctive verb (*dikaiōthōmen*), and with a future indicative verb (*dikaiōthēsetai*). The present indicative and the aorist subjunctive are not communicating anything about the time frame of justification in the context of 2:16. The future verb could simply be a declarative future. But the future verb appears to affirm that justification is ultimately a future verdict declared at the end of history—with current realities in this present evil age—that God will pronounce in the judgment upon those who are united to Christ by faith (2:17, 21). This interpretation seems correct since Paul speaks of both a present (3:29) and a future inheritance in Galatians (4:1, 7; 5:21) and since he speaks of both the experience of the Spirit in the present evil age (Gal 3:1, 14) and of awaiting in the Spirit by faith for the future hope of righteousness/justification (5:5).

The future aspect of justification is supported by Paul's remarks later in the letter that "we await by the Spirit the hope of righteousness" (5:5). This hope of righteousness refers to the future certainty of justification, in which we participate now in this present evil age by faith in Jesus because of his death and resurrection (1:1, 4; 3:13–14, 29). Those who seek justification by law in the current age have been severed from Christ and have fallen from the grace of the gospel (5:4). Those who await the hope of righteousness do so by the Spirit (5:5). To identify righteousness/ justification as a future hope for which we await by the Spirit suggests the future verdict to be pronounced by God on the last day has already invaded this present evil age now through the indwelling presence of the Spirit in the life of the believer (cf. 3:1–14).

The Spirit testifies to the reality that God has imparted the Abrahamic blessing to Jews and Gentiles through Christ's death for them (3:13–14). Jesus' death has delivered Jews and Gentiles from this present evil age (1:4) and from the curse of the law (3:10–13, esp. 3:13). Those who will be justified are already the sons of Abraham and already have access to his inheritance by virtue of their identity in Christ (3:9, 16, 28, 29; 4:7). Yet, Paul speaks of the Abrahamic inheritance as a future inheritance for which we wait in the power of the Spirit as we walk in obedience (5:16–24, esp. 5:16, 21, 22–24).

Fourth, in Galatians, Jesus' death and resurrection achieve justification for those who believe in Christ. God raised Jesus from the dead (Gal 1:1), which assumes his death on the cross (1:4; 3:1, 13). Jesus gave himself "for our sins" to deliver us from this present evil age (1:4). Jewish and Gentile sinners are justified by believing in Jesus instead of by doing works of law (2:16). Jewish and Gentile sinners are seeking to be justified in Christ (2:17). Jesus' death requires righteousness to come by faith instead of by law (2:21). The Galatians experienced spiritual blessings by faith instead of by works of law (3:2–5). Jesus died to redeem Jewish and Gentile sinners from works of law so that both groups would inherit the Abrahamic blessing of the Spirit (3:13–14).[102] If the law was given to create life, then righteousness would come by means of law (3:21). Rather, justification is a forensic verdict whereby God declares Jews and Gentiles in Christ to be not guilty in the age to come, and that verdict has entered into history now by the indwelling power of the Spirit (3:14; 4:5–6; 5:5, 16–26).

Another important statement in 2:16 is the phrase "works of the law." The phrase "by works of law" modifies the verb in the statement "a man is not justified" instead of modifying "a man."[103] The former interpretation highlights a contrast of the origins of justification.[104] That is, "not by works of law a man is justified, but by faith in Jesus Christ" a man

---

102 For Wright's analysis of justification, see recently Wright 2013.

103 Against Seifrid 2003: 217–18; Caneday 2009: 194.

104 Das 2014: 242.

is justified demonstrates that even Jews must be justified by faith in Jesus the same as Gentiles.[105] This affirmation contrasts with the phrase "those from the circumcision" (2:12), with "not from Gentile sinners" (2:15), and with "those from faith" (3:9).

But if Paul wanted to make the phrase "not by works of law" descriptive of "man," he could have stated it more clearly than the way he expresses it in 2:16, as he does in 1:2; 2:12; and 3:9, with an article before the prepositional phrases and in 2:15 with a verb-less clause.[106] Paul's altered text of "living one" to "flesh" in his appeal to LXX Ps 142:2 (MT Ps 143:2) universalizes the verse to include Jews and Gentiles, while the emphasis is on the Jews' need to place faith in Christ to receive justification ("even we ourselves believed in Christ Jesus so that we would be justified by faith in Christ"). The connection with LXX Ps 142:2 links the latter part of Gal 2:16 with the preceding "because we know that a man is not justified by works of law." This connection with the Psalm also pairs the phrases "by faith in Christ and not by works of law" as adverbial modifiers of the statement "so that we would be justified" in 2:16c in order to universalize Torah's inability to justify Jews or Gentiles.[107]

The Psalmist relies upon God to justify him because he knows that no human life can stand righteous in the presence of God (MT Ps 143:1, 11–12; cf. 1 En. 81:5). Paul appropriates the portion about justification to support his primary objection to Peter's inappropriate actions in Antioch (cf. Gal 2:16). Later in Gal 3:1—5:1, Paul universalizes the promise of the Spirit, which fulfills the promise to Abraham and his seed, to include Jews and Gentiles who have faith in Christ (the seed of Abraham). Thus, the phrase "by works of law" modifies the verb "is not justified," so that Paul universalizes the statement to refer to the inability of the law to justify any person (Jew or Gentile).[108]

---

105 Similarly Das 2014: 243. In many Jewish sources, justification comes by works of law. Cf. 2 Bar. 2:2; 14:7, 12; 48:22; 51:3, 7; 63:3, 5; 67:6; 85:2. 2 Baruch says Abraham was justified by works (57:2; 58:1). In Tobit and Sirach, the giving of alms leads to atonement and some form of justification (Tob 4, 10; Sir 3:30; 12:3–7; 17:22; 29:11–13; 40:24). Primary sources in Ziesler 1972: 99–104. For a work arguing for justification by works in early Judaism and in Paul, see VanLandingham 2006.

106 In Galatians, Paul places an article before prepositional phrases to nominalize entire phrases as substantival (2:3; 3:9; 4:29).

107 Ziesler 1972: 99–104.

108 Against Garlington's partisan understanding of "from" (ek). See Garlington 2008: 567–89.

The phrase "by works of law" (*ex ergōn tou nomou*) is Paul's creation in the NT.[109] The phrase occurs in Galatians (Gal 2:16; 3:2, 5, 10) and in Romans (Rom 3:20) without parallel in any Greek text prior to or contemporary with Paul's letters. In earlier scholarship, commentators understood this phrase as a reference to legalistic, self-righteous Jews who sought to earn their way to heaven by keeping the law,[110] "fulfillments of commands,"[111] "duty of the law,"[112] or "comprehensive Torah-observance."[113] Since Krister Stendahl's famous essay in the 1960s and after E. P. Sanders's monumental work in the 1970s,[114] many Pauline scholars have forcefully argued against the legalistic reading of "works of law."[115] Michael Bachmann argues the phrase "works of law" does not refer to the "fulfillment of commands," but rather to the "regulations of the law themselves."[116]

The Dead Sea Scroll 1QS emphasizes the priority of divine action in justification. The scroll identifies God as "my righteousness" (X.13), affirms that God will be praised in distress because of "His salvation" (X.18), that "my justification is with God" (XI.2), that justification is the "source of His righteousness" (XI.6), that "justification is with God" (XI.11), that "justification shall be by the righteousness of God, which endures forever" if one stumbles (XI.13), that God will "judge by the righteousness of His truth" (XI.14–15), that he "pardons sins" (XI.14–15), and the scroll appeals to God to grant the elect to stand before him forever (XI.17). However, the closest ancient Jewish parallel to the phrase "works of law" in Gal 2:16 and the concept of justification occurs in the fragmentary Dead Sea Scroll known as 4QMMT.[117]

4QMMT was written by a leader(s) within the Jewish sectarian community to explain the works that members of the community must perform in order to remain in the community and to experience final

109 For my discussion of "works of law" in Romans, see Williams 2012: 85–87.

110 E.g., Lenski 1961: 104, 114, 119; Burton 1921: 120.

111 From Bachmann 1999: 3. See Bachmann also for scholars who affirm the above views.

112 Bachmann 1999: 3

113 Bachmann 1999: 3

114. Stendahl 1963: 199–215; Sanders 1977.

115 For a survey of scholarship on this issue, see Westerholm 2004.

116 Bachmann 1999: 9.

117 Cf. 4QFlor 1.7; 1QS V.21; VI.18; 1QH IX [=I].26; XII [=IV].31; 2 Bar. 57:2. Das 2014: 248 pointed me to these primary texts.

justification before God at the end of the age. The fragment overtly states God reckons righteousness to the faithful who do the works of Torah.[118]

Debate exists as to what these works of law refer.[119] Further debate pertains to the relationship of this scroll with Paul's remarks in Gal 2:16.[120] The fragment conspicuously states one's performance of works of law results in one's vindication before God at the end of the age. Commenting on the meaning of "works of law" in the sectarian community responsible for 4QMMT, James D. G. Dunn agrees the phrase "works of law" in Gal 2:16 refers to the Torah as a whole, "but in practice" circumcision, food laws, and Sabbath-keeping would prove one's covenant loyalty.[121] These so-called boundary markers are primary for Dunn's interpretation of "works of law."[122] These works also occur in Galatians (Sabbath-keeping [4:10], food laws [2:11–14], and circumcision [5:2, 11; 6:12, 15]).

Yet, in response to Dunn, even in 4QMMT, works of law refer to "immoral behavior" and to those things that are holy and good (4QMMT C 26–27).[123] This suggests works of law include behavior in addition to failure to appropriate the so-called boundary–marking features of the law.[124] Paul uses the phrase "works of law" as long hand for law in Galatians in general without special reference to certain boundary–markers within the law (cf. Gal 2:19, 21; 3:2—4:31; 5:3–4, 18).[125] Much could be said here about "works of law," but I limit my discussion to the following remarks below.[126]

The phrase "works of law" in 2:16 likely refers to the Mosaic law and the stipulations within it, because Paul refers to the need for the entire law to be kept (5:3) and because the second important place where the phrase "works of law" occurs after 2:16 is in 3:10–12.[127] In the latter text, the phrase refers to the deeds required in the Mosaic Covenant as a whole, without a tripartite division of civil, ceremonial, and purity.[128]

---

118 4QMMT=last paragraph in 4Q398 conflated with 4Q399. See also CD 3.14–25; 4Q215 a ii 2–7; 1Q22 2.7–10; 4Q171 2.13–14; Pss. Sol. 3:11–12; 14:2–3, 10; 15:5.

119 For a summary of the debate, see Westerholm 2004; Wright 2015.

120 Westerholm 2004; Wright 2015.

121 Dunn 1993, 1998: 136–37, 155.

122 Dunn 1993, 1998: 136, 155; 2007: 8, 22–26, 43.

123 So Das 2014: 249.

124 Similarly Das 2014: 249.

125 Das 2014: 249.

126 See also my discussion and citation of scholars in Williams 2012: 85–87.

127 Similarly Das 2014: 249.

128 Das 2014: 249; deSilva 2018: 224–27, esp. 227.

Paul suggests that for some Jews, these works were done in obedience to the law of Moses to maintain membership within the people of God, which they thought would have resulted in right standing before God at the end of the age.[129]

In 3:10–12, Paul cites texts from Deuteronomy (21:23; 27:26; 28:58; 30:10) and Leviticus (18:5). In the OT context, Deuteronomy repeats the stipulations given in Exodus, Leviticus, and Numbers and reminds Israel of the life promised to the nation if she obeys Torah in the land. God tells Israel more than once in the OT that obedience to the law results in life (Lev 18:5; 20:22; 25:18), but disobedience results in death (Lev 8:35; 18:5).[130]

Paul's opponents in Galatia seem to have an optimistic view of Torah and of man's ability to achieve the promise of life in it. They appear to have only emphasized circumcision, and perhaps a few additional laws (cf. Gal 2:11–14; 4:9–11), in their preaching to the Galatians as the necessary works they needed to perform to achieve the life promised in the law (Gal 5:2–5), while they ignored other aspects of Torah. Paul's response emphasizes the need for both the Galatians and the opponents to keep the entire law if they sought justification apart from Christ by works of law (5:2–6).

Paul's former Judaism prior to his encounter with Christ on the Damascus Road and the opponents' gospel seem to have two entirely different views of the role of Torah in salvation with respect to Gentiles. In his former manner of life in Judaism, Paul emphasized strict obedience to Torah to receive the life promised in Torah (Gal 1:13–14; 3:10–12; 5:3). However, it would be incorrect to describe Paul's strict obedience to Torah as legalism since by his own testimony he asserts he was keeping the law in accordance with his Jewish heritage (cf. Phil 3:5) and since there is no evidence in Paul's writings that he was seeking to keep the law in order to earn his way to heaven because of a "tortured conscience."[131] His strict Jewish way of life was for the purpose of maintaining covenant membership and to gain future participation in life in the age to come (cf. 1 Bar 4).[132] Paul eventually recognized in light of God's revelation of Jesus

129 See Rom 2:15; 3:20, 28; Gal 2:16; 3:2, 5; 1QS 5.8, 21, 24; 6.13–23; 8.4, 10, 20. Against Wright 1991: 237–38; Dunn 1993: 172. Rightly Moo 1983: 73–100; Schreiner 1984: 151–60; 1985: 245–78; 1993: 975–79.

130 For a discussion of these OT texts in Gal 3:10–12, see the critical commentaries on Galatians.

131 Stendahl 1963.

132 Soteriology in Second Temple Judaism was complex. For essays that highlight the complexity, see Gurtner 2011.

Christ that no one could achieve the life promised in the law by Torah-works (Gal 3:10–12). Perhaps the opponents assumed that after receiving the mark of circumcision, the Galatians would yield to additional Torah requirements. Paul likely emphasizes circumcision because that is what the opponents emphasized in their preaching. Paul's response is justification by faith (=the blessing of Abraham [Gal 3:8]) comes to Jews and Gentiles the same way: namely, by faith in Jesus Christ apart from works of law (2:16).

A third important issue in 2:16 is the meaning of the phrase "faith in/faith of Christ."[133] The two different translations communicate distinct interpretations of the Greek phrase *dia pisteōs Iēsou Christou*. As many scholars have observed, the first translation ("faith in Christ") takes the phrase as an objective genitive and suggests that one is justified by "faith in Christ" apart from works of law. The second takes the phrase as a subjective genitive and suggests that one is justified by the "faithfulness of Christ" apart from works of law. Some advocates of this view have suggested Jesus was the faithful Israelite, who faithfully fulfilled Torah so the Deuteronomic blessings would flow from Jesus to the nations.[134] Thus, Jews and Gentiles become children of Abraham when they believe in Christ because of Christ's faithfulness.[135]

I am not currently convinced one must choose between the objective or subjective genitive readings of *dia pisteōs Iēsou Christou* to discern the meaning of the verse. Instead, the issue is a matter of emphasis. Is Paul emphasizing faith in Christ versus works of law with *dia pisteōs Iēsou Christou* alongside of the verbal clause *episteusamen eis Christon Iēsoun* ("we believed in Christ Jesus")? Or is he highlighting Jesus' faithfulness, Messiah's faithfulness, as the one through whom God has fulfilled the Abrahamic promise for those who believe in Christ. Certainly, both ideas are true in the argument of Galatians (3:1–5:1). I think the phrase *dia pisteōs Iēsou Christou* accentuates faith in Christ versus works of the law as the means by which Jewish and Gentile sinners are justified.

First, Paul uses either the phrase "through faith in Christ" or "by faith in Christ" in Galatians (2:16; 3:22) and in Romans (Rom 3:22). Each time, he pairs the phrase "faith in Christ" with a verb of believing in a context where he contrasts doing works of law (Rom 3:22; Gal 2:16)

---

133 For essays about the debate, see Bird and Sprinkle 2009.

134 Wright 1991.

135 For this precise point, see Wright 1991; 2009, and 2013.

with faith or believing as the means by which one experiences justification (see Gal 3:21–22). The Greek noun *pistis* ("faith") and the verb "to believe" (*pisteuō*) are related to one another, which is not apparent in English translations.[136] The combination of "faith" and "believing" suggests Paul wanted the Galatians to understand the phrases in contrast to justification by works of law (=by doing).

Second, Paul uses the noun for "faith" (*pistis*) instead of the adjective "faithful" (*pistos*). *Pistis* likely means "faithfulness" in Gal 5:22. But there Paul mentions *pistis* as a fruit of the Spirit, whereas in 2:16 he contrasts *pistis* with works of the law. Third, Paul nowhere in Galatians explicitly discusses Jesus' faithfulness. Jesus' faithfulness is implied from Paul's remarks about Jesus' death "for our sins" (1:4), "for me" (2:21), and "for us" (3:13). Rather, Jesus is always either the object of faith (e.g., "we believed in Christ Jesus" [2:16]) or the object of a verb that expresses a faith experience (e.g., "as many of you who were baptized into Christ" [3:27]).

Paul expresses in 2:16 no one will be justified by works of law. Yet, he does not state the reason there. Instead, he explains the reason works of law do not justify later in 3:10—4:7 (esp. 3:10–12 and 3:19). Those of works of law are under a curse, because the law promises life only to those who obey (3:10–12). The law curses everyone under its jurisdiction (3:10). The law was given on account of transgressions (3:19). The law enslaves everyone under its jurisdiction (4:21–26). The law demands obedience (5:3).[137] The law is part of the present evil age (cf. 1:4; 3:15—4:7).[138]

A final interpretative issue in 2:16 is the meaning of the Greek particles *ean mē*. Das suggests there are at least "three different ways" to understand this phrase.[139] However, the third and preferred option is to understand *ean mē* as an adversative ("but") that modifies the entirety of the preceding verse: "because we know a man is not justified by works of law, but [he is justified] by faith in Christ." (brackets mine).[140]

136 See Das's helpful discussion in Das 2014: 250.

137 But no one can obey the law to the fullest in order to achieve the life that it promises (cf. Rom 2:13—3:20).

138 My arguments for the objective genitive are influenced by Schreiner 2010: 164–66, Dunn 1993: 138–39; deSilva 2018: 229–42; and Das 2014: 250–53. For a careful alternative reading, see Hays 2002.

139 For a discussion of the different views, their strengths and weaknesses, and the scholars who maintain them, see Das 2014: 253–54. So also Schreiner 2010: 163. My discussion relies upon Das and Hunn 2007: 281–90. But Das (2014: 254n105) criticizes Hunn for misrepresenting his view in Das 2000: 529–39.

140 DeSilva (2014: 42–43) agrees with my interpretation but argues for an

Admittedly, the third usage is rare in the NT (cf. possibly John 5:19; 15:4). Further, Paul does not appear to use these particles adversatively in his undisputed letters.[141] However, an adversative reading fits the context of Paul's argument in Gal 2–3.[142] He contrasts justification by works with justification by faith in Christ to show that these two paths toward justification (one law and the other faith) are mutually exclusive. This reading leads into Paul's remarks about justification by faith apart from the works of the law in the rest of 2:16. The particles *ei mē* are likewise similarly used in Galatians (Gal 1:7—"but it is not another gospel"; 1:19—"but I saw James, the brother of the Lord").[143]

In 2:17, Paul asks a rather puzzling question: "if while seeking to be justified in Christ we ourselves were found as sinners, then is Christ a minister of sin?" This is puzzling because it appears to enter into the text *de novo*. The verse uses the seemingly non-Pauline phrase of "seeking" to be justified, and it states those seeking justification in Christ are sinners but found not guilty (2:16). Paul's "may it never be!" in 2:17 seems a reasonable statement in response to the question whether Christ is a minister of sin. Paul's previous remarks to Peter that one is born a Jew and not a sinner by association with Gentiles in 2:15 support this interpretation. Additionally, his argument that Torah no longer separates Jews and Gentiles from table–fellowship because both groups are justified by faith in Christ apart from works of law in 2:16 seems to require a negative answer to the question in 2:17.

Justification "in Christ" apart from works of law leads Jews (and Gentiles) away from Torah-observance (2:16). The law curses those under its jurisdiction (3:10). A turn from the law would have caused some Jews to levy the charge of sinner against Jesus (cf. Matt 9:26; Mark 14:64; Luke 7:39; John 8:44; 9:16; 10:33) and against his apostles for preaching a non-Torah-observant gospel (cf. Acts 15). Jewish literature teaches the law leads to life (Lev 18:5; Bar 3–4), but the apostles preached faith in Christ (not the law) leads to life (Gal 3:12, 21). Faith in Christ as the basis upon which Jews and Gentiles are justified serves as the theological

exceptive understanding of the two particles. In agreement with me, see Schreiner 2010: 162–63. So also Hunn 2007: 289–90.

141   Rom 10:15; 11:23; 1 Cor 8:8; 9:16; 13:1; 14:6, 7, 9, 11, 28; 15:36. Texts cited in Das 2014: 253.

142   Longenecker 1990: 83–84.

143   Against deSilva 2014: 42–43. These particles could be understood in a different way.

underpinning to Jew and Gentile unity in the gospel. Justification by faith is antithetical to works of law (Gal 2:16; 3:10–12). Thus, one might conclude as a result that Jesus is a minister (servant) of sin because the gospel of Jesus ignores the Torah-established boundaries between Jews and Gentiles.

One might also think a turn from the law to Christ could, therefore, lead to a licentious lifestyle. This is perhaps one reason Paul spends time in the letter urging the Galatians to walk in the Spirit and not to use their freedom from the law as an occasion for the lust of the flesh (Gal 5:13–26). As I argued earlier, the very definition of a sinner in Second Temple Judaism was either a Gentile[144] or a Jew unfaithful to Torah.[145] An unethical lifestyle would relate to both Gentiles (2 Macc 2:44; 3 Macc 2:17–18) and unfaithful Jews (cf. 1 Macc 1:11, 34). Thus, the charge the opponents could have raised against Paul's gospel is that Christ is a minister of sin because he (per his apostolic messengers) leads Jewish Christ-followers away from Torah-observance, which inevitably leads to ethical anarchy.

Paul offers an emphatic "no!" to this question (2:17). Paul does not deny that "we" (=Jews) were found to be sinners while seeking justification in Christ in their pre-converted state. In fact, contrary to a Jewish understanding of sinner in Second Temple Judaism, Paul affirms Jews were sinners (2:17) (even Torah-observant Jews [3:10]; cf. Rom 3:23) and that Jesus died for their sins (Gal 1:4; 3:13). Jews needed to be liberated from the curse and slavery of the law (3:10—4:7) and from the present evil age (1:4). Those under the law are under the present evil age (1:4), under a curse (3:10), under sin (3:22), under slavery (4:1, 9, 21–25), and under the *ta stoicheia tou kosmou* ("the elemental principles of the world") (4:3). Those under the law will not inherit the kingdom of God (5:16–21) or participate in new creation (6:15). Because they sow in the flesh instead of the Spirit, they will not inherit eternal life (6:8).

Paul rather denies since Jewish sinners seek justification in Christ, this leads to the conclusion that Christ is a minister of sin. The justification of the Jews by faith in Christ is necessary because Jews are sinners under the law in this present evil age and need to be freed from all the effects of the present evil age upon the law. Jews and Gentiles, thus, need to be delivered from every aspect of the present evil age (cf. 3:1—5:1), including (but not limited to) the slavery of Torah (cf. 3:15—5:1). Jews

144 Jub. 22:16–22; Let. Aris. 139, 142.

145 LXX Deut 13:14; 2 Chr 13:7; 1 Macc 1:11; 10:61; 11:21; Sus 1:28, 32.

in Christ were legally/forensically found to be sinners prior to their justification in Christ and prior to the indwelling presence of the Spirit (Gal
3:10—5:26; cf. Sir 44:17; Rom 7:1—8:11; Phil 3:9).[146] But Christ is not a
minister of sin.

In 2:18, Paul grounds (*gar*) his premise in 2:17: "For if I build again
these things, which I destroyed, I commend myself to be a transgressor." The *gar* ("for") in 2:18 connects Paul's remarks in 2:17. In 2:15, he
uses the category of "sinners" to refer to Gentiles versus natural Jewish
identity and in 2:17 to refer to Christ-following Jews seeking justification
in Christ. Now, in 2:18, he refers to a specific kind of sinner: namely, a
transgressor.

A transgressor here refers to a transgressor of the law. A transgressor is a Torah-breaking sinner (3:19; cf. Rom 2:25; Jas 2:11). Paul would
be a transgressor of the law if he reestablished the law as the dividing
wall between Jews and Gentiles (cf. *Let. Aris.* 139–42; Jub. 22:16–22) and
turned away from the gospel, as Peter (Gal 2:11–14), as the opponents
(1:7; 4:17; 5:10; 6:12–13), and as some of the Galatians had already done
(1:6–7; 5:2–4).

The relationship between verses 17–18 is difficult to discern. One
interpretive option is that by the phrase "transgressor," Paul refers to devia-
tion from the gospel.[147] That is, to rebuild the law would mean "to transgress God's will in Christ."[148] Support for this view is Paul does not say
"transgressor of the law" in 2:18, and one could translate a cognate verb
(*parabainō*) of the noun "transgressor" (*parabatēn*) in 2:18 as "to deviate
from."[149] Further, 2:19 talks about co-crucifixion with Christ and death to
the law.[150]

However, Paul does not explicitly say to rebuild the law of Moses
is to "transgress God's will in Christ." Rather, Paul simply says to rebuild
what (=the law) he destroyed makes him a transgressor. The noun "transgressor" occurs in NT contexts to refer to transgressing the law (Rom
2:25; Jas 2:11; cf. Gal 3:19 for the noun "transgression"). Paul explicitly
refers to the works of the law three times in 2:16 and to the law twice in

---

146 Similarly Das 2014: 259; Schreiner 2010: 168–69.

147 For discussion of different interpretive options for 2:18, see Das 2014: 262–66.

148 Das 2014: 262–66; esp. 266.

149 Das 2014: 262–66; esp. 266.

150 Das 2014: 262–66.

2:19. Thus, one can extrapolate from 2:16–19 that "transgressor" refers to transgressing the law.

Paul's statement should be paraphrased in the following way: Christ is certainly not a minister of sin just because we Jews were found to be sinners and sought justification by faith in Christ.[151] Paul (an in-Christ Jew and other in-Christ Jews) would be a transgressor of the law on this side of the cross only if he placed himself under the curse of the law by turning away from the grace of Christ to another gospel (cf. 1:6–7; 2:21; 3:10—4:7; 5:2–4). If Paul (an in-Christ Jew) reestablished Torah as the requirement of membership within Abraham's family and lived his life by that standard and separated himself from the Gentiles because of that standard instead of living as an in-Christ Jew by faith apart from Torah in unity with Christ-following Gentiles, he would prove himself to be a transgressor of the law (=a sinner in the Jewish sense of the term) (2:18; cf. 2:17).[152] As he says later, "as many are from works of law are under a curse" (3:10), and as many are under the law are under sin (3:19–23). Sinners (2:17), transgressor (2:18), and law (2:19) suggest that sinners in this context are those who transgress the law of Moses. Jews were found to be sinners while they were seeking to be justified in Christ because they were under the law until they were found in Christ (2:16–17; 3:22–24; cf. Phil 3:4–10).

Christ delivered those seeking justification in him from the present evil age (Gal 1:4) and delivered Jews and Gentiles from the curse of the law to distribute to them the blessing of the Spirit by faith (3:13–14). Paul and all Jews and Gentiles in Christ are justified (2:16–17). He died to the law through a law, which could not give him life, when he was crucified with Christ (2:19; cf. 3:21), so that he would live (eternally) with respect to God. The law was neither a source of life nor was it ever intended to be. If it were, then God's saving righteousness would certainly be by means of Torah (3:21).

Paul's statements contrast with a Jewish perception of the law in Second Temple Judaism. Paul says rebuilding the law makes one a transgressor (2:18). Early Jews emphasized in different places that disobeying the law makes one a transgressor (1 Macc 1:11, 34; 3 Macc 2:17–19). Law observance promises and leads to life (Lev 18:5; Sir 1:12–28; 3:6; 17:11; 45:5; Bar 3:1—4:2). The author of 2 Macc 7:1–38 says Jews who fought

151 For a helpful discussion of 2:17, see Fee 2007: 88–89.

152 Schreiner (2010: 170–71) and Das (2014: 265–66) take a different view of the verse. Similarly to my view, so Moo 2013: 167.

and died valiantly in obedience to God's law will participate in the resurrection of life and partake of eternal life (2 Macc 7:14, 36). 2 Macc 14 states Razis, an elderly Jew accused of living a Jewish way of life, chose to die nobly by falling on his own sword instead of falling into the hands of Gentiles. As his first attempt at noble suicide failed, his rage moved him to jump off a wall onto the soldiers, rip his guts out, throw them onto the people, and pray to God that he would give them back to him again in the age to come (2 Macc 14:38–46). Razis went to this extreme because of his commitment to a Jewish way of life.[153]

This sort of confidence in the law is not unique to Second Temple Jews. Lev 18:5 promises life to the one who obeys the law. Deut 4:1 likewise promises obedience to the law leads to life (also Deut 4:10; 5:29–33; 6:1–2; 1, 18, 24; 7:12–13). Jews "live to God" by obeying Torah (4 Macc 7:19; 16:25).[154]

However, Paul says he died to the law through the law to live to God because of co-crucifixion with Christ (Gal 2:19–21). Paul's remarks that he died to the law "through the law" are difficult. He at least means that the law did not lead to life (2:19–21; 3:21). But he died to the law (i.e., he lived his life by faith in the Son of God) to attain the eternal life that Torah promised (2:20; 3:11, 21). Because of Christ, death to the law by co-crucifixion with him leads to eternal life both now (2:16, 19–21; 3:21) and in the age to come (2:16; 6:8, 15), not obedience to the law of Moses (3:10–12). Paul's death to the law via co-crucifixion with Christ does not make Christ a minister of sin (2:17–18). Co-crucifixion with Christ ushers in the age of the Spirit and enables all in-Christ people to experience eschatological life now in this present evil age, of which the law is part and from which Jesus died to deliver Jews and Gentiles, as they walk in the Spirit (1:4; 3:13–14; 5:16–26; 6:15). Paul's co-crucifixion with Christ makes him a participant in God's renewing of the cosmos through the cross and resurrection of Christ (cf. 1:4; 6:15).[155]

Co-crucifixion with Christ is a reference to his calling/conversion (1:15–16). This was the moment when God revealed his Son "in" Paul (1:15–16).[156] God led Paul away from his former, violent Jewish manner

153 Similarly Das 2014: 269.

154 Similarly Das 2014: 269.

155 Similarly Schreiner 2010: 170–71; Das 2014: 268; deSilva 2018: 246–47. For further discussion of 2:19–20, see also Moo 2013: 167–71.

156 Similarly Schreiner 2010: 170–71; Das 2014: 268; deSilva 2018: 246–47. For further discussion of 2:19–20, see also Moo 2013: 167–71.

of life, centered on the law, and ushered him into a transformed in-Christ Jewish life, centered on the cross and resurrection of Jesus (1:1, 4; 3:13), faith (2:16, 19–21), and the Spirit (3:1, 14; 4:21—5:6). Christ in Paul via co-crucifixion transformed Paul and directed all of his actions away from the law and toward Christ without erasing or eradicating his Jewish identity (cf. 3:28; see also Rom 9:1; 11:1–2).[157]

In Christ, God's covenantal love, once reserved primarily for Israel (Deut 7:8; Ps 47:4; Hos 3:1; Pss Sol 9:8) and for those who aligned themselves with Israel (Deut 4:37; Sir 4:14), is now reserved for and experienced by Jews and Gentiles in Christ, who loved and gave himself for "me" (Gal 2:20) and for "us" (1:4; 2:19-20; 3:10—4:31).[158] Thus, if God's saving righteousness comes through Torah-observance for Jews or for Gentiles instead of co-crucifixion with Christ (2:20–21; cf. 1:4),[159] then Christ's death would have been worthless and unnecessary (2:21; 3:6–14).[160] Therefore, in 2:15–21, Paul reminds Peter Torah should not divide Jews and Gentiles from sharing table-fellowship with one another, even if the separation occurs because of fear of "those from the circumcision."

157 Though making a point about gift, Barclay 2015: 386 speaks of Paul's "reorientation of the self" and the "reorientation" of his "mode of existence," which Christ "shaped." He also speaks of the "Christ-event" changing Paul's "vision, value, and self."

158 Das 2014: 273. Barclay 2008: 203.

159 For the diversity of righteousness language in Second Temple Judaism and in Paul, see Ziesler 1972. Ziesler (1972: 174) takes "righteousness" in both a forensic and ethical sense in Gal 2:21 since "righteousness" occurs in the context of Paul contrasting his old life in the law with his new life in Christ (2:18–20). This new life is one of righteousness. However, in my view, Paul's law versus grace antithesis reaches back to 2:16 where Paul has argued for a forensic understanding of justification with his by faith not by works antithesis. This suggests "righteousness" should be taken forensically the same way as the verb "to justify" in 2:16–17 without any ethical/behavioral ideas. Of course, Paul talks about the new life in Christ in 2:18–20. And, in Paul's soteriology, justification and new life in the Spirit are closely connected. But Paul does not identify new life in Christ as "righteousness" in 2:17–21, though the term for "righteousness" in 2:21 can have an ethical meaning in Paul (e.g., Rom 6:13, 18–20; 1 Cor 1:30). "Righteousness" in Galatians appears to be reserved as a forensic and relational term when it occurs in conjunction with the verb "to justify" (e.g., cf. Gal 2:16 and 3:21 with 5:3–4).

160 Against Dunn 1993: 149, who suggests that the problem with the law in 2:21 is that it restricts the grace of God to Jewish people. However, in my view, and as others have pointed out, Paul critiques Torah's inability to bring about righteousness (2:21) and life (3:11–12, 21) because the law only leads to a curse (3:10) and is part of the present evil age (3:15—4:7).

Galatians 3

Defense of Paul's Gospel from Scripture and Spiritual Experience (3:1—5:1)

Argument from Experience: Reception of the Spirit by Faith apart from Works of the Law (3:1–5)

Chapter 3 begins the central section of the letter. In 3:1, Paul directly addresses the Galatians for the first time since 1:1. The Genesis and Deuteronomic themes of blessing and curse occur at the beginning and end of the letter (1:1–9; 6:16; cf. Deut 30:19). Paul conflates multiple scriptural citations to highlight the blessing and curse motifs in Genesis (cf. Gen 12:1–3; 15:6; with Gal 3:6–9, 16) and in Deuteronomy (cf. Deut 21:23; 27:26; 28:58; 30:10 with Gal 3:10–14). These themes are prominent in Gal 3:1–14. In 3:1–9, Paul's basic argument is the Galatians received spiritual blessings by faith apart from works of law, just as Abraham received the spiritual blessing of righteousness by faith in God's promise apart from works of law. Therefore, Jews and Gentiles with faith experience the Abrahamic blessing by faith just as faithful Abraham (3:9).

In 3:1–5, Paul asks the Galatians a series of questions. Each question reminds them they received spiritual blessings by faith apart from works of law. He first begins his direct address of the Galatians with a derogatory remark: "O' foolish Galatians" (3:1). Paul attacks not the Galatians' intelligence, but their lack of spiritual discernment. They were contemplating a turn away from his gospel to embrace the law. Law-observance placed them under both an apostolic curse (1:8–9) and under the curse of the law (3:10). This interpretation of Paul's remarks is supported in the OT. There the term "foolish" is applied to those who do not love the one and true living God.[1] "The foolish person has said in his heart there is

---

1 The same adjective (*anoētos*) in Gal 3:1 is applied to Israel's enemies (e.g., LXX Deut 32:31). The term is applied to Jews who renounce a Jewish way of life in 4 Macc 8:17.

no God" (Ps 14:1). "The fear of the Lord is the beginning of knowledge" (Prov 1:7).

The Galatians' contemplative turn away from Paul's gospel, which he received from Jesus Christ and from God, the Father, who raised him from the dead, is foolish. The Galatians owe their experience of the Spirit to God and Christ. Christ gave himself "for our sins to deliver us from this present evil age" (1:4). God raised Jesus Christ from the dead (1:1). God revealed his Son in Paul to announce him as good news amongst the Gentiles (1:15–16). God justifies Jews and Gentiles by faith in Christ apart from works of law (2:11–21). Christ died to deliver "us" from the law's curse by becoming a curse for "us" so that Jews and Gentiles would receive the Abrahamic blessing by faith (3:13–14).

Paul calls the Galatians "bewitched" (3:1). The meaning of this state-ment is unclear.[2] The word *ebaskanen*, translated as "bewitched" or "to cast under a spell," only occurs here in the entire Greek NT. In LXX Deut 28:54, 56; Sir 14:6, 8,[3] the verb refers to someone holding a grudge against someone with an evil eye or disregarding someone in an evil manner or with an evil eye.[4] Plutarch (*Quaest. conv.* 681 A–D) speaks of the power that ancients gave to the evil eye, attributing to the eye power to inflict someone with evil or a sickness.[5]

Paul's presentation of the opponents suggests they were actively en-gaged in persuading and compelling the Galatians to their view by means of preaching and teaching Torah-observance in the Galatians' churches (cf. Gal 5:7–9; 6:12). The opponents preached a contrary message to the gospel that Paul received from God and preached to the Galatians (1:6–9). The opponents preached circumcision (5:2–5). The opponents hindered the Galatians from the truth, and they persuaded them to believe their rival message (5:7–8). Paul identifies the opponents as trouble-makers (5:10). Thus, Paul figuratively uses the language of bewitchment in 3:1 to support at least some of the Galatians have fallen under the spell of the opponents and foolishly began to embrace the opponents' message with their Christian minds. As Martinus De Boer states, the Galatians' con-templation to turn away from Paul's gospel forces him to ask: "Galatians,

2 For an argument in favor of understanding Paul's remarks about the evil eye in light of Deut 28, see Eastman 2001: 69–87.

3 Das 2014: 285. There is an interesting parallel with MT/LXX Deut 28:56 and Gal 3:1. For a discussion, see Eastman 2001: 69–87.

4 Similarly Das 2014: 285. For further discussion, see also deSilva 2018: 266–68.

5 Das 2014: 285.

have you lost your Christian minds [due to] the new preachers who have come to Galatia" (brackets mine).[6] This reading fits with Paul's remarks in 5:7 that the Galatians have been hindered not to obey the truth. This interpretation also fits with the ancient witnesses C, D2, Ψ, and 0278 that include the phrase "not to be persuaded with respect to the truth" as a modifier of the word for bewitched.

Paul asks this question in 3:1 since the opponents have duped the Galatians with their Torah-observant gospel. Their gospel deviated from the cross of Jesus Christ (cf. 6:12). Paul publicly preached Christ before the Galatians' eyes as having been crucified (3:1c). The opponents presented before the Galatians' eyes a distorted, other gospel (cf. 1:6–9).

Interpreters differ on the meaning of *prographō*.[7] Each time Paul uses the verb *prographō* in his letters (Rom 15:4; cf. Eph 3:3), it refers to something written beforehand. In Rom 15:4, it refers to the OT scriptures. In Eph 3:3, it refers to Paul's words. In Gal 3:1 (Paul's earliest use of the verb), the term refers to Paul's gospel proclamation during his first missionary journey with the Galatians (Acts 13–14). On this journey, he preached Jesus' crucifixion as the means by which sinners become right with God by faith (cf. Gal 2:16; 3:10–14).

There are at least four reasons why the above interpretation seems correct. First, Paul emphasizes preaching the good news in Galatians (1:6–11, 15–16). Second, he mentions "previous" preaching to the Galatians elsewhere in the letter (5:21). Third, he uses figurative language earlier in 3:1 when he calls the Galatians "foolish." Fourth, he mentions the cross of Jesus more than once in Galatians. Jesus died for our sins (1:4). Paul refers to his co-crucifixion with Christ (2:19–20). Christ's death was not in vain (2:21). Christ redeemed us from the curse of the law by becoming accursed and hanging upon a tree (3:13). Paul refers to crucifying the flesh's desires (5:24–26). Paul boasts in the cross of Jesus Christ (6:11–17). Paul's emphasis on the cross in Galatians suggests the crucifixion of Jesus Christ was a central aspect of Paul's gospel proclamation to the Galatians. Thus, he identifies them as spiritually dumb if they turn away from his message about the crucified Jesus Christ to the opponents' rival message.[8]

6 De Beor 2011: 171.

7 For a summary and critique of each interpretive option, see Das 2014: 286–88.

8 Perhaps Paul also intends to communicate something about his suffering for the cross. So Das 2014: 287–88. His suffering "embodied the message" of the cross. Paul states in Gal 6:17 that he carries in his body the marks of Jesus. He accuses the

In 3:1b–5, Paul asks a primary question in five distinct ways. The question pertains to whether these Galatians received the blessing of the Spirit and had spiritual experiences by faith or by works of law. Paul's questions are as follows: (1) who bewitched you (3:1b)? (2) Did you receive the Spirit by faith or by works of law (3:2)? (3) Are you foolishly finishing the journey of faith by means of circumcised flesh although you began the journey of faith by faith (3:3; cf. Jer 31:31–33; Ezek 36–37; 2 Cor 8:6; Phil 1:6)?[9] (4) Did you suffer/experience so many things in

---

opponents of preaching circumcision because they were afraid to be "persecuted for the cross of Christ" (6:12). In 4:29, he mentions persecution because of the promise of the gospel. He preached the gospel to the Galatians on a previous occasion because he suffered a weakness in his flesh (4:13–14). Paul's proclamation of the cross of Christ often coincided with his personal suffering for the gospel of Christ. Or perhaps, it's better to say that Paul's suffering often came as a result of preaching the gospel (cf. 2 Cor 11). If the above arguments are correct, Paul would be saying he publicly portrayed Jesus Christ as having suffered crucifixion as he himself suffered for the message of the cross as an apostle (cf. 2 Cor 4:10–11). Paul embodied the crucifixion of Christ to the Galatians both through his preaching and through the visible marks on his body because of his preaching about the cross. If this analysis is correct, Paul's remarks challenge his opponents who preached circumcision (a mark of the flesh) and avoided preaching about the cross of Jesus (which produced marks in the flesh via persecution) because they were afraid to suffer for it (cf. Gal 6:12). Instead, Paul's opponents preach the mark of circumcision and bear that mark in their bodies. For a similar thought, see Hays 2000: 250.

9 The verb translated above as finishing is *epiteleisthe*, which could also be translated "being completed" (1 Esd 8:16, 91; Pss. Sol. 6:6). Paul's appeal to "flesh" (*sarx*) in Gal 3:3 anticipates his discussion about walking in the Spirit and not in the lust of the flesh in 5:16–26. This appeal preludes his polemic against circumcision of the flesh in 5:2–5 and again in 6:12–13. "Flesh" in its negative sense in Galatians refers to a "cosmic power" within the present evil age (1:4; 5:16–21, 24–26). In at least one Jewish source, circumcised flesh helps one overcome an "evil inclination" (1QS V.4–5). Point cited in Das 2014: 294. For additional primary texts, see Bird 2007.

vain (3:4)?[10] (5) Did God give you the Spirit and grant you supernatural,[11] spiritual experiences by works of law or by the hearing of faith (=hearing a message that requires the response of faith) (3:5; cf. Rom 10:14–16, quoting Isa 53:1)?[12]

Argument from Scripture: The Blessing of Abraham (3:6–14)

ABRAHAMIC OFFSPRING BY FAITH (3:6–9)

Paul's answer to the above questions is implicit within each question. But he explicitly states in 3:6–9 the Galatians received the Spirit and had spiritual experiences by faith in Christ apart from works of law, just as Abraham received a blessing (namely, righteousness) from God by faith in his promises. Against the opponents, Paul argues the Galatians' reception of the Spirit by faith proves God had already included them within Abraham's family (cf. Ezek 11:19–20; 36– 37; Joel 2:28–29; MT Joel 3:1–2).[13] In Jub. 1:23–24, Torah-observance leads to the gift of the

---

10   Cf. 4:29 where Paul mentions persecution for the cross. The verb translated as "suffer" above is *paschō*. Some prefer the translation "experience" (e.g., NASB, RSV, NRSV). But *paschō* occurs in numerous texts in the LXX (e.g., 2 Macc 7:18, 32; 4 Macc 9:8; 10:10) and the NT (Matt 17:12, 15; 1 Cor 12:26; Phil 1:29; 2 Tim 1:12; 1 Pet 3:17; Rev 2:10) to mean "to suffer." But *paschō* is used in Josephus (*Ant.* 3.312) to refer to "experience" instead of suffering. "To suffer" seems the right translation in Galatians in light of the theme of suffering (Gal 1:4; 2:19–20; 3:13; 4:14; 6:12) and persecution (a form of suffering) in Galatians (4:29; 5:11; 6:12, 17). However, the immediate context suggests "experience." The "these things" in 3:4 that modify the verb *paschō* might refer to the positive experiences of the Spirit mentioned in 3:2–3. Either way, Paul's point remains the same in 3:2–5: the Galatians received the Spirit and received spiritual experiences by faith and not by works of law. Similarly Das 2014: 296–97. For suffering in Galatians, see Dunne 2017.

11   The Greek text uses the language of "supplying to you the Spirit" and "working powers amongst you" (Gal 3:4; cf. with the phrase "amongst the Gentiles" in 1:16). Paul likely refers to the Spirit's work to do the miraculous through the Galatians or at least in their midst (cf. Matt 11:20–21, 23; Acts 8:13).

12   Schreiner 2010: 182–83. For a list of interpretive options for the phrase "from a hearing of faith," see Das 2014: 289–93. DeSilva states, the head noun "hearing" may "signify the faculty of hearing (as LXX Isa 6:9; Matt 13:14; Mark 7:35; Luke 7:1; Acts 17:20; 1 Cor 12:17; 2 Tim 4:3–4; Heb 5:11; 2 Pet 2:8) or the thing heard, hence 'report' or 'message' (as in LXX Isa 52:7; 53:1; Jer 6:4; 30:8; Matt 4:24; 14:1; 24:6; John 12:38; Acts 28:26; Rom 10:16–17; 2 Thess 2:13; Heb 4:2)." deSilva 2014: 53–54.

13   Similarly Das 2014: 288–89. See also Betz 1979: 132, though I disagree with his comments on pneumatics in Galatians. But he is right to emphasize the Galatians' "experience of the Spirit" happened "outside of the Torah covenant." Betz 1979: 133.

Spirit.[14] However, Paul reminds the Galatians of the opposite truth: their experience of the Spirit was the result of their faith in the crucified Christ, not as a result of Torah-observance.

With the adverb "just as" in 3:6, Paul links 3:6–9 with 3:1–5. He presents Abraham as an example of how God gave his blessing to the Gentiles. Paul's appeal to Abraham is an important rhetorical move on his part. Jewish literature, in both the OT (Gen 12–50) and extra-biblical sources, mentions Jewish heroes (cf. Sir 44–50).[15]

Abraham is perhaps the most important hero in much Jewish literature.[16] Abraham could have been the opponents' chief example to the Galatians as to why they as Gentiles needed to adopt a Jewish way of life. Jewish sources assert Abraham (a Gentile) abandoned idols for Israel's true God (Jub. 11:16–17; 12:2–8, 16–24),[17] call him faithful because he circumcised his children (T. Levi 9:1–14; T. Benj. 10:4; 2 Bar. 57:1–3),[18] and call him perfect for observing the law (Jub. 15:3; 23:10; 24:11) and sinless (Pr Man 8; T. *Ab.* 10:13).[19] Jewish literature also suggests Abraham was reckoned as righteous because God found him faithful when he tested him (1 Macc 2:52; cf. LXX Ps 105:31's remarks about Phinehas).[20] Another Jewish source claims God entered into a covenant with Abraham to bless the nations because he kept the law (Sir 44:19–21).[21] The Dead Sea Scroll CD III.2–3 suggests Abraham was considered a friend of God because he kept God's precepts instead of following his heart's desires.[22] These sources idealize Abraham and present him as a virtually perfect follower of God's laws before there was a written Torah.[23]

See also De Boer 2011: 181.

14 De Boer 2011: 181.

15 Cf. Phineas's faithfulness was reckoned as righteousness in LXX Ps 105:31.

16 For examples of Abraham's prominence in Jewish literature, see Sib. Or. 2:246; T. Levi 6:9; 8:15; 9:12; 15:4; 18:6, 14; 19:5; T. Jud. 17:5; 25:1; T. Dan 7:2; T. Naph. 1:10; T. Ash. 7:7; T. Jos. 6:7; T. Benj. 1:2; 10:4, 6; Let. Aris. 149; Jub. 11:14; 12:12, 14, 26; 15:17; 16:10, 21, 31; 17:16; 18:13; 19:11; 22:4; 3 Macc 6:3; 4 Macc 6:17, 22; 7:19; 13:17; 14:20; 15:28; 16:20, 25; 17:6; 18:1, 20, 23; Pss. Sol. 9:9; 18:3.

17 Das 2014: 302.

18 Das 2014: 303.

19 Das 2014: 303.

20 Das 2014: 303.

21 Das 2014: 303.

22 Das 2014: 303.

23 Cf. also 4QMMT 117–18 [4QMMT C 31–32; 4Q398 Frag. 2.II.7–8; 4Q399 Frag. 1.II.4–5] reference to Gen 15:6. Das 2014: 303–4. See also primary sources cited

Paul, however, emphasizes Abraham's exemplary faith to reinforce to the Galatians the importance of their faith in Jesus as their entry point into an initial and ongoing experience of the Spirit (3:1–5). Just as Abraham's faith brought him the blessing of a conferred status of righteousness by God (3:6; cf. Gen 12:1–13; 15:1–6), the Galatians' faith granted them the gift of the Spirit (3:1–9, 14). Paul's use of Abraham highlights the error of the opponents' Torah-based message. God is likely the theological subject of Gal 3:6 since in the Abrahamic narrative, God initiates and preempts Abraham's response of faith by establishing a covenant with him (cf. Gen 12:1—17:14).

The reckoning of righteousness in this context communicates a forensic idea (cf. LXX Ps 105:31). When God reckons someone as righteous, he considers something to be true that was previously untrue (LXX Gen 15:6). Paul would agree circumcision and Torah were necessary and important for the people of God prior to the revelation of God in Christ (cf. Lev 12:3; Gal 1:13–16). He would, however, strongly disagree that Torah grants one access to the Spirit or life in the age to come (cf. Gal 2:16–21; 3:21; contra Gen 17:4–14; Bar 4:1). Instead, "now" since Jesus' death delivers "us from the present evil age" (Gal 1:4) and distributes the Spirit to Jews and Gentiles (3:13–14; 4:4–6), neither circumcision nor Torah functions as the sign of the Abrahamic covenant or as a mark of those who will receive life in the age to come (Gal 3:6–9; cf. 1:4; 5:21; 6:15).

Faith is the pathway to the Abrahamic blessing for Abraham (3:6), for Jews (2:16), and for Gentiles (3:6—4:31). Abraham "believed God" (Gal 3:6), and "those from faith" are the "sons of Abraham" (3:7). And the mark of the Spirit, which Jews and Gentiles receive via Christ's death and resurrection by faith, sets apart and lives within those who are part of Abraham's offspring (3:6–14; 4:6). To live in accordance with the flesh is to live "according to the values and desires of the present evil age" (1:4),[24] because "flesh is primarily a power" in Galatians (cf. 5:16–26).[25]

Paul continues his argument from 3:6–7 in 3:8 with comments about the inclusion of the Gentiles within the Abrahamic promise. He asserts God's justification of the Gentiles was foreseen in the scripture when the scripture announced the good news in advance to Abraham that "all the nations will be blessed by/in you" (3:8). The scriptures' foreknowledge

---

in Keener 2018: 128–34.

24 Das 2014: 295.

25 Das 2014: 295.

refers to God's plan for the families of the earth before it unfolded in history since Paul says the scripture foresaw and announced in advance the good news that "God will justify the *ethnē* by faith" (3:8). God's plan to bless many different people with salvation through Christ apart from works of law was announced beforehand in the scriptures to Abraham (Gen 12:1–3; cf. Gal 3:22, 27; 4:30).

Paul's statement in 3:8 about God's promise of the justification of the Gentiles is possibly a conflation of LXX Gen 12:3; 18:18, 22:18, 26:4, and 28:14.[26] His exegesis likely contrasts with his opponents' exegesis of the Abrahamic narratives and their interpretation of the role of works of law in the laws of God's covenant people. LXX Gen 12:3 states "all the tribes" (*phylai*) of the earth will be blessed, whereas Paul states all of the "nations" (*ethnē*) of the earth will be blessed (Gal 3:8). The specific reason for the difference between the two textual traditions could be coincidental (i.e., Paul could have used a different LXX version from our current LXX traditions) or intentional (i.e., Paul could have intentionally switched the words to make his remarks more appropriate to the Gentiles in Galatia). Paul possibly changes the wording from "tribes of the earth" in LXX Gen 12:3b to "all the Gentiles" in Gal 3:8 to fit his precise argument against the opponents in favor of the Gentile-inclusive nature of his gospel.[27]

Paul may have simply conflated multiple texts from Genesis regarding God's promise to bless Abraham (LXX Gen 12:3; 18:18; 22:18, 26:4, 28:14).[28] LXX Gen 18:18 and 22:18 specifically assert all of the *ethnē* will be blessed. LXX Gen 18:18 asserts all of the nations will be blessed "in him" (i.e., Abraham). LXX Gen 22:18a states all of the nations will be blessed in "your seed." Paul does not introduce the concept of "seed" (*sperma*) into his argument until Gal 3:16 (cf. also LXX Gen 26:4). The promise of God's universal blessing for Jews and Gentiles because of Abraham's seed emerges in Paul's argument in Gal 3:16–29.[29]

---

26 For further discussion of *ethnē*, see Williams and Moss 2019. For a grammatical comparison of the LXX texts with Gal 3:8, see Das 2014: 308.

27 Regarding Paul changing the wording of the LXX, a similar thought in Moo 2013: 199.

28 For Paul's use of scripture, see Hays 1989; Watson 2015.

29 In the DSS, Jewish attitudes toward Gentile groups are negative. Gentiles are called "idol worshipers without God" (1QpHab XII.13; XIII.3–4), "enemies of God" (1QM XII.8–9), and "objects of God's judgment at the hands of his elect" (1QpHab 5.4). For these texts and others and for the preceding description, see Silva 2014: 2.90.

Paul's appeal to scripture strengthens his argument as to why the Galatians should not embrace the opponents' Torah-observant gospel. God announced beforehand to Abraham the good news that all the Gentiles (i.e., all of the families of the earth) will be blessed by means of Abraham.[30] This statement is a sharp rhetorical jab against Paul's opponents because Abraham, the uncircumcised Gentile and father of the Jews from Ur of the Chaldeans, was the agent through whom God would bless all people, Jews and Gentiles. The Galatians received the Abrahamic blessing by faith in Jesus Christ. Jesus died to deliver all people from the curse of the law (3:10–14). Jesus is Abraham's offspring, through whom God promises to bless all of the ethnically distinct families of the earth (3:16). Thus, by faith in Christ and apart from the works of the law, Jews and Gentiles are more like Abraham, who received God's blessing by believing in his promise, than Paul's Jewish opponents, who preached a rival gospel based on Torah apart from faith alone and who believed they would receive the blessing of Abraham by Torah-observance. Paul concludes, therefore, "those from faith" (Jews and Gentiles in Christ) are blessed with faithful Abraham (3:9). Those who have faith in Christ (2:16), Abraham's offspring (3:16), experience the Abrahamic blessing promised to Abraham and his offspring (cf. Gen 12–50).

THE CROSS, THE CURSE, AND THE SPIRIT (3:10–14)

In Gal 3:10–14, Paul provides the reason for his inference in 3:9: Jesus delivered "us" from the curse of the law in order to impart to Christ-following Jews and Gentiles the Abrahamic blessing of the Spirit by faith. That 3:10–14 exegetically grounds 3:1–9 is supported by the *gar* ("for") in 3:10. The argument can be summarized as follows: those from faith are blessed with the Abrahamic blessing (3:1–9), because the law does not lead to eschatological life but to an eschatological curse (3:10–12). But Christ delivered Jews and Gentiles from Torah's curse by becoming a curse for them so that they would receive the Abrahamic blessing of the Spirit by faith (3:13–14).

---

30 Das (2014: 309) thinks *ethnē* only refers to non-Jews in Gal 3:8 because of the Jew and non-Jew distinction in the context of Galatians. But he agrees that *ethnē* in the original source in Genesis refers to all people without Jewish and non-Jewish distinctions.

There are at least four major exegetical issues in this verse.[31] The first is Paul's use of LXX Deut 27:26; 28:58. Paul seemingly conflates these verses to mean something entirely different from what they mean in their original context of Deuteronomy. Second, how should one translate the two *hoti*-clauses that begin and conclude the verse? Third, how does Paul use LXX Hab 2:4, specifically his use of the phrase "by faith?" Does "by faith" modify "the righteous one" or "will live?" Fourth, does the verb "will live" refer to eschatological life? Is the statement an eschatological-soteriological declaration or is it a temporal promise? I discuss these issues in the exegesis below.

In 3:10, Paul makes a shocking statement: "for as many are from works of law are under a curse." These words are shocking because they state the opposite of what the OT actually says about Torah-observance (e.g., Lev 18:5), and Paul's conclusion in 3:10 ("because everyone who fails to do all the things written in the book of the law is cursed") does not appear to support his premise in 3:10a. Paul also cites in 3:10b–12 as scriptural proof for his assertion in 3:10 a conflation of OT texts that affirm the opposite of what he asserts. In 3:10b–12, Paul conflates LXX Deut 27:26; 28:58 (Gal 3:10); Hab 2:4 (Gal 3:11); and Lev 18:5 (Gal 3:12).

Paul's citations from LXX Deut 27:26 and 28:58 provide the most immediate support for his remarks in 3:10a since he introduces his scriptural proof with *gar* ("for") in 3:10. Deut 27:26 occurs at the end of a detailed section about the curses of those who do not obey the law. The Lord states in no uncertain terms "Cursed be anyone who does not conform to the words of this law by doing them" (Deut 27:26, ESV). The curse comes to those who disobey, not to those who obey. Furthermore, after concluding a discussion about the curses that will come upon those who do not obey the law in the land, Deut 28:58–59 states "If you are not careful to do all the words of this law that are written in this book, that you may fear this glorious and awesome name, the Lord your God, then the Lord will bring on you and your offspring extraordinary afflictions, afflictions severe and lasting and sicknesses grieving and lasting" (Deut 28:58–59). Deut 30:10 emphasizes the importance of obeying the words written in the book of the law. The obvious question, then, is why in Gal 3:10a does Paul state the opposite of what Deuteronomy actually says about those who rely upon works of law?

---

31 For a discussion of the important exegetical and theological issues in the text, see Das 2014: 312–36; Moo 2013: 201–23; Longenecker 1990: 116–26; Betz 1979: 144–53; Witherington 1998: 231–40.

Paul seems to use Deut 27:26 as his base text within the scriptural conflations since Paul's words are closer to this text than to the others.[32] In Deut 27–30, the curses of the law refer to the specific judgments of God that will come upon non-Torah-observers in the land. Moses recapitulates the law to Israel to remind them of their covenant with YHWH at Sinai before they entered into the promised-land (Deuteronomy). He especially tells the people they must obey "all" of the law to the fullest when they enter the land (cf. Deut 27:3, 8; 28:1, 15, 58; 31:12). Otherwise, they would receive the curses promised to those who disobey (Deut 27:1–28:68).

YHWH promised long life in the land only to those who comprehensively obeyed his commands (Lev 18:5).[33] Multiple Jewish texts in the Second Temple Period applied this promise of temporal life to eternal life in an age to come (Pss. Sol. 14:1–10; Bar 3–4; 2 Bar 41–51). According to 2 Baruch, the righteous are those who observe God's law and consequently participate in the age to come (cf. 2 Apoc. Bar. 24:1; 48:19, 22, 24; 51:3, 4, 7).[34] Those who obey Torah receive the promise of eternal life (32:1; 38:1; 48:22; 51:3, 4–7).[35] The expectation of obedience to Torah leading to life is one reason Paul cites Lev 18:5 in Gal 3:12. Contrary to the promise of life in Lev 18:5 and repeated throughout Deut 27–30, Paul emphasizes in Galatians to be under the law is to be under a curse (Gal 3:10),[36] not to receive life (3:11, 21). Israel's disobedience in the land resulted in a curse in the land but their obedience would result in divine blessing in the land (Deut 27–32).

Hays says to suggest Paul refers to the "unfulfillability" of the law in Gal 3:10–11 when he identifies those of the law are accursed "is such a ridiculous caricature of Judaism, however, that it could hardly have been taken seriously as a persuasive argument in Paul's time."[37] Yet, against Hays, certain Jewish sources support comprehensive obedience to the law was expected in order to achieve the life that it promises (CD

32 See Das (2014: 312) for similarities and differences between Paul and the scriptural conflations from Deuteronomy.

33 For the function of Lev 18:5 in early Judaism and in Paul, see Sprinkle 2008. Sprinkle argues in Gal 3:12, Paul thinks the promise in Lev 18:5 is a dead end because it prioritizes human agency.

34 So Gurtner 2011: 114–26; esp. 124–26.

35 Gurtner 2011: 124–26; Das 2014: 323–24.

36 Contra Josephus, *Ag. Ap.* 2.210.

37 Hays 2000: 257.

II.15–16; 1QS III.21–23; IV.18–22).[38] As I stated earlier, Jewish literature idealized Abraham. Jubilees mentions the perfection of Abraham's conduct (Jub. 23:10),[39] the perfection of Jacob, Leah, and Joseph (Jub. 27:17; 36:23; 40:8),[40] and the perfection of Noah by stating "he did not transgress anything" God ordained (Jub. 5:19).[41] Philo says Moses was a "living and reasonable" law (*Mos.* 1.162) and sinless (*Mos.* 1.28).[42] But, in Paul's view, "as many are from works of law are under a curse" along with disobedient Israel (Gal 3:10–4:31).

The curse of the law refers to eschatological judgment in Galatians, which Paul describes as failure to participate in the Abrahamic blessing of the Spirit (3:14) and failure to inherit the kingdom of God (5:21). He begins the letter highlighting this curse by wishing an anathema upon anyone (human or angel) preaching a gospel contrary to his gospel (1:8–9). Paul appropriates the Deuteronomic curses to the Galatians in light of his revelation of God in Christ (1:15–16), just as he appropriates the physical land promises to refer to eschatological judgment versus eschatological life (5:21). The question, however, still remains: why does Paul cite texts from Deuteronomy to prove an antithetical point to the original Deuteronomic texts in Gal 3:10?

Hays, following Wright, suggests Paul is placing those under the curse of the law "whose identity" derives from the law.[43] The law was given to Israel as a nation, and it promised covenantal blessings to the nations if they obeyed.[44] Those within the covenant were subject to the sanctions of the covenant.[45] Israel's disobedience to the covenant did not lead to the blessing set forth in Deut 28.[46] Moses explicitly promises Israel the nation would "turn aside" from Torah-observance after his death (Deut 31:29) and "God's anger" would rest upon them.[47] This prediction is celebrated in Deut 32.[48] Thus, "Paul warns the Galatians that those whose identity

38 Das (2014: 314) pointed me to these texts.
39 Das 2014: 314–15.
40 Das 2014: 314–15.
41 Das 2014: 314–15.
42 Das 2014: 314–15.
43 Hays 2000: 258. See also Wright 1991.
44 Hays 2000: 258.
45 Hays 2000: 258.
46 Hays 2000: 258.
47 Hays 2000: 258.
48 Hays 2000: 258.

is grounded in the Law are under a curse, he is in effect saying to them 'If you affiliate yourself with those who place their hope in obeying the Law (i.e., the Missionaries), you are joining a losing team'—not because obedience is theoretically impossible, but because Israel historically has failed and has in fact incurred the judgment of which Deuteronomy solemnly warns.'"[49] In other words, God sent Israel "into exile."[50] "Despite the return," the nation "has never" experienced the national blessing promised in Deuteronomy.[51]

However, against Hays, in my view Paul seems to offer a threefold curse pronouncement of those who subscribe to Torah. First, those who associate with Torah as a mark of covenant membership are subject to Torah's curse, because Christ died to redeem those under Torah's curse from the curse of the law (3:13). Torah curses those who do not obey (LXX Deut 27:1—29:20). Second, no one obeys or fulfills the law unless one has the indwelling presence of the Spirit (Gal 3:14; 4:5–6; 5:13–21; 6:2), but Torah still demands obedience beyond circumcision for all people under Torah's jurisdiction regardless of whether one has the Spirit or not (Gal 5:3; cf. LXX Deut 27:1—29:20; CD II.15–16). Since this latter point is explicitly stated in both LXX Deut 27:1—29:20 and in Gal 5:3, it could be the implicit premise of the scriptural conflations from Deuteronomy in Gal 3:10.[52] That Paul desired the Galatians to supply an implicit premise based on his scriptural conflations is possible.[53] The scriptural conflations in Gal 3:10 from Deut 27:26 and 28:58 point in this direction when the verse states that "everyone is cursed who does not abide by all things written in the book of the law in order to do them."

Third, Paul also intends to communicate the law curses because it is under the present evil age (Gal 1:4; 3:15—4:11) since he says "as many are from works of law" instead of saying "those who do the works of law" are under a curse (cf. Rom 2:13).[54] Of course, failure to do the law brings a curse in Deuteronomy (cf. Deut 27–28). Paul emphasizes this point in

---

49 Hays 2000: 258–59. See also discussion in deSilva 2018: 288–90.

50 Hays 2000: 259.

51 Hays 2000: 259.

52 For examples of implicit premises in ancient sources, see Das 2014: 312n203. See also Kennedy 1984. For an article arguing for a "modified implicit premise" in Gal 3:10, see Young 1998: 79–92; esp. 86.

53 Justin, *Dial.* 95.1; Chrysostom, *Hom. Gal.* (NPNF 13:26–27) agreed that 3:10 has an implied premise. Sources cited in Das 2014: 312n204.

54 For the law as part of the present evil age, see Wakefield 2004.

Gal 3:10–12 when he appeals to texts in Deuteronomy, which mention the requirement of doing all things in the book of the law, and when he contrasts the life inherited by the righteous by faith versus by doing the law. This latter point highlights the necessity of obedience to the law in Gal 3:12 with his appeal to Lev 18:5 that too talks about doing the things of the law to receive the life that it promises. Thus, failure to obey the law explains in part why those who identify with the law are under a curse (3:10).

Still, in Galatians, the law is also under the present evil age (1:4). It enslaves those under its jurisdiction to the elements of the world (4:8–11). The law places them under a curse (3:13), under sin, and under slavery (3:19—4:31). The certainty of the law's curse upon those under its jurisdiction, human inability to obey the law, and the law's position under the present evil age make it impossible for those of works of law to achieve the life that it promises in Galatians. The way of the law is the way of the curse and, thus, leads to a spiritually dead end in Galatians (3:10), whose end is enslavement (3:15—4:31). The law guarantees that those who subscribe to it as a way of life are destined to receive its curse.

We cannot know for certain, but scholars have suggested the opponents may have argued obedience to the law grants access into the Abrahamic covenant to bolster their argument that the Galatians should receive the mark of circumcision. The opponents may have used Gen 12:1–3; 15:1–6; and 17:1–14 as their starting point to compel the Galatians to embrace circumcision. The Abrahamic narrative, Lev 18:5, Deut 27:26; 28:58; and 30:10 may have compelled the Galatians to be circumcised. But Paul argues the opposite premise from these texts in light of Christ: namely, law does not lead to life but to a curse. Furthermore, Paul begins his scriptural appeal to Abraham with Gen 15:6, not with Gen 12:1–3. Whereas the opponents emphasized circumcision as the pathway to life for Gentile Christ-followers, Paul emphasizes Jews who compel Gentiles to be circumcised place themselves and those Gentiles under Torah's curse, because Torah demands obedience and is under the present evil age.

The opponents could have preached along these lines to the Galatians:

> Galatians, get circumcised, just as Abraham was circumcised, because circumcision is the eternal sign of the Abrahamic covenant. And the eternal sign of the Abrahamic covenant made its way into the law. And the law leads to life and thus to the

universal blessing that God promised to Abraham, the father of
the Jewish people.

Paul likewise uses portions of the Abrahamic narrative related to
Abraham's faith (cf. Gen 15:6; with Gal 3:6), the universal blessing of the
Gentiles through Abraham (cf. Gen 12:3; 18:18; with Gal 3:7–9), and the
promises spoken to Abraham and his seed (cf. Gen 13:15; 18:8; 24:7; with
Gal 3:16–17, 29). He allegorizes the narratives about Isaac and Ishmael
(cf. Gen 16:15; 21:2, 9–10; with Gal 4:21–24), while conflating his allegory with a reference to LXX Isa 54:1. He conflates these narratives with
texts from LXX Deut 27:26; 28:58 (Gal 3:10), LXX Hab 2:4 (Gal 3:11),
and LXX Lev 18:5 (Gal 3:12) to emphasize the Galatians are children
of the promise, just as Isaac, because of their faith in Christ. He emphasizes Jews and Gentiles are children of the promise by faith in Christ (Gal
4:28–5:1). The law curses everyone under its jurisdiction, because the
law must be comprehensively obeyed (Gal 5:3).[55] Receiving the mark of
circumcision would make the Galatians responsible to obey the whole
law (5:2–6, 8, 11, 13, 15).

Paul's remarks about law-observance leading to a curse contrasts
with his opponents' view of the law and with the views of other Jewish groups in the Second Temple period (T. Levi 13:1; T. Jud. 26:1; T.
Dan 5:1; T. Ash. 6:3; Let. Aris. 127).[56] Both Lev 18:5 (cf. Gal 3:12) and
Deuteronomy affirm obedience to the law leads to life but disobedience
leads to a curse (Deut 27:1—29:29). Certain Jewish texts also emphasize
obedience to Torah leads to life.

Baruch asserts that wisdom, long life, and length of days come from
observance of the law (Bar 3:14—4:37). 1 Maccabees states the law needs
to be preserved so that it will bring glory to Israel (1 Macc 14:29). 4 Maccabees demonstrates that religious devotion to the law conquers all human desires by glamorizing the martyrdom of faithful Torah-observant
Jews at the hands of a non-Torah-observant Greek Tyrant. Sirach states a
"sensible person will trust in the law" (Sir 33:3). Jubilees declares the Lord
gave Israel the law and testimony "as an eternal law for their generations"
(Jub. 2:33). The Letter of Aristeas acknowledges "the good life" consists
in "observing the laws" (Let. Aris. 127). 2 Baruch (54:5, 21; 59:2) and 4
Ezra (6:27, 28; 9:7–13) declare that faith in God is to live in accordance

---

55 So also Lev 18:5; Deut 27–30.

56 For contrasting views of law-observance and the curse, see sources cited in
deSilva 2018: 288n64.

with the law. 4 Ezra adds that perfect obedience to the law leads to life (7:88–101).[57]

Pseudo-Philo (*LAB*) suggests that the eternal law brings light into the world, forms a covenant with the Lord's people, and judges the ungodly (11:1–5). The Testaments of the Twelve Patriarchs state that all who obey the law shall be honored all the days of their lives (T. Levi 13:2–3). And the same tradition urges the audience "to do righteousness on earth" (=doing the law) so that righteousness would be attained in heaven (T. Levi 13:5). The Testament of Judah says the law provides hope for all who observe it in its entirety (T. Jud. 26:1).[58]

Paul's opponents in Galatia appear to have a similar understanding of Torah as the Hebrew Bible and some of their Second Temple Jewish contemporaries. This view seems similar to Paul's understanding of the law prior to God's act of revealing his Son to him so that he might "preach the gospel" among Gentiles (cf. Gal 1:14–16). Because of the revelation of God in Christ (Gal 1:14–16), Paul now instead argues the law brings a curse to everyone under its jurisdiction (Gal 3:10). He offers his reason in 3:11: namely, law does not justify but the righteous one by faith will live. The following are the two different translation options for the hoti-clauses in 3:11:

> Now because no one is justified by law before God, it is evident that the righteous one by faith shall live.

> Now that no one is justified before God by the law is evident, because the righteous one by faith shall live.

The difference between the two options is a matter of emphasis. The first emphasizes the righteous one by faith shall live. This assertion is true because Paul has already asserted justification comes by faith apart from works of law (2:16, 2:21) and has empirically established in 3:10 the law brings a curse. Therefore, because justification comes by faith apart from works of the law and the law brings a curse upon all people, that no one is justified by law before God is clearly established in 2:16, 21; and 3:10. The second option emphasizes that no one is justified before God by law is evident,[59] because "the righteous one by faith shall live." This interpre-

---

57 For a list of Jewish texts, see Das 2014: 310–16.

58 For more primary texts, see Bird 2006. For a discussion of Jewish sources, see Das 2014: 310–23; Schreiner 2010: 212–14; Sprinkle 2008: 27–130; Gathercole 2002: 126–45; Keener 2018: 138–39, and the essays in Gurtner 2011: 1–261.

59 For the different translation options for *dēlon* in 3:11 ("it is evident"), see Oakes

tation takes the second *hoti* as providing the scriptural proof from Hab 2:4 for the premise regarding justification apart from Torah-observance.

Much has been made of these two translations.[60] This first option seems most likely given the context of the statement.[61] But this commentator fails to see how a choice between the two would change Paul's basic thesis in the verse. Paul's basic point in 3:11 is the following: because (*hoti*) no one is justified (declared to be in the right) in God's law court by doing the law (since the law brings a curse [3:10]), that (*hoti*) the righteous one shall live by faith is clear.[62] Paul's intent here is to say law does not lead to the Abrahamic blessing. But, as he will say in 3:13–14, faith in Jesus Christ, the liberator, brings the blessing of Abraham to Jews and Gentiles.

This interpretation seems plausible since Paul has already argued in 2:16 that a man is justified by faith apart from works of law and that "we believed in Christ Jesus so that we would be justified by faith in Christ and not by works of law, because by works of law not any flesh will be justified." In Gal 2:20, he affirms that he lives by "faith in the Son of God" and in 2:21 that righteousness through the law would render Jesus' death vain. Righteousness would only come through law if the law was able to give life (3:21).

In Gal 3:1–5, Paul argued the Galatians had miraculous experiences with the Spirit by faith and not by works of law, "just as Abraham believed God and it was counted to him as righteousness" (3:6). In 3:7, he reiterates the importance of faith/believing in 3:7–9 by asserting "those from faith" are Abraham's sons (3:7); the scripture foresaw that "God would justify the Gentiles by faith;" the scripture proclaimed to Abraham in advance that "all the nations will be blessed by means of you" (3:8), and by asserting that "those from faith" are blessed with faithful Abraham (3:9). Then, in 3:10–14, Paul provides the reason for his remarks in 3:1–9: namely, law brings a curse unless obeyed, but Christ liberates "us" from

---

2015: 111.

60   For a helpful discussion of the issues and a bibliography of secondary literature, see Das 2014: 316–21. Moo 2013: 205–6 prefers the traditional reading of the syntax that takes Gal 3:11b as the scriptural proof of the premise in 3:11a.

61   For a list of interpreters against this reading, see De Boer 2011: 202. De Boer 2011: 202 affirms the first position.

62   For this understanding of the *hoti dēlon hoti* construction in the Greek text, see Jos. *Ag. Ap.* 2.13. The phrase "before God" (*para tō theō*) reinforces the forensic nature of justification (cf. Luke 1:30; Rom 2:11, 13; 2 Thess 1:6).

the law's curse to distribute universally the blessing of Abraham. Thus, justification comes to the one who has faith in Christ apart from works of the law.

That the verb "shall live" refers to eternal life is likely since Paul associates justification with eternal life in Galatians (6:8) and since he interprets the promises to Abraham being realized by means of justification by faith in Christ (2:16), the seed of Abraham (3:16), the reception of the Spirit (3:2–14; 5:5, 16), deliverance from the curse of the law (3:10), and new creation (6:15). He also synonymously uses "righteousness" and "to give life" (3:21) and connects the Spirit with God's action in Christ (1:4; 3:1–14; 4:4–6; 5:5; 16–26). These soteriological blessings are realized because Christ "gave himself for our sins to deliver us from the present evil age" (1:4).

Another important element of Paul's exegesis of scripture in Gal 3:10–12 is his citation of Hab 2:4. His reading of this text adds to the viability of my above interpretation of Gal 3:10 (that the law requires full obedience, no one obeys, the law is part of the present evil age, and therefore, law only leads to a curse now that Christ has come). In the context of Hab 2:4, the prophet questions God for allowing evil to fall upon Israel. YHWH asserts the proud one is inflated with arrogance and his soul is not upright within him (Hab 2:4a). But, in MT Hab 2:4b, YHWH declares the righteous will experience life because of "his" faithfulness.

Paul's use of Hab 2:4 in Gal 3:11 is striking because it does not reflect any known textual tradition. The Hebrew text translates as "and the righteous one will live by *his faithfulness*." LXX Hab 2:4 could be translated as "and the righteous one will live by *my faith*."[63] The Dead Sea Scroll Habakkuk commentary renders the verse to refer "to faith in or loyalty to the community's teacher" (1QpHab VII.14–VIII.3).[64] The phrase "righteous one" occurs as a reference to Jesus in the NT (cf. Acts 3:14; 7:52; 22:14; 1 Pet 3:18; 1 John 2:1).[65] The title "righteous one" also occurs in Jewish sources to refer to "the long awaited eschatological deliverer" (1 En. 38:2).[66]

Paul's rendering of Hab 2:4 emphasizes the importance of one's individual faith in contrast to works of law as the means by which one

---

63 For the different readings in the LXX versions, see Moo 2013: 219.

64 Das 2014: 318.

65 Hays 2000: 259.

66 Hays 2000: 259.

inherits life: "the righteous one by faith shall live."[67] In the argument of 3:10–12, Paul appears to use the Habakkuk text to reinforce to the Galatians the importance and the necessity of their personal faith in Christ as the means by which they will inherit eternal life. Paul redefines the righteous one as one with faith in Christ and not by works of law, whereas the Hebrew Scriptures (Ps 1) and Jewish sources (1 Macc 1; Bar 3–4) identify the law-observant as righteous.

The above interpretation of Paul's remarks in 3:10–11 fits with his citation of Lev 18:5 in Gal 3:12: "the one who does them will live by them." "Them" refers to the works of the law (cf. Gal 2:16; 3:10). This citation, along with Hab 2:4 in Gal 3:11, suggests Paul pits believing in Christ versus doing the works of law against each other in 3:10–12.

In its original context, Lev 18:5 promises Israel temporal life in the land if the people obeyed Torah (Lev 18:1–30).[68] YHWH required Torah-obedience from Israel in the land to set apart his people and their land as holy, but he promised the land would spew Israel out if the people violated Torah (cf. Lev 18:25–30). But the required obedience of the "one who does" the law cannot actually be achieved by doing the law. These things suggest one's personal faith apart from one's Torah-works is necessary to achieve the life promised in the law.

The promise of life in LXX Lev 18:5 is not a conditional promise of salvation within a legalistic soteriological frame. Rather, it was a conditional promise of temporal life in the land based on the people's obedience to Torah, a people with whom the Lord had already entered into a covenant relationship before giving them the law at Sinai (cf. Gen 12–Exod 19). Commentators have rightly observed that certain Second Temple Jewish texts interpret this conditional promise of temporal life to continue in the age to come if Torah was obeyed to the fullest.[69] Das rightly points out that 1QS IV.6-8 "refers to everlasting blessing and eternal joy in life without end as an extension of the long life and fruitfulness enjoyed in the present for the righteous (Dan 12:2; Wis 2:22; 2 Macc 7:9; 4 Macc 15:3; 17:12)."[70] Das continues Pss. Sol. 14:1–10 links "the destruc-

---

67 Even Hays (2000: 259) affirms this.

68 For the function of Lev 18:5 in Second Temple Judaism and in Paul, see Sprinkle 2008.

69 For examples, see Das 2014: 323.

70 Das 2014: 323. Cf. Bar 4:1; 1QS IV.6–14; CD 3.14–20; Let. Aris. 127; Pss. Sol. 14:1–10; Philo, *Congr.* 86–87.

tion of the sinner with the inheritance" of the righteous and eternal life with language similar to Lev 18:5.[71]

That Pss. Sol. 14:1–10 applies Lev 18:5 to eternal life is strengthened by the Psalm's connection of the righteous walking in the righteous ways of the Lord's commandments with the promise that the righteous will live by the law forever, that they possess the Paradise of the Lord and the tree of life forever, and that they will receive an inheritance of joy from the Lord (Pss. Sol. 14:2–5, 10). Lawless ones, however, will not receive this life, because they walk in the ways of sinners. They will receive the inheritance of Hades and destruction as a result (Pss. Sol. 14:6–9).[72]

Paul's appeal to Deut 27–30; Lev 18:5, and Hab 2:4 within the same argument supports the covenantal context of his statements. Even while many Jews in the Second Temple period lived in the Diaspora outside of the holy city and without regular access to the temple, they performed Torah-works because this is what the covenant required (e.g., LXX Lev 18:5, Deut 27–30, Daniel; Tobit; Philo, *Special Laws*; 4QMMT).[73] If the people broke the stipulations of the covenant, YHWH would execute the appropriate judgment against the guilty. If the people maintained and honored the covenant by their fidelity, then YHWH distributed the rewards and blessings of covenant-obedience (Lev 18:5; Deut 27–30).

Paul's contention in 3:10 is that no one is able to do Torah-works in a sufficient way to achieve the life that Torah promises, because it curses everyone. Israel constantly lived in this tension of blessing when they obeyed and curse when they disobeyed. Disobedience was inevitable and the curses of disobedience were certain (cf. Deut 31:29). Paul suggests this latter point is proven by the conditional promise of life in Lev 18:5. This is why he cites this verse to show that life/righteousness comes apart from Torah-works through Christ (Gal 3:10–14).[74]

The above analysis provides a reason Paul states in Gal 3:12 that "the law is not from faith." Paul sharply pits faith against law here with his believing versus doing antithesis. Doing the law is not living on the basis of faith (3:12).[75] Abraham and other Jews prior to Christ had faith (cf. 3:6).[76]

71 Das 2014: 323.

72 Similarly Sprinkle 2008: 93–100; Das 2014: 323.

73 Barclay 1996.

74 Wright 1991; 2013 has especially emphasized the importance of covenant in Paul's theology.

75 Oakes 2015: 112.

76 Oakes 2015: 112.

Paul's point is that "the way of life under Jewish law was life dependent on doing the law."[77] His remarks accentuate the blessings of Torah came by means of faithful obedience. This faithful obedience included faith, but it is faithful obedience nevertheless (hence, his citation of Lev 18:5). Certain Jews understood that if the law was obeyed, then one was proven to be in the right (=justified) in YHWH's court of law (4QMMT),[78] while others believed that Torah-works would only be possible if God granted divine enablement, mercy, and repentance (1QH; Pr Man). Although the term legalism might be too anachronistic to describe early Jewish perceptions of the relationship between soteriology, the law, and divine and human agency in the soteriological experience in certain Jewish sources or in Gal 3:12, numerous examples exist in early Jewish sources supporting Jewish moral optimism and an emphasis on human agency in Jewish soteriology (cf. Jubilees; Sirach; Tobit).[79]

Saul, the Pharisee, would have agreed that Torah-obedience results in a positive verdict in YHWH's law-court since these sorts of statements are in the Hebrew Scriptures (LXX Deut 25:1; 1 Kgs 8:31–32; Ps 50:6; Isa 43:26) and in Second Temple Jewish texts (Pss. Sol. 9:2). Torah-obedient Jews were rendered righteous because of their faithful obedience to Torah (Wis 4:1—6:5, 17–21). Those who disobeyed Torah were declared unrighteous/wicked (Wis 6:1—12:27) or "renegades" (1 Macc 7:5) because of their disobedience to Torah.

The reason Paul denies justification by Torah-works in Gal 3:11 is assumed from Gal 2:16 and 3:2–9: namely, since the law brings a curse, no one can be justified by works of law but only through faith in Jesus Christ. Law leads to a curse, but faith leads to a blessing (cf. 3:9–10). God invaded the present evil age in and through Jesus Christ (Gal 1:4; 1:15–16), but Paul's opponents were proclaiming circumcision (Torah-works) as the mark of covenant membership within the people of God to Gentile Christ-followers in Galatia (Gal 5:2–3; 6:12–13; cf. 1:6–7). The apocalypse of God in Christ included Jesus' death and resurrection (Gal 1:1, 4; 3:13) and the revelation of God's Son in Paul on the Damascus road (1:15–16).

---

77 Oakes 2015: 112.

78 Cf. LXX Deut 25:1 and 4QMMT with Gal 3:11 and Rom 2:13.

79 E.g., see the numerous examples in Gathercole 2002. Against Dunn 1998: 152–54.

Each of these events provided Paul with a Spirit-driven, interpretive shift.[80] Once God rescued Paul from the present evil age (1:4), delivered him from the curse of the law (3:13), and gave him the blessing of the Spirit (3:14) by means of the apocalypse of God's crucified, resurrected, and exalted Son (1:1, 4, 15–16; 2:17–21; 3:13), God transformed his understanding of Torah-works, the covenant, Jew and Gentile relations, and how Gentiles related to the covenant.[81] He contends in Gal 3:10 those subscribing to Torah-works are accursed and in 3:11 that no one is justified by Torah since the law requires obedience. Paul's citation from Lev 18:5 assumes that no one can adequately perform the law. Paul instead asserts the Messiah (*Christos*) has come to redeem those under Torah's curse from its curse by becoming a curse for them (Gal 3:13).

Justification "not by works of law" is Paul's way of saying that right standing before God is not by means of Torah, but by exclusive faith in Jesus Christ (Gal 2:16—3:29).[82] This is the reason for the Hab 2:4 citation "the righteous one by faith will live." Namely, the righteous one is the justified one, and this one shall live by faith (=shall receive eternal life by faith) (cf. John 11:25; Rom 1:17; Heb 10:38), because no one is justified by means of the law (cf. Gal 3:11).

---

80 For a discussion of Paul's hermeneutic of faith, see Watson 2015. For a recent work on reading Paul with the Reformers, see Chester 2017.

81 I disagree with certain aspects of Wright's exegesis of Gal 3:10–14, but he rightly agrees Paul's revelation of Christ transformed his understanding of these things. Wright 1991; 2013.

82 Regardless of whether the term "legalism" applies here, it must be stressed that Paul is critiquing the idea that human action precedes divine action in the distribution of God's soteriological blessing. If the Galatians pursued justification by Torah-works, they would have been trusting in their effort to justify them. Their effort should be criticized as contrary to the gospel of justification by faith, because God revealed his Son in Paul as the means by which Jewish and Gentile sinners can be justified. Torah-works are no longer relevant for demarcating the people of God from the non-people of God, but faith in Christ since now in the new age the apocalypse of God in Christ has invaded the cosmos via the incarnation, death, and resurrection of Jesus. The law emphasized obedience in the old age, but Paul emphasizes faith in Christ now that Christ has come. However, if the Galatians pursued Torah-works alongside of or in addition to faith in Christ, then they would render the grace of God revealed in Christ as null and void (Gal 2:21). Justification "not by works of law but by faith in Christ" proposes one viable option to life: namely, faith in Christ now that Jesus has invaded this present evil age to deliver Jews and Gentiles from the curse of the law (Gal 1:4; 3:13). Faith in Christ and only faith in Christ is the pathway to the Abrahamic blessing that leads to life (Gal 3:14), not Torah-works (2:16; 3:10—4:7).

Torah-observant Jews performed the law in order to live in the present age (Deut 4:1; 8:1; Ezek 20:11, 13) and in the age to come (Bar 4:1; 1QS IV.6–12; CD III.14–20; Let. Aris. 127).[83] In 4 Macc 17:12, Jews, who faithfully endured suffering for the sake of God's law, were given the reward of "immortality" and "long lasting life." Paul argues Jews and Gentiles are justified by faith in Christ apart from works of law (Gal 2:16), and the law does not give life (3:21). Life comes through Christ (cf. Gal 2:16, 19–20). One must experience a death to the law by co-crucifixion with Christ to receive the life promised in, but unattainable by, the law (2:19). In 3:10–12, Paul "interprets the saving actions of God . . . in view of what God has done in Christ (Deut 30:12–14)."[84] In light of God's apocalypse in Christ, Paul understands the life-giving promises of the law to point to and to be fulfilled in Jesus Christ. His remarks in 3:13–18 support this point.

Paul's reference to Jesus as the *Christos* in 3:13 is significant. God promised Abraham that he would bless the nations through him (Gen 12:1–3; 15:1–5; 18:19). God likewise promised David a seed to reign forever over his kingdom (2 Sam 7:12–14). These promises both to Abraham and to David are realized in Jesus, the seed of Abraham and the Son of David (Gal 3:16; Rom 1:3). The former is evident in Galatians when Paul calls Jesus the seed of Abraham (Gal 3:16). The latter is evident by Paul's numerous references to Jesus as the Christos/Messiah in Galatians (Gal 1:12, 22; 2:4,16–17, 20–21; 3:1, 13–14, 16, 26–28; 4:19; 5:1–2, 6).[85]

Gal 3:10–14 has its main verbal clause in 3:13. The verse lacks an explicit connecting particle. But it appears to assume an adversative connection since the content of 3:13 contrasts with 3:10–12. Paul's point appears to be law brings a curse to all (3:10–12), "but" Christ redeems "us" from the law's curse.

The law is aligned with a curse in Galatians. It gives a curse (3:10, 13). Paul here seems to come very close to identifying the law as a curse.[86] If so, the latter point does not in any way, shape, or form intend to communicate an anti-Jewish attitude in Galatians. Rather, Paul communicates an anti-Torah attitude in the letter. To be under the law is equivalent to being under a curse (3:10, 13), under sin (3:22–23), and under the *ta*

83 So Das 2014: 322–23.

84 Das 2014: 324.

85 So also Gal 3:22, 24, 29; 5:4, 24; 6:2, 12, 14, 18; 4:14.

86 Agreeing with Schlier (1989: 136), Betz (1979: 149) says the law gives a curse and is a curse.

stoicheia tou kosmou in Galatians (4:3, 5, 9). Paul's anti-Torah tone in the letter is already anticipated in 1:13–14 when he talks about his "former manner of life in Judaism." Paul speaks this way because his devotion to Judaism and the law prior to his faith in Christ represented the old age. Torah-observant Judaism apart from faith in Christ only leads to a curse (3:10). But Christ "redeemed us from the curse of the law" (3:13).

The verb *exagorazō* ("I redeem") in 3:13 refers to buying time (LXX Dan 2:8; Eph 5:16; Col 4:5). A cognate verb (*agorazō*) refers to buying grain (LXX Gen 41:57; 42:5) or to buying unspecified things (1 Macc 13:49). Since Paul uses slavery and freedom motifs in Galatians (4:1–9, 21–31; 5:1), *exagorazō* has a slavery connotation and thus communicates the idea of redemption/emancipation. Jesus redeems (purchases) Jews and Gentiles from the law's curse.[87] Those of works of law are already under its curse, but Jesus liberates them "from" this curse (cf. 4:5). This interpretation is confirmed by Paul's later remarks about the law.

He asserts the law imprisons those under its jurisdiction (3:15—4:7). In 4:1–4, Paul compares life under the law to a child under the instruction of a pedagogue until the set time of the father. During this time, the child is no different than a slave until he reaches the age of maturity, although he is Lord over the inheritance (4:1). In 4:4–5, Paul asserts God sent his Son to be under the law to redeem (*exagorazō*) those under the law so that they would receive adoption. This redemption results in sonship (4:5). This sonship results in an inheritance of the Spirit for those whom God redeemed through his Son (4:6). In Gal 3:19–29, Paul argues the law was given as a guardian and a pedagogue because of sin to enslave, to guard, and to oversee those under its power so that they would be justified by faith in Christ and become heirs of Abraham's inheritance. But, in 4:1–7, Paul suggests Jesus redeemed those under Torah's mastery so that they would in fact become sons and heirs of God's promises to Abraham.

In the OT, a person could redeem slaves (LXX Exod 12:44), land (LXX Lev 25:24), a victim of a murder (LXX Exod 21:30), property (LXX Lev 25:18–32), and the firstborn (LXX Num 3:46).[88] Paul identifies those under the law as slaves (cf. Gal 3:19—4:7). He establishes Christ as the liberator of those under the law's slavery, stating he paid the price of his life to redeem those from bondage under the law to extend to them the blessing of Abraham (Gal 3:14) and to liberate them from the *ta stoicheia*

---

87 For different uses, see BDAG, 271.
88 For a discussion of redemption, see Silva 2014: 1.139–40.

tou kosmou and the law (3:19—5:1). Paul's remarks about the law strongly contrast with his opponents' proclamation about circumcision (1:8–9; 5:10–11).

By possibly appealing to texts like Gen 12, 15, and 17; Lev 18:5; and Deut 27:26, Paul's opponents were seeking to persuade the Galatians to pursue justification by Torah since they believed it would lead to life (Gal 5:3). Paul was seeking to dissuade the Galatians from pursuing justification in Torah because he believed it would only lead to a curse (Gal 1:8–9; 3:10). But Christ, Paul suggests, delivered those under the curse of the law from the curse by becoming a curse (3:13).

In his famous Galatians commentary, J. Louis Martyn argued central to Christ's death in Gal 3:13 is "apocalyptic warfare."[89] Martyn's apocalyptic reading highlights some important aspects about the death of Jesus in Galatians.[90] He emphasizes Jesus' death was God's victory for those under the curse of the law (Gal 3:13).[91] "God's victory in Christ" resulted in emancipation from the present evil age (Gal 1:4; 4:21—5:1). Paul begins the letter with this latter point in Gal 1:4 and continues to discuss victory and freedom in Christ in Gal 3:1—5:1.

In Gal 5:16–21, Paul's discussion about walking in the flesh versus walking in the Spirit further highlights Jesus' deliverance of us from the current cosmological powers of the present evil age. Walking in the flesh represents the present evil age. Walking in the Spirit represents the new age in Christ, the age of the indwelling presence of the Spirit (Gal 3:13–14). And only those who walk in the Spirit will inherit the kingdom of God (Gal 5:21), that is, will experience deliverance from slavery to the weak idols of the present evil age from which Jesus died to deliver and redeem them (Gal 1:4; 3:13—5:21). Jesus' death has inaugurated this kingdom now and has begun the process of new creation (Gal 6:15).

However, an apocalyptic reading alone of Gal 3:13 fails to take seriously Paul's appropriation of the Deuteronomic curses to Jesus' death and the benefits that his death accomplished for those under Torah's curse. Paul states Jesus redeemed us "by becoming a curse" in Gal 3:13 and that his death distributed the Abrahamic blessing to Jews and Gentiles. The apocalyptic deliverance that Martyn rightly affirms can only be a reality

---

89 Martyn 1997: 318n110.

90 For a detailed discussion of Martyn and other apocalyptic readings of Paul, see Wright 2015.

91 Martyn 1997: 318n110.

via Jesus' curse-bearing death for all (Jews and Gentiles) under Torah's curse (3:13; 4:4–6).

In Gal 3:13b, Paul grounds his statement about Jesus' redemption of "us" from the curse of the law in a scriptural citation from LXX Deut 21:23.[92] Scholars have made much of the identity of the "us" in Gal 3:13. A trend in scholarship has been to interpret the "us" to refer to Jews due to the Jew and Gentile distinctions in chapter 2 and because of *ta ethnē* in 3:14 and a switch to the first plural in 3:14b.[93] Support for this reading in both the Hebrew Bible (Isa 45:20–23) and in Second Temple Jewish literature (Tob 14:4–7) suggests that Israel's restoration precedes Gentile abandonment of idolatry.[94] Thus, Christ redeemed Jews so that the blessing would extend to Gentiles (and Jews) (Gal 3:13–14).

The "us" in 3:13 likely includes both Jews and Gentiles since Paul's argument in 3:6–9 is that God promised to Abraham before there was a Jew and Gentile distinction that he would justify all of the families of the earth by faith (3:8). Those from faith, as opposed to those from works of law, are blessed with faithful Abraham (3:9). Paul also emphasizes again that the law brings a curse to all and that justification comes to the one who has faith (3:10–12).

The context of LXX Deut 21:23 is not crucifixion. But, along with the authors of the Dead Sea Scroll (DSS) 11QT LXIV.6–13 (cf. 4QpNah 1.7–8), who applied the verse to crucifixion,[95] Paul applies LXX Deut 21:23 to Jesus' crucifixion. LXX Deut 21:23 occurs in a context about the punishment of a rebellious son. Moses states the parents should bring the rebellious son before the elders at the gates of the city, accuse him before the elders, and then all of the men would stone him to death (LXX Deut 21:18–21). Stoning functioned to purge the evil one from the midst of the community and to put fear within the hearts of the people to detour them away from disobeying Torah (LXX Deut 21:21). Then, LXX Deut 21:22–23 instructs the people not to leave on the tree the dead body of

92 With the exception of two words, Paul's citation of Deut 21:23 agrees verbatim with the LXX.

93 See Donaldson 1986: 94–112; Witherington 1998: 236. Specifically referring to 3:13, so also Wright 1991: 151–53.

94 Das 2014: 330; Schnabel 2002: 35–57.

95 McLean (1996: 132–33) does not think 11QT LXIV.6–13 refers to crucifixion. For references to crucifixion in Second Temple sources, see Jos. *Ant.* 12.255–6; 13.380–83; 20.102; 20:129; *Bellum Judaicum* 1.97–98; 2.75; 2.241; 2.253; Philo, *Flacc.* 72, 83–85; *Ios.* 96, 98, 156; *Somn.* 2.213–14; *Spec.* 3.151.

a person who committed a capital crime (LXX Deut 21:22). The community likely hanged the dead body on a tree as a public spectacle so that everyone would see what would happen to those within the community who violated the stipulations of the covenant.

In a similar way as Paul, 11QT LXIV.6–13 seems to interpret Deut 21:23 to refer to a death by crucifixion.[96] To my knowledge, Gal 3:13 and 11QT LXIV.6–13 are the only Second Temple texts that identify the crucified person as cursed.[97] Many Jewish texts talk about crucifixion, but they do not render the crucified person as accursed (Jos. *Ant.* 12.255–56, 380–81; *Ant.* 18.64; T. Mos. 6:9; 8:1).[98] But both 11QT LXIV.6–13 and Gal 3:13 assert the crucified victim was accursed.

Deuteronomy urges that instead of leaving the dead corpse on a tree, the people should bury it the same night so that the corpse would not defile the entire community, because the person hanged on a tree is cursed by God (LXX Deut 21:23). Paul leaves off the phrase "by God" from the word "cursed." But the context of Deut 21–30 and Paul's appropriation of this section in 3:10–13 with the words "law" and "curse" link 3:10 and 3:13 with Deut 21–30 to support that God cursed Jesus and Jesus identified as an accursed breaker of the law.

By applying the curse of the law to Jesus, Paul demonstrates that the Torah only leads to a curse (Gal 3:10–12). One should not separate the curse of the law from the curse of God in general, but Paul seems to do so here in order to distance the law from God in his argument.[99] In his remarks in Gal 3:19, Paul even says that the law was appointed through angels. To disobey God's law was to receive God's curse that he promises within the law (cf. Deut 27–32). Christ became accursed by the law by representing those under its curse, and he liberated them from its curse (Gal 3:13). Christ became cursed by the law by virtue of being born into the present evil age under the slavery of the law (cf. 1:4; 3:15—4:7). Gal 3:13–14 suggests the curse and blessing of the law kiss each other in the cross of Jesus Christ (cf. 1:4; 6:14–15).

In Gal 3:14, Paul states with two clauses the purpose(s) for which Christ redeemed "us" from the curse of the law: "so that the promise of

96 For a discussion about crucifixion and the curse of God, see Das 2014: 325–27; O'Brien 2006: 55–76.

97 For crucifixion in the Mediterranean world, see Chapman 2008; O'Brien 2006: 55–76, esp. 64; Cook 2014.

98 Das 2014: 326.

99 Similarly De Boer 2011: 213; Martyn 1997: 321, 326.

Abraham would come to the Gentiles in Christ Jesus, so that we would receive the promise of the Spirit through faith." This verse reiterates his earlier remarks about the Spirit, faith, and the blessing of Abraham from 3:1–12. The entire section of 3:1–14 focuses on the means by which Jews and Gentiles participate in the blessing of Abraham and receive the Spirit.

Interpreters debate the relationship between these two "so that" clauses (also called *hina*-clauses because of the Greek word *hina*).[100] One option is the second *hina*-clause should be interpreted to explain the first purpose clause.[101] This interpretation understands the two clauses to communicate one truth about Jesus' death in 3:13: "so that the blessing of Abraham would come to the Gentiles in Christ Jesus, that is, so that we would receive the promise of the Spirit through faith."[102] This interpretation also understands the blessing of Abraham and the promise of the Spirit to refer to the same thing: namely, eternal life in Christ and the realization of God's promise to Abraham through God's invasion of the world in Christ and the distribution of the Spirit.

The second interpretation of the relationship between the two purpose clauses suggests the first one provides the purpose of redemption in 3:13, whereas the second provides the result of the first purpose clause.[103] This interpretation suggests the following: "Christ redeemed us from the curse of the law by becoming a curse for us . . . so that the blessing of Abraham would come to the Gentiles in Christ Jesus, [and the blessing comes to the Gentiles in Christ Jesus] so that we would receive the promise of the Spirit through faith" (brackets mine). A third option is to interpret both purpose clauses as coordinate with the main verb in 3:13, but to interpret them as producing two different effects: (1) the blessing of Abraham to the Gentiles and (2) Jewish and Gentile reception of the Spirit.[104]

De Boer understands all who believe (Jews and Gentiles) as recipients of the blessing of the Spirit.[105] Ben Witherington's interpretation distinguishes between the blessing of Abraham to the Gentiles and the

---

100 For a discussion, see Moo: 2013: 214.
101 The Greek syntactical category is called epexegetical. Moo 2013: 214.
102 So Moo 2013: 214; Longenecker 1990: 123; De Boer 2011: 214.
103 Lightfoot 1957: 140; Caneday 1989: 205–6.
104 Hays 2000: 262.
105 De Boer 2011: 214.

Jews (="we") who receive the promise of the Spirit.[106] It suggests Gentiles receive the blessing of Abraham, but "we" (=Jews) receive the promise of the Spirit through faith. Witherington's interpretation fits with his view that the pronouns "we/us" in 3:13 specify Jews. He says, "If Paul is being consistent in his use of 'we' in this passage, Paul will be seeking to emphasize that Christ's death not only opened the door for the Gentiles to receive the blessing but for Jews to receive the Spirit, just as he had already said the Galatian converts did at 3:5 (cf. Acts 2.32)."[107]

The first interpretation of the purpose clauses seems right.[108] Both clauses are coordinate,[109] and modify the main verb "to redeem." The second clause clarifies or further defines the first purpose clause. Christ's redemption of "us" from the curse of the law is redemption for both Jews and Gentiles from the law's curse. This redemption results in the blessing of Abraham coming to the *ethnē* (i.e., all the families of the earth), which is a universal distribution of the promise to Jews and Gentiles (cf. Gal 3:8 with Gen 12:1–3).

Paul begins this section in 3:2–5 strongly suggesting the Gentiles received the Spirit by faith with a series of questions. He says "those from faith" (Jews and Gentiles) (cf. 3:2–5) are blessed with faithful Abraham (3:6–9). This statement contrasts with "as many are from works of law are under a curse" (3:10). Blessing and curse are universalized in 3:2–10. Those who have faith like Abraham (Jews and Gentiles) are blessed (3:6–9), but those who subscribe to works of law (Jews or Gentiles) are cursed (3:10). The opponents in Galatia are preaching the law to the Galatians. If they embrace law, they place themselves under the curse and forfeit the promise originally given to them when they believed after Paul initially preached the cross to them (3:1–2, 5; 5:4).

In 3:6–9, Paul asserts further the Galatians' experience of the Spirit and of numerous additional spiritual experiences were by faith apart from works of law, just as Abraham believed God's promise and he reckoned his faith to him as righteousness. In 3:7, Paul states all people from faith are sons of Abraham. In 3:8, he supports this assertion with reference to the justification of the *ethnē*, citing Gen 12:3 as scriptural proof. He infers in 3:9 that all from faith are blessed with the faithful Abraham.

---

106 Witherington 1998: 240.

107 Witherington 1998: 240.

108 Rightly Martyn 1997: 323; Schreiner 2010: 219; deSilva 2014: 64.

109 So Matera 1992: 120.

Gal 3:10–14 offers reasons that (1) the law brings a curse (3:10); (2) the law does not justify (3:11–12); and (3) Christ redeemed both Jews and Gentiles from the law's curse (3:13). This redemption was for the intended purpose-result of distributing the blessing of Abraham (which Paul has already stated twice comes to all those from faith, whether Jew or Gentile) (3:7, 9). Thus, the universal distribution of the Spirit to Jews and Gentiles in 3:14 fulfills the promise to bless the *ethnē* through faith in Jesus Christ. This universal distribution of the Spirit upon all flesh (=Jews and Gentiles) is the fulfillment of what the prophets anticipated (Isa 40–66; Joel 2:28; cf. Acts 2:1–40).[110] Isa 44:3 specifically parallels "Spirit" and "blessing" and "seed."[111]

Fusing the Horizons: The Importance of the Cross and the Spirit in the Christian Life

The cross of Jesus Christ makes the law no longer necessary for Jews or Gentiles aspiring to be part of the people of God and the family of Abraham (3:10–13). This does not mean, however, that Jews neither can nor should any longer practice a Jewish way of life in Galatians. Instead, the cross makes the practicing of the law irrelevant as a marker of the people of God and as a marker of those who are welcomed into the Christ-following assemblies. Christians deeply need to understand who they are in light of the cross and the Spirit, whom God distributes to Jews and Gentiles by faith through the cross and resurrection.

When we truly live cross-centered lives as Christians, we will live Spirit-empowered lives as Christians. And then, and only then, Christians will be in a position to pursue with urgency the kind of Christ-centered unity and love for one another for which Jesus died and for which Paul labored amongst the Galatians and other Christian assemblies. The cross-centered and Spirit-empowered life will enable Christians to love one another and so fulfill the law of Christ (5:13–14; 6:2). This cross-centered and Spirit-empowered love for one another will manifest itself in Christian communities through specific actions. We will resist the lust of the flesh, such as quarreling with one another, being divisive with one another, engaging in

110 E.g., see Isa 4:2–6; 11:1–2; 32:15–17; 44:1–5; 59:21; 61:1; Jer 31:31–34; Ezek 11:14–21; 36:22–27; 37:1–14; Joel 2:28–29 (MT 3:1–2). Similarly Das 2014: 334n318.

111 Similarly Hays 2000: 261.

selfish rivalries with one another, and being at enmities with one another (5:20–21). Instead, we will display love toward one another by showing peace, patience, kindness, goodness, faithfulness, compassion, and self-control toward one another (5:22–23). We will show love toward one another as Christians by bearing the burdens of one another, helping fellow believers when they fall into transgression, honor those who teach us the word, and by doing good toward all people, especially toward those within Christian communities (6:1–10). The cross is not an abstract historical event void of practical value for the Christian life. The historical fact of the cross in Galatians turns the ages from the old age to the new age and is the means by which God grants by faith in Christ to Christians the Spirit who enables them to live in unity with their brothers and sisters in Christ as they together live out in their churches in the Spirit co-crucifixion with Christ and co-crucifixion to the world (2:19–20; 6:14).

The Superiority of the Promise over the Law (3:15—4:11)

In Gal 3:15—4:11, Paul emphasizes the superiority of God's promise to Abraham over his giving of the law to Moses. In 3:15–18, he uses an illustration about the certainty of a man-made covenant. This illustration argues God's covenant with Abraham is not abolished as a result of the law. In 3:19—4:7, he explains the law's purpose in light of God's promise to Abraham. In 3:19–22, he asserts the law was given because of sin until Jesus, the seed of Abraham, should come into this world to fulfill the promise. In 3:23—4:7, he argues the law was a temporary guardian until the fullness of time when Jesus would come to redeem those under the law. Paul's entire discussion about the superiority of the promise over the inferiority of the law serves to dissuade the Galatians from turning away from his law-free gospel to his opponents' Torah-observant gospel.[112]

The Temporary Nature of the Law (3:15-18)

In 3:15–18, Paul discusses the certainty of his promise to Abraham in order to defend the superiority of his gospel and the inferiority of his opponents' gospel to dissuade the Galatians from turning away from his gospel. He begins this discussion with an illustration about man-made covenants, which the words "I am speaking in a human way" support

112 Similarly Schreiner 2010: 223–25.

(3:15). He introduces the illustration in 3:15a, elaborates it in 3:15b, and applies it to God's covenant with Abraham in 3:16–18. By repeating the verb *atheteō* ("to nullify") in 3:15, Paul links 3:15 with his conclusion in 2:21: "I do not nullify (*atheteō*) the grace of God; for if righteousness comes through the law, then Christ died needlessly" (brackets mine).[113] Paul rejects justification by Torah-works and avoids nullifying the grace of God (2:21). God does not nullify God's covenant with Abraham as a result of his giving the law to the Jewish offspring of Abraham (3:15–18).

Some debate exists as to whether Paul refers to a covenant or a will/ testament with the word *diathēkē* in 3:15.[114] The idea of will/testament is perhaps Paul's background when he introduces the man-made covenant in 3:15, especially since he speaks of "adding a codicil" to this man-made covenant. However, since Paul discusses the superiority of God's covenant with Abraham over the Mosaic covenant (3:15—4:7), since he connects the Abrahamic "covenant" with language of God's promise of a multitude of offspring (cf. Gal 3:8 with LXX Gen 15:18; 17:2, 4–6) and specifically with the language of seed (cf. Gal 3:15–17 with LXX Gen 17:7–10, 12, 19), and since LXX Gen 17:2–21 specifically mentions God's *diathēkē* with Abraham, Paul likely uses *diathēkē* in Gal 3:15 to refer to a human covenant. This term leads into his discussion of the superiority of God's promise to Abraham over the Sinai covenant with Israel.[115] James M. Scott says covenant is basically an "agreement" or a "pact"

---

113 Similarly Hays 2001: 263–64.

114 See discussion in Das 2014: 345–49.

115 Hays 2000: 263. For a few examples of *diathēkē* as covenant, see Gen 6:18; 9:9; Exod 2:24; 6:4–5; 16:34; Lev 2:13; 16:13; 24:3; Num 1:50, 53; 4:5; 7:89; Deut 4:13, 23, 31; 5:2–3; 7:2, 9, 12; Jdg 2:1–2, 20; 20:27; 1 Sam 4:3–5; 18:3; 20:8, 16; 23:18; 2 Sam 3:12–13, 21; 5:3; 15:24; 23:5; 1 Kgs 3:15; 6:19; 8:1, 6, 9, 21, 23–24; 11:11; 19:10, 14; 2 Kgs 11:4, 12, 17; 13:23; 17:15, 35, 38; 18:12; 23:2; 23:3, 21; 23:2–3, 21; 1 Chr 11:3; 15:25–26, 28–29; 16:6, 15–17, 37; 17:1; 22:19; 28:2, 18; 2 Chr 5:2, 7, 10; 6:11, 14; 7:18; 13:5; 15:12; 21:7; 23:3, 11, 16; 24:6; 29:10; 34:30–32; Ezra 10:3; Neh 1:5; 9:8, 32; 13:29; Job 31:1; 41:4; Ps 25:10, 14; Prov 2:17; Isa 24:5; 28:15, 18; 42:6; 49:8; Jer 3:16; 11:2–3, 6, 8, 10; 14:21; Ezek 16:8, 59–62; 17:13–16, 18–19; 20:37; 34:25; 37:26; 44:7; Dan 9:4, 27; Hos 2:18; 6:7; 8:1; Amos 1:9; Zech 9:11; 11:10; Mal 2:4–5, 8, 10, 14; 3:1; Jdt 9:13; Wis 1:16; Sir 17:12; 24:23; 28:7; 39:8; 42:2; 44:20, 22; 45:5, 7, 15, 24–25; 47:11; 1 Bar 2:35; Pr Azar 1:11; 1 Macc 1:11, 15, 57, 63; 2:20, 27, 50, 54; 4:10; 11:9; 2 Macc 1:2; 7:36; 14:20, 26–27; 4 Ezra 2:5, 7; 3:15; 7:46; 10:22; Matt 26:28; Mark 14:24; Luke 1:72; 22:20; Acts 3:25; 7:8; Rom 11:27; 1 Cor 11:25; 2 Cor 3:6, 14; Gal 3:17; Heb 7:22; 8:6–10, 13; 9:1, 4, 15, 18, 20; 10:16, 29; 12:24; 13:20; Rev 11:19. See Schreiner 2010: 227. Das (2014: 345–49) discusses the evidence for covenant, but argues for the meaning of will/testament.

between at least two parties.[116] The Hebrew Bible speaks explicitly of the Noachic covenant, the Abrahamic covenant, the Sinaitic covenant, the Deuteronomic covenant, and the Davidic covenant.[117] Paul's main point is covenants were meant to be kept, not broken.

Paul applies the analogy of a man-made covenant to the law of Moses. He emphasizes the law does not nullify the covenant with Abraham since the law came 430 years after the promise. If man-made covenants are intended to be kept and not broken, then how much more will God keep his covenantal promises to Abraham? Paul wisely develops the idea of the "promises" instead of the covenant in order to keep separate the law and the promises to Abraham in the rest of chapter 3.[118] Numerous Jewish texts conflate the Abrahamic promise with the law of Moses (Sir 17:11–13; 24:23; 28:7; 39:8; Jub. 6–44; 4 Ezra 3:32–33; 7:24, 46; 8:27).[119] Sirach asserts the Lord gave Israel the law as an "eternal covenant" and as the "law of life" (Sir 17:11–12).[120] Sirach even goes as far as suggesting Abraham kept the law of God (Sir 44:19–20).[121] However, Paul starkly distinguishes between these two covenants. He accentuates the law is neither the fulfillment of nor the pathway to the blessing of Abraham.

Paul refers to the "promises" of Abraham (3:16), saying the "promises were spoken to Abraham and to his seed." The word "promises" (*epaggelias*) forges a link with Paul's earlier remarks about Abraham's faith/faithfulness in 3:6–9 and Abraham's blessing in 3:14. The "promises" especially forge a link with 3:14b where the singular "promise" (*epaggelian*) occurs. The promise in 3:14 refers to the blessing of Abraham, which is the Spirit. Paul further explains the "promise" in 3:14 with his comments about the "promises" in 3:16.[122] Genesis does not actually mention the word "promise" when God makes promises to Abraham (cf. LXX Gen 13:15; 15:18; 17:1–9; 24:7), but this is an insertion by Paul ("promises" in Gal 3:16, 21; "promise" in Gal 3:14, 17–18, 22, 29; 4:23, 28).[123] Gen 17:1–27 links the terms circumcision, covenant, blessing, seed, and the

---

116 Scott 2010: 491–94.

117 Scott 2010: 491–92.

118 Thought from Das 2014: 342–44; 349–50.

119 Das 2014: 342–43.

120 Das 2014: 342.

121 Das 2014: 342–43.

122 Betz 1979: 156.

123 Betz 1979: 156n31.

concept of promise, suggesting that the promises and the blessing are directly related to Abraham's fulfillment of circumcision. In Gal 3:8–16, Paul links covenant, blessing, Spirit, promise, promises, and seed, but he ignores the reference to circumcision in Gen 17 and focuses on the "promises" (cf. Gen 15:5–6 with Gal 3:6; Gen 12:3; 18:18 with Gal 3:8).[124]

The promise of the Spirit in 3:14b is another way of talking about the blessing of Abraham in 3:14a.[125] The universal distribution of the Spirit to Jews and Gentiles as a result of Jesus' death made God's universal promise to Abraham a reality. When Paul refers to the "promises" to Abraham, he likely refers to the entire Abrahamic narrative where God gave multiple promises to Abraham regarding land, seed, and universal blessing and where he repeated the same promises more than once (cf. Gen 12:1–3; 13:14–17; 17:4–8; 24:7; 26:2–5).

Although God made "promises" to Abraham, Paul summarizes them as a singular "blessing" because they were fulfilled by means of the singular distribution of the Spirit to Jews and Gentiles (Gal 3:14).[126] Paul interprets the promises to Abraham regarding land, seed, and universal blessing in light of Jesus Christ and in light of the apocalypse of God in Christ (1:4, 15–16; 3:13). The "promise" is Paul's way of summarizing God's work to deliver Jews and Gentiles from the present evil age (1:4), to deliver them from the curse of the law (3:13), to pour out his Spirit on all flesh (3:14; cf. MT Joel 2:27–28), and to renew creation through Christ (Gal 6:15; cf. Isa 65:17–25). This interpretation fits with Paul's earlier statements about God revealing his Son in him "that he might preach him as good news amongst the Gentiles" (Gal 1:15–16) and with his assertion in 3:16 that Jesus is the "seed" of Abraham instead of identifying Isaac as Abraham's seed.

God promised the land to Abraham and to his seed (LXX Gen 12:7; 13:15; 15:18; 17:8).[127] The land promise is only one of the many promises to Abraham (cf. LXX Gen 12:1–3). In LXX Gen 22:17, God promises to bless Abraham by increasing his seed (*sperma*) because he did not withhold from offering his only son (*huios*) Isaac as a sacrifice to him on the altar (cf. LXX Gen 22:1–18). God promises in LXX Gen 22:17 to make Abraham's seed (*sperma*) as the stars of heaven and as the sand of the sea

124 Betz 1979: 156n31 and 157.
125 Similarly Das 2014: 350; Schreiner 2010: 219; Keener 2018: 142–43.
126 Similarly De Boer 2011: 224; Das 2014: 350.
127 deSilva 2018: 308–9.

as a result of his faithful obedience to God. He further promises Abraham his seed "will inherit" (*klēronomēsei* [same verb in Gal 5:21 to refer to inheriting the kingdom of God]) other cities (i.e., land). LXX Gen 22:18a brings together the promise of the universal blessing of the *ethnē* through Abraham's seed (*sperma*) and the inheritance that his seed will inherit into one statement: "And all of the families of the earth will be blessed in your seed."[128]

God reiterates his covenant with Abraham to Isaac (his promised son). In LXX Gen 26:3–4, God promises Isaac he will bless his "seed" (*sperma*) by giving it "all of the land" that he promised to Abraham (LXX Gen 26:3).[129] He continues saying he would multiply Isaac's seed (*sperma*) as the stars of heaven, that he would give to his "seed all of this land," and that "all of the nations of the earth will be blessed in your seed" (LXX Gen 26:4; cf. LXX Gen 18:18; 22:18).

Paul uses this language when he refers to the promise of universal blessing in Abraham in Gal 3:8. He clarifies his point by asserting the promises were spoken to a singular "seed" of Abraham instead of to a plurality of "seeds" and by identifying Jews and Gentiles who have faith in Christ as the seed of Abraham and heirs of his promises (Gal 3:16, 29). Gal 3:29 affirms there would be many heirs of a singular promise for those in Christ, the seed of Abraham: "If you are Christ's, then you are the seed of Abraham, [namely], heirs according to the promise" (brackets mine). God fulfills all of his promises to Abraham only through Jesus Christ, the true seed of Abraham.[130] "Christ is the one true heir of Abraham, and Christ's people share in this inheritance only by becoming incorporated into his life (cf. 2:20; 3:26–28)."[131] And through the universal distribution of the Spirit, God's promises to Abraham are realized in all of the families of the earth (cf. 3:14).

The late (and possibly) second century CE Jewish text 4 Macc 18:1 refers to the Israelites as those born of the "seeds of the Abraham people" with a plural form of *sperma* (*spermatōn*). The author connects the "seeds" (*spermatōn*) of Abraham with Israelites. Paul, however, goes out of his way to highlight the promises to Abraham were not spoken to

---

128 For further discussion of Paul's remarks here and the different nuances, see Das 2014: 350–51; Longenecker 1990: 130–31; De Boer 2011: 218–25; Moo 2013: 228–30; deSilva 2018: 308–10.

129 Cf. LXX Gen 12:1–13; 15:1–5; 17:1–14; 18:18; 22:1–18.

130 Hays 2000: 264.

131 Hays 2000: 264.

"seeds" (*spermasin*, plural) as referring to many, but to a singular "seed" (*sperma*), who is Christ (Gal 3:16).[132] Paul merges the concepts of Davidic seed when he calls Jesus Christ (cf. 2 Sam 7:12–14; Ps 89:3–4) and seed of Abraham into a singular statement.[133]

Jesus is both the "seed" of Abraham and the Christ (cf. 1:1, 3; 2:16–17, 19–21; 3:1, 13–14, 16, 26–29; 4:19; 6:12, 14, 18). Paul pits the singular seed of Abraham, the Christ, against the many seeds/descendants/offspring of Abraham, namely circumcised Jews, to lead into his argument in Gal 3:28–29 that circumcised Jews and uncircumcised Gentiles in Christ are part of Abraham's family (cf. also Gal 2:11–16). This interpretation seems right because there is "neither Jew nor Greek" in Christ (Gal 3:28) and because "If you all are Christ's, then you all are the seed [sperma, corporate singular] of Abraham" (3:29) (brackets mine). Paul concludes with a similar sentiment in Gal 6:15: "neither circumcision nor uncircumcision is anything but new creation."

LXX Deut 4:37 identifies the "seed" as elect Jews ("And because [God] loved your fathers, he chose their seed [*sperma*] after them, and he himself led you out by his strong hand from Egypt" [brackets mine]). Paul interprets the identity of the "seed" in light of Jesus and the Spirit (Gal 3:2–3, 5, 13–14; 4:6, 29; 5:5, 16–22, 25). The uncircumcised, Gentile Abraham inherits a universal offspring of descendants through his singular seed/offspring, Christ. Through the Christ, Jews and Gentiles become part of the seed/offspring of Abraham by faith in Christ (Abraham's seed) apart from Torah-works and circumcision (cf. Gal 2:11–16).

Paul returns to the theme of covenant in Gal 3:16–17. The law of Moses, which came 430 years after the promise, does not nullify a covenant that was ratified by God so that it would abolish the promise (Gal 3:19). Gen 15:13 states Israel spent 400 years in Egypt. 430 years could refer to the number of years the Israelites were slaves in Egypt (Exod 12:40–41).[134] Once more, 430 years could be a general time frame from the last reference to God's promise to Abraham in Gen 48:20 before slavery in

132 Cf. also Williams 1997: 95.

133 Hays (2000: 264) asserts Paul's exegesis builds upon the Jewish tradition of "the messianic seed of David." This seed will inherit an eternal covenant corresponding to God's covenantal promise with David (2 Sam 7:12–14). Cf. 4QFlor. I.10–13; 4 Ezra 7:28.

134 For a similar understanding of the 430 years as Paul and later Rabbis, see Jos. *Ant.* 9.1, 204; *J.W.* 9.4, 382. Das 2014: 353 pointed me to these sources.

Egypt.[135] Thus, 430 years could refer to the general time frame after the promises to Abraham and continue through Egyptian slavery until the time YHWH delivered Israel from slavery.[136] Regardless, though, of how one takes the 430 years, Paul's basic point is the law, which came years after the promise to Abraham, does not abolish the promise, which God gave to Abraham before he gave the law to Israel. Rather, the chronology of the promise supports it is superior to the law, because the former came first and the latter came hundreds of years after the promise.

In 3:18, Paul supports the preceding assertions about the superiority of the promise over the law based on chronology: "for if the inheritance is from the law, then it is no longer by means of a promise. But God freely gifted Abraham through a promise."[137] This verse connects the concept of inheritance and promise with Abraham (cf. LXX Gen 26:3–5). LXX Gen 26:5 links God's promises to Abraham with his faithful obedience (LXX Gen 26:5), neither with circumcision (LXX Gen 17:1–14) nor with Torah-works.

Second Temple Jewish literature suggests otherwise. In Jubilees, Abraham's calling and blessing are subsequent to his obedience (Jub. 12:1–5, 12–14, 19–20, 22–24).[138] 1 Macc 2:52 states Abraham was reckoned as righteous because of his faithful obedience to the test. Sir 44:19–21 states God entered into a covenant with Abraham and promised to bless the nations through his "seed" (*sperma*) because he "treasured the law of the Most High One."

Jewish ideas contemporary with Paul speak of the eternality of the law (Wis 18:4; 4 Ezra 9:37; 1 En. 99:2; Jub. 3:31; 6:17; Bar 4:1; 2 Bar. 77:15).[139] But Paul shockingly says the law is both temporal and inferior to the promise (Gal 3:17–18, 21). And, more than this, Paul suggests Abraham's inheritance was given by grace through a promise apart from the law ("For if by law the inheritance [is], then no longer by means of a promise. But to Abraham through a promise God freely gifted Abraham."). Here grace and law are mutually exclusive. This, however, is not a reference to or a critique of legalism. Rather, Paul's remarks critique the

---

135 Das 2014: 353; Schreiner 2010: 230–31n37.

136 Schreiner 2010: 230–31n37.

137 For recent work on grace as gift, see Barclay 2015.

138 For divergent pictures of Abraham in Second Temple Judaism, see Bowley 2010: 294–95.

139 Das 2014: 354.

prominent Jewish belief in Second Temple Judaism that God's gracious action of blessing Abraham was subsequent to his obedience to Torah.

Like LXX Gen 26:5, Paul links the blessing of Abraham with his faith and faithfulness (Gal 3:9). He associates Abraham's faithfulness with faith (Gal 3:5–9; cf. LXX Gen 15:6), not with the necessity to uphold the eternal sign of circumcision (LXX Gen 17:1–27).[140] This suggests Paul is still basing his argument against the opponents largely on the Abrahamic narrative. This narrative permeates with faith in/faithfulness to God's promises (Gal 2:16–3:29; cf. LXX Gen 12:1–23:20). Throughout Gal 3:6–18, he refers to several important themes in the Abrahamic narrative: "believing/faith/faithful" (3:6–9; cf. LXX Gen 15:6), "blessing" of the *ethnē* (3:8–9, 14a; cf. LXX Gen 12:1–3; 15:1–5; 18:18; 22:17–18), "promise/promises" (3:14b, 16–18; cf. LXX Gen 12:1–3; 15:1–5; 17:1–14), "covenant" (3:15, 17; cf. LXX Gen 17:1–14), and "inheritance" (3:18; cf. LXX Gen 22:10, 17; 26:4). In Abraham's day, this inheritance referred to land (LXX Gen 12:1–3; 26:3–4), but the promises included land and many descendants (LXX Gen 12:1–3). In LXX Gen 21:10, the translators use a verbal cognate (*klēronomesei*, "he will inherit") of the noun *klēronomia* ("inheritance") to assert that Ishmael will not inherit with Isaac. Jewish communities on occasions interpreted inheritance as a reference to eternal or eschatological life (Pss. Sol. 14:5, 9–10; 15:10–11; 17:23; cf. also 1 Pet 1:4; 3:9; Rev 21:7).[141] Jews also interpreted the inheritance in terms of inheriting the entire cosmos (cf. Ps 22:27–28; Sir 44:21; Jub. 22:14; 32:19).[142]

Certain Jewish texts associated promise and inheritance with the law (2 Macc 2:17–18; Pss. Sol. 12:6; 2 Bar. 14:12–13).[143] Paul associates the promise and the inheritance with faith in Christ and separates them from the law (Gal 2:16—3:29). He synonymously interprets the inheritance and the promise as realized by faith in Christ through the singular distribution of the Spirit via his death and resurrection (Gal 3:13–29;

---

140 Similar to LXX Gen 17:1–27, Jub. 15:23–33 links the blessing of Abraham with the covenant sign of circumcision, and both texts identify circumcision as an eternal covenant (LXX Gen 17:7, 13, 19; Jub. 15:28). Jub. 23:10 speaks of Abraham's perfection of ways. Postdating the NT, later rabbinic literature states Abraham "obeyed the entire Torah, even before it was written" (*m. Qidd.* 4:14) and that God preserves the world because of Abraham's "merit" (*m. Tanh.* Exod 34). Bowley 2010: 295 pointed me to these texts. Preceding comments in note are influenced by him.

141 Das 2014: 355.

142 Schreiner 2010: 231.

143 Similarly Das 2014: 356.

4:5). Paul contends the promise, and other promises, were given to Abraham and Jesus, his seed (Gal 3:16). He has already identified the promise as the Spirit in Gal 3:14b ("the promise of the Spirit"). The promise of the Spirit and the promises to Abraham are realized in Jesus and in the giving of the Holy Spirit to Jews and Gentiles who have faith in Jesus Christ (Gal 3:1–14). The promises are fulfilled by means of the death of the Christ who delivered Jews and Gentiles from the present evil age and from the curse of the law (Gal 1:4; 3:13–14). The promise of the Spirit inaugurates the new age (Gal 1:4) and envisages the additional promises given to Abraham by transforming them into promises related to eternal life (cf. Gal 5:16—6:9). Eternal life in Galatians includes the realization of Isaiah's new creation (Gal 6:15; cf. Isa 65:17–25).

In Gal 4:21–31, Paul allegorizes the verse about Isaac and Ishmael and Sarah and Hagar in LXX Gen 21:10 to show the Galatians that they (Gentiles in Christ) are children of the free woman (=Sarah). They are citizens of the heavenly Jerusalem because they are in Christ, whereas the opponents (and non-in-Christ Jews) are children of the earthly Jerusalem (=subject to the law of Moses). This is Paul's way of saying Gentiles in Christ are delivered from the curse of the present evil age (1:4), the curse of the law, and the slavery that it produces (3:13; 4:21—5:1). The opponents and non-Christ following Jews are under the law's curse and its bondage (3:10-4:7).

Paul emphatically asserts in Gal 4:28 the Gentile Galatians are children of the promise (=Abraham's spiritual offspring), if/because they are Christ's (3:29). And if/because they are Christ's, then they are heirs (*klēronomia*) of the blessing of Abraham. As children, they have access to Abraham's inheritance, which is ultimately soteriological in nature (i.e., justification by faith, the reception of the Spirit, eternal life, the kingdom of God, and new creation [2:16, 19; 3:14, 29; 5:21; 6:15]).

Paul confirms this point lexically in 5:21 when he says that those who walk according to the flesh instead of according to the Spirit will not inherit (*klēronomesei*) the kingdom of God. Those who do not have the Spirit will fall short of inheriting Abraham's (soteriological) inheritance. The Galatians were part of Abraham's family by virtue of their faith in Christ and their experience of the Spirit. Their embrace of circumcision (i.e., the law) would have placed them under the law's curse (3:10), under slavery (cf. 3:23—4:7), without the Spirit (cf. 3:14), and excluded them outside the kingdom of God and from participating in new creation (cf. 5:21; 6:15).

The Law's Purpose (3:19–25)

With his remarks in 3:18, Paul concludes his discussion of the Abrahamic narrative. He now begins to answer an important question in 3:19–4:7: If the law is not the pathway to the Abrahamic blessing (3:2–18), but Christ's death and faith in Christ (3:13–18), then why did God appoint the law? Paul's answer is simple, even if the way he presents it is not. God appointed the law "because of transgressions" (3:19).

With the words "what then?" in 3:19, Paul introduces the Galatians to a question he will later answer. The question is "what's the purpose of the law?" Paul's answer occurs in 3:19b—4:7. The law was appointed/added (*prosetethē*) "on account of transgressions" (3:19).

Shockingly, on the one hand, Paul might be distancing God from the law here with the passive verb in 3:19a (*prosetethē*).[144] If so, this distancing adds to Paul's argument that his gospel, which fulfills the promise, is superior to the opponents' gospel, which focuses on Torah. Of course, Paul knows God appointed the law. However, on the other hand, one must not press the passive voice of *prosetethē* too much since Paul asserts in 3:16 with the passive verb that "the promises were spoken to Abraham and to his seed." It would be grossly incorrect to argue that Paul distances God from the promises to Abraham because of the passive form of the verb "were spoken."

Instead, Paul's basic point here is not who appointed the law (he assumes God) but why the law was appointed. He asserted earlier the law was appointed 430 years after the promise (3:17). The law's appointment did not intend to abolish the promise by adding to the initial covenant (cf. Gal 3:15 with 3:17–18). Now, he states why the law was appointed: "on account of transgressions" (3:19).

"Transgressions" (*parabaseōn*) is a technical word for violating God's revealed commands.[145] When one disobeys Torah, he commits the sin of transgression (cf. Rom 2:23). The meaning of the phrase "on account of transgressions" is unclear because of the preposition *charin* ("on account of") attached to it. The preposition could be interpreted

---

144 Similarly Hays 2000: 267. Against Hübner 1984: 24–36; Martyn 1997: 356–57, who argued angels acted without God and gave the law.

145 E.g., LXX Ps 100:3; Rom 2:23; 4:15; 5:14; Heb 2:2; 9:15. Paraptōma is Paul's typical word for transgression (e.g., Rom 4:25; 5:15–16, 20; 11:12). For discussion of the textual variants, see Das 2014: 338–39; Moo 2013: 245.

in at least seven ways.[146] But I briefly discuss the most likely meaning in Galatians and argue for my interpretation.

First, God appointed the law to increase the power of sin.[147] This view understands the verse as analogous to Paul's argument in Rom 4:15 and 7:1–25.[148] Second, God appointed the law to curb evil through sacrifices.[149] Third, the law was given to identify sin as transgression.[150] Positions one and two are theologically accurate descriptions of the law, but do not seem to represent Paul's point in Gal 3:19. Here Paul neither discusses the law's function in increasing the power of sin nor its function to curb evil. Position three is true in Rom 4:15, but finds no exegetical basis in Paul's argument in Galatians. Instead, the statement God appointed the law "on account of transgressions" refers to the temporary, pedagogical guardianship of the law over those under its jurisdiction to identify sin as transgression until Christ came to fulfill the promise.[151] The law still identifies sin as transgression now that Christ has come. But Paul's point is now that Christ has come, the law is no longer the pedagogue (3:19—4:7). Rather, Christ and the Spirit are (cf. 3:14; 5:5, 16–26). Since I think Paul's discussion of the law in Gal 3:19–4:7 supports this interpretation, I will support it below in my exegesis of this section.

In 3:19b, Paul adds a temporal clause to communicate the temporary and inferior nature of the law in comparison to the eternal and superior nature of the promise: "until the seed should come, to whom he gave the promise." His discussion of the temporary guardianship of the law continues throughout 3:20—4:7. This is evident by the numerous temporal markers: "*Before* faith came" (3:23), "imprisoned *until* the faith was revealed" (3:23), the law became a pedagogue "*until* Christ" (3:24), "*after* faith came" (3:25), "*as long as* the heir is an infant" (4:1), "*until* the set *time* of the father" (4:2), "*when*" we were infants (4:3), and "*when* the fullness of *time* came" (4:4).[152] Gal 3:22 asserts the scripture imprisoned "all things" under sin until Christ would come. The scripture imprisons by identifying sin as transgression and placing those under the law under

146   For a discussion of options, see Das 2014: 358–61.

147   Betz 1979: 165 for support of this view.

148   Betz 1979: 165.

149   Dunn 1993: 189–90.

150   Matera 1992: 128; Longenecker 1990: 138–39 with qualification. Hays 2000: 266n164 pointed me to these texts.

151   Contra Das 2014: 360–61. Das emphasizes the converting function of the law.

152   The italicized temporal markers are based on my translation of the Greek text.

a curse and sin (cf. 3:10–12, 22, 23). Many Jewish sources in the Second Temple period suggest Torah is eternal (Sir 24:9; Wis 18:4; 4 Ezra 9:37; 1 En. 99:2; As. Mos. 1:11; Jos. *Ag. Ap.* 2.38; Philo, *Mos.* 2.14).[153]

Paul declares God temporally appointed the law because of transgressions "until the seed" would come (3:19b). The seed (*sperma*) is a reference to Christ (cf. 3:16). His coming brings the guardianship of the law to its end (cf. 4:1–7). In 3:19c, Paul adds the "seed" is the one "to whom he has given a promise." Along with "seed," the concept of promise recalls Paul's remarks in 3:16: "now the promises were spoken to Abraham and to his seed . . . who is Christ." His remarks in 3:19c further aid his premise that the coming of the seed resulted in the expiration of the law, given because of transgressions, because God gave a promise to Abraham's seed apart from the law. Still talking about the law's inferiority, Paul states the law "was appointed through angels by the hand of a mediator" (3:19d).

At first, Paul's remarks about angels serving as agents through whom the law was appointed might seem odd. However, they are supported in the LXX and in at least two places in the NT besides Gal 3:19c. In LXX Deut 33:2, the translator states the Lord appeared to Moses at Sinai with angels. In Acts 7:53, before his death, Stephen preached the Jews received the law as "ordinances from angels."[154] Hebrews 2:2 speaks of the "word spoken through angels." Paul argues for the superiority of the promise over the law by the way the law was transmitted to Israel. The law was appointed through angels, revealed to Moses (the mediator) (Gal 3:19c; cf. Acts 7:53), and then given to the people, whereas the promise came directly from God to Abraham without a mediator (cf. LXX Gen 12:1–3).[155]

In Gal 3:20, Paul continues to discuss the inferiority of the law in comparison to the superiority of the promise by elaborating on the role of the "mediator." The mediator in Gal 3:19c is Moses (Lev 26:46; Num 15:23; 36:13; LXX Exod 34:29). Paul suggests mediation is an inferior act of communication.[156] He remarks that a "mediator is not [the mediator] of one, but God is one" (brackets mine). Moses was the mediator between God and Israel (e.g., Exod 20:1—Deut 33:29).[157] Moses represented more

153 Texts cited in Betz 1979: 168n48.

154 *Diatagas* in Acts 7:53 is a nominal cognate of the participle *diatageis* in Gal 3:19c. Second Temple Jewish apocalyptic literature is latent with examples of angels giving revelations from God (e.g., Jub. 1:17—2:1; 1 Enoch, 2 Baruch, 4 Ezra).

155 Similarly Schreiner 2010: 243.

156 Cf. also Philo, *QG* 1.55.

157 For specific texts, see Exod 20:19, 21–22; Lev 26:46; Deut 5:4–5, 22–23, 27, 31;

than one party. He mediated as a third party for at least two additional parties (God and Israel).[158]

Mesitēs ("mediator") occurs in LXX Job 9:33 to refer hypothetically to someone who would mediate between Job and God. With the exception of Gal 3:20, each time the term "mediator" (*mesitēs*) occurs in the NT, it always refers to Jesus as the mediator between God and man (cf. 1 Tim 2:5; Heb 8:6; 9:15; 12:24). Paul's point with this analogy is the mediator represents other people, but God does not. He represents himself. But Moses (=the one mediator) represents God and the people (see Exod 20:1–Deut 32).[159] "But God is one!" With the latter statement about God's oneness, Paul appeals to "the very law" from which he endeavors to distance God and the Galatians.[160]

A similar statement occurs in LXX Deut 6:4 ("Our God, namely the Lord, is one Lord") to accentuate Israel must love her one and only God with all of her heart by obeying the law. Paul seems to appeal to LXX Deut 6:4 (i.e., the law) to emphasize oneness for the purpose of highlighting Gentile inclusion (cf. also Zech 14:9).[161] There is one seed of Abraham (Gal 3:15–19). There is one God (3:20). Jewish and Gentile Christ-followers are one in Christ (3:28), and they are the many heirs that make up the one seed of Abraham (3:29). However, the law with its many commandments separates Jews from Gentiles.

The Lord expected Israel to show love for and faithfulness to him through Torah-observance. Neither in LXX Deut 6:4 nor in Gal 3:19c–20 is this statement an abstract appeal to Jewish monotheism. Rather, in both places the statement is a Jewish way of expressing the supremacy of God over all things and his demand of all to worship him, for he is the one and true God (monotheism) of Jews and Gentiles.[162] In Gal 3:19c, the statement "God is one" specifically communicates that Israel's one God, who represents himself, gave a promise that sits in authority over the law.

33:2; Acts 7:38, 53; Heb 2:2; 9:15.

158 Similar to Moo 2013: 237; Lightfoot 1881: 146–47; Burton 1921: 190; Longenecker 1990: 142. Against Wright 1991: 157–74, who sees "one" as a reference to the people of God.

159 Cf. Lev 26:46; Num 36:13. Contra Cosgrove 1988: 66, who argued the first occurrence of "one" in 3:20 refers to Christ in 3:16.

160 Similarly Hays 2000: 267.

161 Bruno 2010.

162 For this point, see Bruno 2010. On monotheism in Second Temple Judaism and early Christianity, see Bauckham 2008.

God represents himself. He directly gave a promise to Abraham to bless the nations through him without a mediator, but he gave the law to Israel through the mediation of angels and Moses. Paul's opponents represent themselves (Gal 6:12–13), but Paul's gospel comes directly from God (Gal 1:1, 11–12). His gospel from God emphasizes the promise, which Abraham received directly from God, instead of Torah-works, which Israel received from God, through angels, and from Moses.

In 3:21a, Paul restates the question in 3:19 with another question related to the law: "is the law contrary to the promises of God?" He answers with an emphatic "No!" Paul again uses the plural "promises" to refer to the relationship between the law and the promise. Given the context, it seems right to understand the phrase "promises of God" as a reference to the promises God gave to Abraham (Gal 3:16). God fulfilled these promises when Jesus died and universally distributed the Spirit upon Jews and Gentiles who have faith in him (Gal 3:13–14). Paul is not asking whether the law and promise are different, for he's already established they are (cf. 3:1–20). Rather, Paul's point here is to deny emphatically that the law leads to life. This is why he asserts in 3:21c, righteousness would come by means of law if law leads to life. If law leads to life, then the law would be contrary to the promises.

Both the Hebrew Bible (Lev 18:5) and Second Temple literature (Bar 3:9, 13–14; 4:1; Sir 17:11; 45:5; 4 Ezra 14:30) teach obedience to the law will lead to life. The Jewish texts interpret temporal life in the land in Lev 18:5 as eternal life in this world and the next (Bar 3:9; 4 Ezra 14:30).[163] The law promises life to those who obey it (Gal 3:10–12; cf. Lev 18:5; Deut 6:24; 30:15–20; 32:47; Sir 17:11), but the promise promises life to those who believe it is fulfilled in Christ (Gal 3:5–9, 29).

Paul interprets the promise of life in the law as a promise of eternal life. He also interprets it in light of the death and resurrection of Jesus to poignantly assert, against his opponents, that eternal life comes only through belief in the fulfilled promise in Christ (2:11—5:1). Paul's verb for "give life" in 3:21 (*zōopoieō*) refers to God's act and Jesus' act of resurrecting the dead (John 5:21), to the resurrection of the dead without specifying the agent of the resurrection (1 Cor 15:22, 36), to Jesus' resurrection (1 Pet 3:18), to eternal life and Spiritual resurrection (Rom 4:17;

---

163 For a work on soteriology and the theological diversity in early Judaism, see Gurtner 2011.

8:11), and it refers to the Spirit's act of creating eternal life (John 6:63; 2 Cor 3:6).[164]

Paul's concern in 3:21a pertains to whether the law works against or "nullifies" the promise. In Gal 2:21, Paul says he will not "nullify" the grace of God by subscribing to Torah-works as a means to justification. In Gal 3:15, he states no one "nullifies" a covenant put into effect. In Gal 3:21b–22, he affirms that if the law was given to lead to life, then righteousness comes by means of law (Gal 3:21; cf. Gal 2:21). Paul concludes life does not come by means of law so that the promise would come "by faith in Jesus Christ to those who believe" (3:22; cf. 3:2–5).

Paul uses "scripture" (*graphē*) instead of "law" (nomos) in Gal 3:22 to expound the purpose of the law. *Graphē* could refer to specific scriptural references (cf. Mark 12:10; Luke 4:21). Paul likely identifies the law as scripture since he refers to the law's role to imprison those under its jurisdiction in Gal 3:23—4:7 and since *graphē* refers to the law elsewhere in the NT (cf. 1 Tim 5:18; 2 Tim 3:16; Jas 2:8).[165] Instead of nullifying the promise, the law/scripture "shut up all under sin so that the promise would be given by faith to those who believe" (Gal 3:22).

The opponents in all likelihood appealed to the law/scripture as support for their gospel of circumcision. Paul uses the law/scripture against them by saying law/scripture actually imprisoned all until Christ came. The opponents were attempting to lead the Galatians away from Christ to the law/scripture, which enslaves them (3:15—4:7), and they were apparently experiencing some success (1:6). Paul attempts to lead the Galatians away from the law to Christ, who redeems/liberates them from the law (Gal 3:13—5:1).

In 3:23—4:7, Paul continues his discussion about the inferiority of the law. He links 3:23 with 3:22 by using *sugkleiomenoi* ("being imprisoned").[166] The law universally imprisons all things and all people. Paul negatively speaks of the law saying "now before faith came, we were held in custody under the law, because we were imprisoned to the faith about to be revealed." To be under the law is equivalent to being under a curse (cf. 3:10) and under sin (3:22). The law, Paul says, did not liberate those with current faith who were once under its jurisdiction. Rather, it

164 For similar discussions of the verb, see also De Boer 2011: 233; Das 2014: 367; Moo 2014: 238–39; Betz 1979: 174n104.

165 Cf. also Exod 32:16; Deut 10:4; 1 Chr 15:15; 28:19.

166 Cf. sunekleisen in 3:22.

imprisoned and held them in custody as a guardian until a temporary period of time.

Paul's reference to faith continues to contrast the promise and the law (cf. 3:2–22). "Faith/trust" refers to "faith in Christ" (2:16; 3:2–29), for Jesus delivered "us" from the present evil age and from the curse of the law (1:4; 3:13). "Under the law" communicates slavery to the law's power, which "being imprisoned" and "held in custody" support (3:22–23). To be under the law is explicitly identified as slavery in 4:21–22 (cf. also 4:1–8; 4:21—5:1). In Galatians, to be "under the law" (3:23; 4:5, 21) is also equivalent to being "under a curse" (3:10), "under sin" (3:22), under demonic powers (4:3), and within the present evil age (1:4).

For Paul, the present evil age includes life without the Spirit and life under sin, under the law, under the elements of the world, under a curse, and under slavery. The phrase "elements of the world" (*ta stoicheia tou kosmou*) is connected to the "weak" and "poor" "elements" (*stoicheia*) to which the Galatians were contemplating a turn to serve as slaves (4:9). Gal 4:8 suggests these "elements" at least refer to the idols worshipped as gods by the Galatians prior to their faith in and liberation by Jesus (cf. 4:2–7).[167] *Stoicheia* occurs in the plural in Second Temple Jewish literature to refer to the elements of the universe without the accompanying phrase "of the world" (Wis 7:17). In Galatians, the phrase *ta stoicheia tou kosmou* ("elements of the world") refers to the old age (1:4) enslaved under sin (3:22) and under the law (4:3–5).

The "world" is another way of talking about the "present evil age" in Galatians (cf. 1:4 with 6:14), for Paul asserts the world has been crucified to him and he to the world (6:14). In 2:19–20, he speaks for the first time of his co-crucifixion with Christ as a death to the law so that he would live to God. Thus, "world" encompasses "law" and the "present evil age." But Jesus' death delivered "us" and liberated "us" from the bondage within the present evil age under the law by bringing about the age of the Spirit (1:4; 3:13–14).

The Spirit leads to life (3:10–14; 5:16–26), deliverance from the curse of the law (3:13–14), and grants status within Abraham's family (3:29—4:7). This new life in Christ is simultaneously "life" in the kingdom of God (5:21) and a death to the world/the law/the present evil age (1:4; 2:17–21; 4:2–7; 6:12). Prior to God's invasion of this world in Christ (1:4, 15–16), Jews and Gentiles were held in custody under the law and

---

167 Oakes 2015: 135.

imprisoned to the faith, "which is about to be revealed" (cf. 1:4, 15–16; 3:13–14). But once that faith was revealed, that is, once Christ came in the fullness of time (4:4), liberation from the imprisonment and the guardianship of the law came to those with faith in Christ (1:4, 15–16; 3:13—4:6).

"Therefore," Paul infers "the law has become our pedagogue until Christ so that we would be justified by faith" (3:24). Paul's argument pertains to the ending of one age (pedagogue/law) and the beginning of another (=Christ). The turning of the ages includes both individuals and the cosmos. This is in fact how Paul began the letter in 1:4: "[Christ] gave himself for our sins so that he might deliver us from the present evil age" (brackets mine). In the fullness of time (4:4; salvation-history), Christ died for our sins (1:4; 3:14; 4:5; anthropology) to deliver us from the present evil age (1:4; apocalyptic). And again in 3:13–14: "Christ redeemed us from the curse of the law, so that the blessing of Abraham would come to the Gentiles, so that we would receive the promise of the Spirit through faith." In 4:4–5, he says Christ was born under the law "so that he would redeem those under the law, so that we would receive the adoption." In 6:15, he specifically refers to "new creation."

Paul reinforces justification by faith apart from the law in 3:24 by underscoring the law's temporary nature (cf. 2:16). He identifies the law as a "pedagogue."[168] The ancient pedagogue had many functions.[169] One of those functions was to serve as a temporary guardian over the child until the appointed time of the father.[170] This seems to be Paul's use of the pedagogue in 3:23—4:7, for he discusses the temporary nature of the law as a guardian from 3:19—4:7. The law served as a temporary guardian until the coming of Christ into the cosmos to identify sin as transgression so that justification would be experienced by faith (3:24). Although Paul is negative toward the law in Galatians, "the Law is not an adversary of God's redemptive purpose; rather, God has used the Law to illuminate Israel's condition—and therefore *a fortiori*, the universal human condition—of bondage to the power of Sin (Rom 7:7)."[171] The law, then, temporarily imprisoned all under sin so that God would fulfill what

---

168 Pedagogue is an English transliteration of a Greek word.

169 For primary sources, see Das 2014: 374; Longenecker 1982: 53–61.

170 For a list of sources that discuss the function of the pedagogue, see Hays 2000: 269n172.

171 Hays 2000: 269.

he promised to Abraham through Jesus Christ, his offspring (cf. Gal 3:16, 25–27).

Sons of God and Abraham's Offspring (3:26–29)

Paul further highlights the priority of the promise over the law: "Because faith has come, we are no longer under a pedagogue" (3:25). In 3:26–27, he supports his premise in 3:26: "for you all are sons of God through faith in Christ Jesus." In Christ Jesus through faith, Jews and Gentiles are sons of God, not through Torah-works (cf. 1:22; 2:4, 17; 3:14; 5:6). In the Hebrew Bible, YHWH identifies Israel as his son (e.g., MT Exod 4:22; Deut 14:1–2; Hos 11:1).[172] Jewish literature likewise identifies Israel as God's sons (Jub. 1:23–25).[173] But now, in the new age of the Spirit inaugurated by Christ's death and resurrection for "us" (Gal 1:1, 4; 3:13–14),[174] Gentiles become God's sons in Christ and by faith (Gal 3:26).

In the OT, Israel is called God's son (Hos 11:1). In the NT, Jesus is identified as God's son (Gal 1:15–16; 2:20).[175] The status of sonship comes to Gentiles, Paul says, because the Galatians put on Christ when they were baptized into Christ (Gal 3:27). Paul closely connects baptism and faith in Gal 3:26–27. The Galatians' baptism symbolically represented they put on Christ (i.e., identified with him), participated in a co-crucifixion (=a death),[176] and became part of the family of Abraham by faith (Gal 3:26–29). This baptism likely refers to water-baptism, for water-baptism was the moment in early Christianity wherein Christians put on Christ in a visually symbolic way (cf. Rom 6:2–11). The Galatians' allegiance to Christ by faith and their sonship were confirmed when they were baptized in water (cf. Rom 6:2–11).[177] Jews and Gentiles receive a

---

172 Cf. with LXX Exod 4:22; Hos 11:1. The latter calls Israel "children" instead of "sons." For a similar point about Jewish texts on Israel as God's son, see Schreiner 2010: 256; Dunn 1993: 202; Das 2014: 378; deSilva 2018: 334n216.

173 See sources in previous note.

174 Since Paul begins the letter with a reference to Jesus' resurrection (1:1) and since he speaks of the new life that Christ's death accomplishes for those who have faith in him (2:20; 6:8), I think he assumes Christ's resurrection from 1:1 throughout the entire letter. Because Jesus lives, those in Christ will experience the life-giving power of the Spirit (cf. 3:13—5:22).

175 Cf. Matt 3:17; 4:3, 6; 8:29; John 1:34.

176 Cf. Gal 2:19–20 with Rom 6:2–11.

177 Many scholars agree that Paul refers to water baptism in Gal 3:27. For an exception, see Hunn 2003–2004: 372–75.

new, transformed identity when they put on Christ by being baptized into him without the total eradication of their old identities. The status the opponents promised the Galatians with their other gospel of circumcision is already realized by faith in Christ apart from works of law, which the Galatians' baptism into Christ proves.

In 3:28, Paul clarifies that in Christ, their social identities do not open up for them the pathway to the Abrahamic blessing or superiority over others in the assemblies of God. In Christ Jesus, no social boundary should either exclude or include those with certain social markers from sharing in an equal portion of the blessing of Abraham ("There is neither Jew nor Greek, neither slave nor free, neither male and female"). The reason for this transformation of social boundaries is "for you are all one in Christ" (3:28b). The clause "for you all are one in Christ" explains the meaning of Paul's denial of distinctions in Christ. Paul does not teach the obliteration of social distinctions in Christ,[178] but the transformation of social distinctions in Christ in the assemblies of Galatia.[179] The distinct groups mentioned in 3:28a are all one in Christ. That is, they are unified in Christ (cf. 2:11–14). These distinctions are not determinative for Abrahamic sonship.

God's covenant with Abraham in Gen 17:9–14 prioritizes males as the recipients of the covenantal sign of circumcision (cf. Gen 17:15–16). Only males could be circumcised in the old covenant. Both males and females could receive baptism as the sign of the new covenant in Christ (cf. 3:28). One of Sarai's roles in the Abrahamic narratives was to give birth to Abraham's offspring. However, Paul says that union with Christ, the seed of Abraham (Gal 3:16), includes Gentiles, Jews, male and female, slave and free within the family of Abraham regardless of social distinctions: "for they are all one in Christ" (Gal 3:28). This oneness is transformation in Christ.[180] Paul's reference to the Jewish and Gentile distinctions between Jewish Christ-followers and Gentile-Christ followers in 2:11–14 support this reading, as well as Paul's argument throughout the letter that Gentile Galatians in Christ do not need to embrace Jewish Torah-works to become part of Abraham's family (e.g., 2:1—5:12).[181] In Christ, social

178 Against Betz 1979: 189–201.

179 Against Fee 2007: 142.

180 For a helpful discussion and for secondary sources, see Das 2014: 384–87 and sources in n. 267.

181 Christ's liberation of Jews and Gentiles from this present evil age (1:4) and from the curse of the law (3:13) and his universal distribution of the Spirit to Jews and

distinctions neither include nor exclude one from Abraham's family, but acceptance or rejection of Abraham's seed determines one's status within Abraham's offspring (Gal 3:28–29). Social distinctions remain for those in Christ (cf. 2:15). But, in Christ Jesus, these social distinctions do not constitute one's access to the privileges of Abraham in the assemblies of God (cf. 2:14).

Paul conspicuously makes the above point in 3:29: "now if you are Christ's, then you are Abraham's seed, namely, heirs according to the promise." He again returns to the concept of promise (3:14, 16, 18). Gentiles in Christ (and Jews in Christ) are part of the family of Abraham apart from circumcision and apart from Torah-works. They put on Christ, the seed of Abraham (3:16), who (Jesus) delivered Jews and Gentiles from the present evil age and from the curse of the law (1:4; 3:13–14).

Paul redefines the offspring of Abraham in 3:29, suggesting that only those in Christ (regardless of social distinctions) are transformed into God's offspring and that only they are heirs of his promises to Abraham. Jesus endowed Jews and Gentiles with the promise of the Spirit. The Spirit is the proof that all the promises to Abraham are realized in Christ Jesus (cf. 3:14). This point is sustained by Paul's link of "promise" and "heirs." These concepts are from the Abrahamic narrative (cf. LXX Gen 12:1–3; 15:16; 17:2–23; 18:18). In Christ Jesus, the Galatians received the Spirit (Gal 3:14), became children of Abraham, and sons and daughters of God along with Christ-following Jews (Gal 3:13–14, 28–29; 4:6).

Fusing the Horizons: Honoring Women and Hating Misogyny in the Church Honor the Gospel

In the United States, certain churches have created a culture of dehumanizing, exploiting, shaming, and objectifying women. This misogyny crosses

---

Gentiles in Christ incorporate distinct social groups into the family of Abraham as they place faith in Christ and put him on via baptism. There were still social distinctions between Jews and Gentiles, slaves and free, and male and female in the first century within the assemblies of Christ (cf. 1 Cor 7, 11, 14). Otherwise, Paul's acknowledgment of these distinct groups would have had no rhetorical effect in a letter written to dissuade Gentiles from embracing a Torah-observant gospel preached by Jewish teachers. In Gal 3:28, Paul does not suggest an in-Christ identity void of social identities in the Christ-following community. He affirms the unity of a transformed in-Christ community filled with people from distinct social communities. Compelling Gentile Christ-followers to be circumcised fractures that unity.

denominational, racial, ethnic, cultural, theological, social, educational, economic, and geographical boundaries. Certain churches have overtly or covertly created an abusive culture toward women. This abuse is verbal, physical, and emotional. In egalitarian and complementarian contexts, brave women are coming forward to tell their stories of and experiences of being abused in egalitarian or in complementarian contexts.

In Gal 3:28, Paul reminds us that women have the same access to the spiritual blessings of Abraham as men and that neither their God-given identity as women nor the social barriers that often disadvantage them in society because they are women disqualify them from the spiritual blessings of Abraham that they have in Christ. Sadly, too often, in certain kinds of egalitarian and complementarian churches, and in the homes of the families that attend them, women are viewed as honorable only in so far as they serve as the means by which husbands satisfy their sexual desires within the context of marriage or in so far as they are agents through whom they bear children for their husbands. Certainly, child-bearing is a beautiful (and biblical!) stewardship, and indeed God ordains sexual intimacy within the context of marriage between one man and one woman as a good thing.

However, any man (or woman) who thinks a woman's sole purpose for existence is to be used as a means by which men satisfy their sexual desires or only as a means to procreate dishonors the gospel and dehumanizes women as fellow image-bearers. Some women will never marry. Some women who marry will never be able to bear children and, therefore, will never be parents. And, at some point in many marriages, husbands and wives will be incapable of engaging in sexual intimacy with one another as their bodies age and change as a result. But these realities don't make a woman less of a woman. Woman is a woman by virtue of God's good creation of her as a woman.

Although in my view the bible teaches that God creates men and women as ontologically valuable and with ontological dignity because both male and female are created in the image of God, the bible teaches God gives men and women distinct gender roles. In my view, this at least means that although God gives men a unique stewardship of leadership in the home and in the church, women and men share in the same ontological stuff that makes them the climax of and most important creatures within God's good creation. Because they are created in God's image, women are worthy of the dignity that they should receive as image-bearers.

Misogyny is present in both complementarian and egalitarian church communities. Those who hold to either position need to heed the exhortation to honor women. Misogynist churches must stop baptizing their misogyny in a scandalous exegesis of biblical texts in order to twist the bible into supporting any form of misogyny or abuse against women. Misogyny is anti-gospel!

Christian churches should intentionally and urgently honor women in ways that are consistent with the gospel and the church context and communities in which these churches exist. They should intentionally create a culture where racially, ethnically, socially, educationally, diverse women with diverse personalities and with diverse gifts are constantly celebrated, appreciated, valued, honored, and supported to use their gifts in ways that are consistent with the bible's teaching. Honoring women in our churches and in society honors the gospel. And hating misogyny in our churches and in society honors the gospel. Gospel-believing churches should be safe spaces of fellowship and community for diverse women. They should be spaces where women are valued as fellow image-bearers of God, the Father, as co-heirs of his Son, Christ, and as co-citizens of the kingdom of God. May gospel-believing churches honor the gospel by honoring women and by hating misogyny.

Galatians 4

Paul defends His Gospel by means of Scripture and Spiritual Experiences, cont. (3:1—5:1)

Out of Slavery to Adoption in Christ (4:1–7)

In 4:1–7, Paul mixes metaphors. He rhetorically moves from the metaphor of a pedagogue to using the metaphor of stewards and managers. He compares the temporary guardianship (the pedagogue in 3:24–25) of the law to the heir under stewards and managers over his household until the set time of the father (4:1–2). He applies the illustration in 4:3–7 to those in Christ. When Jews and Gentiles were infants under the law, they were enslaved (4:3). But now that God's appointed time has come to bring liberation in Christ (4:5), he lived and died under the law (4:4) and died to redeem Jews and Gentiles under the law, so that they would now in this present evil age be adopted as sons into God's family. In Christ and by the Spirit, God is the Father of Jews and Gentiles (cf. 1:1, 3; 4:2, 4, 6, 31).[1] Just as a child, when he reaches the age of maturity, Jews and Gentiles in Christ have access to the Father's inheritance through the Spirit, who lives in their hearts, because they are sons (4:6). "Therefore," because they are sons, they are no longer slaves, but heirs through God (4:7).[2]

Turning to the Law Leads the Galatians to Idolatry (4:8–11)

In 4:8–11, Paul concludes his argument regarding the superiority of the promise over the law. Here Paul expresses great fear that he labored in vain amongst the Galatians. He fears they were in danger of walking away from the freedom they received by faith in Christ and by his liberating

---

1 For God as father of Israel, see Deut 32:5–6; Isa 63:15–16.

2 For a similar summary with varying exegetical nuances, see amongst many commentators Schreiner 2010: 263; Das 2014: 401–2; Hays 2000: 280–81.

work in order to embrace special days and months and seasons and years related to the law (4:10–11).[3]

In 4:8, Paul reminds the Galatians they formerly before their faith in Christ served idols ("the natural things which are not gods"), because they did not know the true God of Israel. In the OT, knowledge of God and sonship in his family were privileges experienced only by Israel or by those who identified with Israel (Exod 20–Joshua; 1 Sam 3:7; Ps 9:10; Wis 2:13).[4] But in Christ Jesus by the Spirit, the Galatians have "now" been adopted by Israel's true God as sons and heirs (3:13–14; 4:2–9). Their experience of the Spirit because of Jesus' death testifies to this fact (3:13–14; 4:5–6).

Some Jewish sources betray Gentiles as idolaters (Jub. 22:16–22; Wis 14:1–29). Paul likewise identifies the Galatians as idolaters (Gal 4:9–11; cf. Rom 1:18–32; 1 Thess 4:5; 2 Thess 1:8–9). In 4:8–11, he communicates Gentile idolatry in a most shocking way in comparison with his Jewish contemporaries. He contends the Galatians' turn from Christ toward works of law is equivalent to a return to idolatry.[5]

One way that Gentile idolatry would have manifested itself was by means of polytheistic worship. This could have been woven within the social and civic structures of the Greco-Roman world.[6] When the Galatians did not know God, they were idolaters and served their idols as slaves (Gal 4:8–9). But now that they know God, rather are known by God, Paul asks why they were turning again to the "weak" and "poor elements" (Gal 4:9). He calls the Galatians "brothers" (3:15; 4:12; 6:1) and "my children" (4:19) elsewhere in the letter. Both titles suggest that not all of the Galatians had apostatized. In 4:9, he is concerned they are in the process of turning away from eternal life and spiritual freedom in Christ to the curse and the slavery of the law (cf. 3:10—5:1).

The "weak" and "poor" elements in this context refer to the idols mentioned in 4:8, which Paul identifies as "the natural things which are not gods." The term "elements" (*stoicheia*) recalls the phrase "elements

---

3 Similar summary in Schreiner 2010: 275.

4 Das 2014: 419.

5 Keener 2018: 194. My interpretation does not mean to imply that the Galatians' turn to Judaism was ontologically the same as their previous lives in paganism. Rather, if the Galatians turn from Christ to Judaism, they would again be enslaved to the present evil age as they were prior to their faith in Christ. Similarly Witherington 1998: 301-2; Longenecker 1990: 181; Das 2014: 422–25.

6 For primary literature, see Ferguson 2003.

of the world" (*ta stoicheia tou kosmou*) (4:3). Paul identifies the *stoicheia* as weak here but affirmed earlier they have the power to enslave (4:3; cf. Wis 13:18–19). I interpreted the latter above to refer to the old age (1:4), which is enslaved under sin (3:22) and under the law (4:3–5). The Galatians were idolaters prior to their faith in Christ (4:8–9), worshipping the natural things that were not gods at all. But now in the life-giving age of the Spirit inaugurated by Christ's death and resurrection (1:1, 4; 3:13–14), Paul associates the Galatians' turn to Torah as a return to Gentile idolatry.

Prior to God's invasion of this world through Christ (1:4, 15–16), Jews and Gentiles were held in custody under the law and imprisoned to the faith, "which was about to be revealed" (cf. 1:4, 15–16; 3:13–14). But once that faith was revealed, that is, once Christ came in the fullness of time (4:5), liberation from the imprisonment and the guardianship of the law came to those with faith in Christ (1:4, 15–16; 3:13—4:6). Instead of walking in the Spirit and not fulfilling the lust of the flesh (5:16), the Galatians were "observing days and months and seasons and years" (4:10).

These special days likely refer to observance of the calendrical days outlined in the law of Moses (e.g., Sabbath, Yom Kippur, etc. [see Exod 20:1—Deut 33:29]). These would have been clear Jewish identity markers. Jews celebrated both feasts (Lev 23, 25) and festivals (Exod 13:3–10; 23:14–17).[7] Factions within Second Temple Judaism focused on special days and seasons corresponding to the appropriate Jewish calendar (e.g., Jub. 2:9; 1 Enoch 72–82; esp. 82:7–9).[8] Jews widely acknowledged Sabbath as a special day (Exod 31:15–17; Deut 5:12–15; Philo, *Mos.* 2.3).[9]

Observance of the Jewish calendar proves to Paul the Galatians are serious about embracing a Jewish way of life. Yet, in Paul's view, their fixation on special days is an act in step with the present evil age (Gal 4:11), an age under a curse (3:10), under sin (3:22), and under bondage (3:23—4:3). Thus, Paul is shocked (1:6) and genuinely puzzled (4:9) why the Galatians would turn away from freedom in Christ to slavery under the law. Moreover, he feared maybe the Galatians did not really believe the gospel when he preached the crucified and resurrected Christ to them

---

7   For specific Jewish texts, see Das 2014: 424n140.

8   Cf. Das 2014: 424; Schreiner 2010: 279; Dunn 1993: 227; Bruce 1982: 205. Similarly, but with clarifying cautions, see Burton 1921: 234; Longenecker 1990: 182. Against Betz 1979: 217–18.

9   Even non-Jews recognized the uniqueness of the Jewish Sabbath (Juvenal, *Sat.* 14.96). So also Das 2014: 423. For primary texts, see Donaldson 2007.

the first time: "I fear for you lest in vain I labored among you" (4:11; cf. with 1 Cor 15:1–2). He further expresses his concern in 4:12–20.

Argument from Hospitality and Friendship (4:12–20)

In 4:12–20, Paul makes an emotional and motherly appeal to the Galatians not to turn away from his gospel.[10] His appeal is based on his friendship with the Galatians. He urges them to imitate his faith in and faithfulness to Christ, just as he imitated them. He reminds the Galatians he did not impose Jewish regulations on them. He instead lived in a Gentile manner of life when he was with them (4:12). He reminds them their reception of the gospel was evident by the way they treated him when he was "weak" (4:13–14a). They received him as a messenger from God as if he were Christ himself (4:14b).

Paul, then, hyperbolically declares the Galatians' love for him was apparent when they received him and his gospel in spite of his weakness. He says they would have plucked out their eyes for him if possible (4:15). Their love for him in his weakness proves he is not their enemy because he speaks truth to them (4:16). He warns them against the opponents who were seeking them in the wrong way and for the wrong reasons (4:17–18). Finally, he appeals to the Galatians with maternal language, stressing he would suffer labor pains once again for them until Christ would be fully formed in them (4:19). He wishes he could be with them in person and change his tone with them, because he is deeply despondent about their spiritual situation (4:20).

Having argued the pathway to the Abrahamic blessing is faith in Christ instead of law, Paul now appeals to himself as an example. He urges the Galatians to "become as I, because I also became as you!" The desperation in Paul's appeal is evident with his words: "Brothers, I urge you!" This is an emphatic appeal with both the imperative ("become as I") and the verb of volition ("I urge you").

With this appeal, Paul recalls a motif that emerged in 2:11–14 when he records his confrontation of Peter in Antioch. When Peter withdrew from table-fellowship, Paul reminded him he was not living in a Jewish manner of life but in a Gentile manner of life. Consequently, Paul argued it was wrong to compel Gentiles to become Jewish since Jews are Jews by

---

10 For emotion and different kinds of rhetorical devices in the NT, see Kennedy 1984: 15–16. For a primary text, see Quintilian, *Inst.* 6.2.20. Das 2014: 450n30; Witherington 1998: 305.

nature and not sinners by association with Gentiles (2:11–15). In 4:12, Paul commands the Galatians to become like him. He was not a Torah-observant Jew, but a law-free Christ-following Jew (2:19–21). Paul lived in a Gentile manner of life apart from strict observance of Torah when he was with them ("because I [became] as you") by dying with Christ (1:14—2:21) (brackets mine).

A Motherly Reminder that the Galatians Received Paul's Gospel (4:12b–20)

In 4:12b–16, Paul reminds the Galatians of their deep love for him. This rhetorical strategy serves to emphasize they received his gospel when he ministered to them. He says "you did not mistreat me" (4:12b). They received his gospel, evident by their love for him. He reiterates the Galatians' love for him: "And you know that because of a weakness of the flesh, I announced the good news to you formerly" (4:13).

In 4:13, Paul refers to a personal weakness without identifying it. In Rom 6:19, the phrase "weakness of the flesh" appears to refer to spiritual weakness since the chapter emphasizes Jesus' deliverance of sinners from the power and mastery of sin. The term for "weakness" (*astheneia*) often refers to physical weakness in the NT (John 5:5; 11:4; Rom 8:26; 1 Cor 2:3; 15:43; 2 Cor 12:9). This seems to be Paul's referent in Gal 4:13.

Paul's weakness (not sickness) forced him to stay in a specific area in Galatia. This weakness may refer to his personal suffering and afflictions because he preached the gospel of Jesus Christ (Gal 6:12, 17; cf. 2 Cor 4:10; 6:4–5; 11:23–25; 12:7–10).[11] Because of this weakness, he preached the gospel to them (cf. Acts 13–14). This weakness was not burdensome to the Galatians. Rather, they received him as Christ Jesus himself, demonstrating they received his gospel. Or as Gal 4:14 suggests "your temptation in my flesh, you did not despise or spit on."

To spit on someone was a form of dishonor in the ancient world (cf. Matt 26:67; 27:30; Mark 15:19; Luke 18:32). Those in antiquity spat to deter sickness, sorcery, "demonic threats, or an evil eye" (Mark 7:33; John 9:6).[12] The Galatians received Paul and his gospel as they would have received a "messenger of God," as "Christ Jesus" (Gal 4:14). "Messenger" (*aggelos*) is the same term Paul uses in Gal 1:8 to anathematize messengers who preach a false gospel and in 3:19 to refer to agents through

---

11   Goddard and Cummins 1993: 93–126. Cited in Hays 2000: 293n207.

12   So Das 2014: 463; Witherington 1998: 311; Keener 2018: 201.

whom God gave the law. The only other occurrence of the phrase "angel of God" in the NT refers to a divine angel from heaven (Acts 10:3).

Angel (or messenger) of God represents the authority of God. Angels delivered messages from God himself (Matt 1:20, 24; 2:13, 19; Luke 1:13, 19; Gal 1:8). With the phrase "as Christ Jesus" (Gal 4:14), Paul might be identifying Jesus as a messenger from God. However, the three uses of *hōs* ("as, like") in 4:12 and 4:14 make it likely that the fourth *hōs* ("as, like") in 4:14 is comparative. The Galatians received Paul when he was weak in his flesh in a like manner as they would have received a divine angel and much more as they would have received Christ Jesus if he were with them and weak in his flesh. His emphasis is the Galatians received Paul's gospel. A parallel with Paul's comments here is Jesus' statement in Matt 10:40: "The one who receives you receives me and the one who receives me receives the one who sent me."[13]

"Therefore," Paul concludes "where is your blessing" (4:15a)? Paul expresses deep concern for the Galatians' status in the kingdom of God. The context suggests the "blessing" pertains to the Abrahamic blessing, which Paul has argued since 3:1 is fulfilled in Christ and of which Jews and Gentiles participate by faith in Christ (3:1—4:11). The only other occurrence of *makarismos* ("blessing") in Paul is Rom 4:6, 9. There the term also occurs in context of circumcision and Abraham. Paul specifically states the blessing of justification in Rom 4:8 (namely, not having one's sins reckoned to one's account) comes to both the circumcision (=Jews) and to the un-circumcision (=Gentiles) by faith apart from circumcision (Rom 4:9), just as righteousness was reckoned to Abraham by faith apart from circumcision (Rom 4:1; cf. also Rom 4:1–25). But, in Gal 4:15, the blessing could also refer to the Galatians good treatment of Paul.[14]

In Gal 4:15b, Paul again returns to highlighting the Galatians' acceptance of his gospel by reminding them of their love for him when he was with them. He hyperbolically asserts they would have gouged out their eyes and given them to him if possible. The hyperbole is apparent by the conditional statement "if possible" (*ei dunaton*).[15] Das points out the gouging out of the eyes was a "torture technique" in the ancient world (LXX 1 Kgs 11:2).[16] With these remarks of gouging out eyes, Paul

13 De Boer 2011: 280.

14 So Das 2014: 465.

15 For additional hypothetical examples, see Matt 24:24; 26:39; Mark 13:22; 14:35.

16 Das 2014: 465–66. For the metaphor of friends plucking out their eyes for each other, see Lucian (Tox. 40–41). Source cited in Das 2014: 466; Moo 2013: 286; deSilva

hyperbolically demonstrates the Galatians identified with Paul's suffering and the social shame that would come as a result. He speaks to the deep friendship that Paul and the Galatians once shared because of the gospel.[17]

"Therefore," Paul asks the Galatians why they made him their enemy because he speaks truth to them (Gal 4:16). If the Galatians identified with his suffering by receiving him when he suffered and if they were willing to show their friendship by plucking out their eyes for him, then he wonders why they treat him as an enemy because he speaks the truth to them now? Truth in Galatians always relates to the gospel (2:5, 14—refers to the truth of the gospel; cf. 5:7).

Paul suggests the reason the opponents pursued the Galatians was to shut them out (Gal 4:17), not to build them up in the truth. He likely means to shut them out of the family of Abraham, which would result in their exclusion from the kingdom of God.[18] Paul has already argued that Jesus fulfills the Abrahamic blessing and distributes the Spirit to Jews and Gentiles (3:1–29). He later suggests those who fail to walk in the Spirit will not inherit the kingdom of God (5:21). Paul reminds the Galatians of the good (honor) that comes from being zealously pursued (4:18), not only by Paul when he was present with them (4:18). But the opponents sought the Galatians with wrong motives so that the latter would pursue the former (4:17). Later Paul charges the opponents with pursuing the Galatians for the purpose of winning converts to Judaism because they wanted to boast in their (the Galatians') circumcised flesh and because they were afraid to be persecuted for the cross of Christ (6:12–13).

With an apocalyptic punch,[19] Paul's concern for the Galatians takes on a maternal tone. He uses the language of birth pains to describe his desire to see Christ fully formed in the assemblies of Galatia ("in you") (4:19).[20] Paul presents the Galatians' spiritual birth as incomplete. He is

---

2018: 382n22. However, Moo, as Dunn 1993: 236, is open to the possibility that the verse could support that Paul had an eye disease and that the Galatians loved him so much that they would have willingly given him their own eyes—if it were possible.

17 Betz 1979: 228; Longenecker 1990: 193; Das 2014: 466; deSilva 2018: 381–82.

18 Similarly Schreiner 2010: 288.

19 See LXX Isa 13:8; 21:3; 45:10; Jer 4:31; 1 En. 62:4; 2 Bar. 56:6; 4 Ezra 4:2; 1QH 3.7–10; Matt 24:8; Mark 13:8; Rev 12:2. For these and additional primary and secondary sources, see Das 2014: 470–72; De Boer 2011: 284; Martyn 1997: 423–29; Keener 2018: 209n971–74.

20 Against Kahl 2000: 37–49.

genuinely concerned maybe he labored amongst them in vain (4:11). Hence, he expresses despondency about them (4:20). He wishes he could be present with the Galatians and change his sharp tone of concern for them (4:20; cf. 1:6–9; 3:1–5; 4:8–11; 5:12). In 4:21–31, Paul pushes the imagery of childbirth further in an effort to win the Galatians back to his gospel.

Argument from Scripture and an Exhortation (4:21—5:1)

In 4:21—5:1, to advance his argument against the opponents, Paul again mentions Abraham and his descendants (cf. 3:6, 14, 16, 18, 29). The main thought in this section is as follows: Jews and Gentiles in Christ should stand firm in the freedom of the gospel, a freedom provided by Christ. Paul communicates this point in five different ways. First, the Galatians are spiritual children of Abraham (4:28). Second, Jews and Gentiles are spiritual children of the free woman, Sarah, not children of the slave woman, Hagar (4:31). Third, Christ freed Jews and Gentiles to live freely from the law (5:1a). Fourth, the Galatians should stand firm in Christ (5:1b). Fifth, the Galatians should not subject themselves again to a yoke of slavery, which they would do if they subjected themselves to works of law (5:1c). Paul makes his argument with an allegorical interpretation of the Sarah and Hagar story, which he interprets to refer to two covenants (Sarah=new covenant in Christ and Hagar=Mosaic covenant) (4:21–26; cf. with Gen 16:1–16; 21:1–14). Paul also interprets LXX Isa 54:1 to refer to Jews and Gentiles in Christ (Gal 4:27).

In a recent informative monograph, Matthew Thiessen argued Paul's allegorical use of Genesis 16–21 in Gal 4:21–31 serves his argument that "Gentile Judaizing" was wrong. Gentiles in Christ are already children of Abraham and heirs of the promise apart from the mark of circumcision. Thiessen says Gen 17:9 specifically requires circumcision on the eighth day, but neither Abraham nor Ishmael was circumcised on the eighth day (Gen 17:23-26). However, Abraham circumcised Isaac, the promised child, on the eighth day (Gen 21:4). Gentiles in Galatia who received the mark of circumcision would have been more akin to Ishmael, who was not circumcised on the eighth day and who was not the promised child, than with Isaac, who was circumcised on the eighth day and who was the promised child.[21]

21 Thiessen 2016: 73–100.

Thiessen's monograph is a helpful corrective to interpretations that present a caricature of Judaism and the law. He also accurately highlights that Paul's target in Galatians is Gentiles who are in danger of receiving Jewish marks of identity. However, Paul speaks negatively of the law and against those who attempt to keep it from Gal 2:16—4:31 and then again in 5:3–4.

In 2:16, he says no one receives justification by works of the law. In 2:21, he says righteousness does not come by means of law. In 3:1–5, he says the Galatians experienced the Spirit and other supernatural experiences by faith and not by works of the law. In 3:10–14, he says the law brings a curse, and Jesus died to redeem us from that curse. In 3:18, he says the inheritance does not come to its heirs by the law. In 3:19, he says the law was given because of transgressions and that it was appointed through angels. In 3:21, he says the law does not give life. In 3:23, he says the law held us under bondage. In 3:24—4:7, he says the law was a temporary guardian until the seed should come. In 4:8–11, he says if the Galatians turn to the law, this would be analogous to returning to pagan idols. In 4:21–31, he says the law is equivalent to slavery (cf. 5:1). In 5:3–4, he says if one receives circumcision, he is obligated to keep the whole law and that those who seek justification by law have been cut off from Christ and have fallen from grace. Thus, Paul seems to offer a sharp critique of the law and non-Christian Judaism. His remarks in Gal 4:21–31 confirm this interpretation.

In 4:21, Paul reminds the Galatians of the slavery the law produces for all under its jurisdiction (cf. 3:21—4:7): "You who wish to be under the law, tell me: do you not hear what the law says" (4:21)? To be under the law is another way of talking about being under a curse (3:10) and under the bondage of sin in Galatians (3:22–23). The interpreter might expect Paul to quote, echo, or allude to a text from Deuteronomy or another text from the Mosaic law as he reminds the Galatians what the law says. However, he surprisingly appeals to the Sarah and Hagar narrative in Genesis (Gen 16, 21).

After asking whether the Galatians know what the law says, Paul now offers a provocative allegorical interpretation of the Sarah and Hagar narrative. The reasons Paul appealed to this narrative are unclear. Perhaps he did so because the opponents used the Abrahamic narrative to argue Gentiles in Christ had to be circumcised in compliance with

Genesis 17.[22] Nevertheless, Paul uses Abraham one final time in the letter to argue against his opponents' gospel.

Paul could be identifying this story as part of the traditions identified as law (=Genesis–Deuteronomy) since the Hebrew Bible is divided between law (Genesis–Deuteronomy), prophets (Isaiah–Malachi), and the writings (Joshua–2 Chronicles). However, since Paul explicitly identifies his interpretation of the narrative as an allegory (*allēgoroumena*) in 4:24, Paul likely begins his allegory in 4:21 to underline the law produces slavery and those who identify with it are slaves, not the heirs of the promises. This point would parallel with the way Hagar (a slave) and her son (Ishmael) failed to inherit the land with the free woman (4:30; cf. LXX Gen 21:10), for Paul begins 4:22 with the formula "for it has been written." And then he begins to tell the story of Sarah and Hagar from 4:22–24, calls it an allegory in 4:24, and applies the story both to Jews under the law without faith in Christ and to Jews and Gentiles in Christ (4:25–26).

An important issue in Gal 4:24 relates to Paul associating the Sarah-Hagar story with an allegory. The verb "to speak in an allegorical way" occurs nowhere else in the NT. Philo (*Leg.* 2.5) and Josephus (*Ant.* 1.24) use the verb.[23] Philo uses the term both to speak of an allegorical interpretation and "to speak allegorically" (cf. also his allegorical exegesis of Isa 54:1 in *Rewards* 1:158).[24] Without saying Gen 16–21 is an allegory, Paul seems to use the ancient method of allegorical interpretation in his application of the Sarah and Hagar narrative to the Galatian crisis in order to contrast between two covenants: law and Christ, slavery and freedom.[25] Paul's meaning of allegory is close to what some would call typology.[26] An allegorical-typological understanding is likely since Paul says the two women are two covenants (4:24). Paul seems to confirm this interpretation with statements about the two women corresponding to two covenants and two Jerusalems (Gal 4:24–26).

In 4:22–23, Paul allegorically retells the Sarah and Hagar story (cf. Gen 16:1–16; 21:1–12; *Jub.* 16:16–18). Paul asserts Abraham had two sons, one with the free woman and one with the slave woman (Gal 4:22).

22 See discussion in Das 2014: 483–90.

23 Moo 2013: 299.

24 Moo 2013: 299. Cf. also Philo, *Migr. Abr* 82.

25 For an article analyzing patristic exegesis of Gal 4:21–31, see Kepple 1977: 239–49.

26 Martyn 1997: 436; Moo 2013: 300; Schreiner 2010: 300.

Gen 25:1–5 reinforces Paul's allegorical exegesis. We know from Gen 25:1–5 that Abraham had more than two sons. But Paul picks up the part of the Abrahamic narrative that features the child born to the slave woman apart from the promise and the child born to the free woman in accordance with the promise (cf. Gal 4:22–23 with Gen 16–21). Even Gen 25:5 makes it plain that Isaac was the promised child by asserting Abraham gave all that he had to Isaac when he died instead of to the many sons he bore to Keturah, his second wife, and instead of to the sons of his concubines (Gen 25:1–5). Although he gave gifts to the sons of his concubines, he still sent them away from Isaac eastward to the east country (Gen 25:6).

The free mother gave birth to the promised child ("through a promise") (Gal 4:23). In the Genesis narrative, Isaac's conception and birth happen because of God's promise (Gen 21:1–2). The text says "The Lord visited Sarah just as he said and he did just as he spoke" (Gen 21:1). After the Lord's visitation, "Sarah conceived and bore a son to Abraham in his elderly age in the appointed time that the Lord spoke with him" (Gen 21:2). Contrary to the Hagar-Ishmael narrative (Gen 16:1–4), the text says nothing about Abraham entering into Sarah to give birth to Isaac (cf. Gen 21:1–2). But rather, Gen 21 and Paul highlight God's "divine action" to fulfill his promise (cf. Gen 21:1–2 with Gal 4:29).[27] Isaac was born through a divine means (according to the Spirit), but Ishmael through a human means (according to the flesh) (Gal 4:29).[28]

In 4:24, Paul tells the Galatians the Hagar-Sarah comparison is allegorically speaking, even though the allegory likely begins in nascent form in 4:22 because of the statement "for it has been written." Paul elaborates upon this allegory saying Hagar, namely, Mt. Sinai (=the law of Moses) is a mountain in Arabia.[29] She corresponds to the present Jerusalem, by which Paul means Jews under the law without faith in Christ (4:25). "Hagar, Sinai, and Jerusalem are all in the slavery column."[30]

Paul's point is not to make a precise geographical argument, but he wants to associate Hagar with Mt. Sinai and Mt. Sinai with slavery since this is where the law was given.[31] This seems right because Paul says "for

27 Similarly Thiessen 2016: 89.

28 Thiessen 2016: 89.

29 For the syntax of Gal 4:24, see Das 2014: 496–97.

30 Hays 2000: 303.

31 Similarly Das 2014: 497–99; Schreiner 2010: 302; Witherington 1998: 330; deSilva 2018: 397–98.

she is patterned after the present Jerusalem, for she is in slavery with her children" (4:25). In Galatians, slavery is connected to life under the law (3:21—4:7; 5:1). But Sarah represents the Jerusalem from above, for the Greek particle "men" ("indeed/on the one hand") introduces a contrast with Hagar, the slave-woman (4:23), but ends with a reference to the "Jerusalem from above," who is both free and who is "our mother" (4:26).[32]

Das explains that from a Diasporic Jewish perspective, Jerusalem was also the "mother city" (Philo, *Leg.* 281–83; Strabo, *Geogr.* 16.2.28).[33] In Greco-Roman thought, both Greek (Plato, *Resp.* 9.592A–B) and Roman (Seneca, *Ot. Sap.* 4.1; 6.4; 8.1–3) authors contrasted the "earthly city" with the "heavenly city."[34] Das may be right that Paul could be invoking each of these cultural images to contrast the earthly Jerusalem of non-Christ following Jews and Gentiles with the heavenly Jerusalem of Christ-following Jews and Gentiles (contrast with Pss. Sol. 1:6; 4 Ezra 9:38—10:59).[35] However, references to Sinai, Abraham, and covenant would have more likely invoked the images of the Torah-covenant versus the Abrahamic covenant, for Paul appeals to these images in the context of arguing for the superiority of the Abrahamic promise over the law and the Gentile-inclusive nature of the Abrahamic covenant (cf. 3:1—4:31) as he urges the Galatians not to return to idolatry by subscribing to Torah-obedience (cf. 4:8–9).[36]

Martyn argues 4:21—5:1 contrasts two Gentile missions, one pursued by Paul and the other by the teachers.[37] The heavenly Jerusalem represents the "true church of God."[38] The Jerusalem from below represents the church in Jerusalem on earth, "at present satisfied to house the False Brothers with their ungodly support of the enslaving Law-observant mission to Gentiles."[39] Those born according to the flesh into a "state of slav-

32 For the Greco-Roman background behind Paul's remarks, see Das 2014: 495–498; Elliott 2003: 120–23, 258–86.

33 Das 2014: 490.

34 Das 2014: 490; deSilva 2018: 398.

35 Das 2014: 490. See also Jewish sources cited in Das 2014: 499-500. For a discussion of Jewish texts discussing the heavenly Jerusalem, see Martyn 1997: 440; Keener 2018: 220-22.

36 Similarly deSilva 2018: 391–406, although he does not emphasize the idolatry point.

37 Martyn 1997: 431–66.

38 Martyn 1997: 441.

39 Martyn 1997: 440–41.

ery" refer to the "work of the teachers in their Torah-observant mission to Gentiles."[40] Martyn claims, "the circumcision-free mission produces Isaac-like churches, begetting them by the power of God's promised Spirit, and giving birth to them via Sarah, the free woman, the Jerusalem from above."[41]

However, Das points out, "In 4:21–31, Paul associates the Torah-covenant with Hagar, a mother, and a mountain, Sinai."[42] Mother Mt. Sinai is in slavery with her children (4:25). Das and Elliott point out that in 5:12, Paul employs the imagery of mutilation to indict the opponents for teaching circumcision. If the analysis and observations of Das and Elliott are correct, then Paul's words against the slave woman, Hagar, would have likely evoked in the Galatians the reality that to embrace the law of Moses would be their "equivalent" to returning to a life of mutilating idolatry.[43] This interpretation seems plausible in light of Paul's previous warning in 4:8–9: namely, the Galatians were slaves to false gods and to weak and poor elements before they both knew God and were known by God. However, Paul digresses in 4:25–27 without finishing the allegorical explanation of the two covenants. Context suggests, though, that he associates the Abrahamic promise with the free-woman, who brings freedom to Jews and Gentiles in Christ (4:24, 26–27).

In 4:27, Paul conflates the allegorical explanation of the Sarah and Hagar narrative with a fresh appropriation of LXX Isa 54:1 to include both Jews in Christ and Gentiles in Christ within the covenant personified by the free woman and her child. He likely uses Isa 54:1 to highlight that Gentiles in Christ (along with Jews in Christ) should rejoice, although they are ethnically without a husband (=God).[44] The context of LXX Isa 54 focuses on the joy YHWH would bring to Israel when he delivers her from desolation at the hands of the Gentiles because of her sins.[45]

---

40 Martyn 1997: 453.

41 Martyn 1997: 452.

42 Das 2014: 489.

43 Das 2014: 489; Elliott 2003: 120–23, 258–86.

44 Since Paul conflates his allegorical interpretation of the Sarah and Hagar narrative with an appropriation of LXX Isa 54:1 to the Gentile situation in Galatia, perhaps Paul too allegorizes LXX Isa 54:1 to show further the Galatians the difference between the two covenants.

45 For a discussion of Paul's use of Isa 54:1, see De Boer 2011: 303–5.

The personification of Jerusalem as a mother also appears in LXX Ps 86:5 and 4 Ezra 10:7 (cf. 4 Ezra 9:38—10:59).[46] Apocalyptic writers in the Second Temple period, writing after Rome's invasion and destruction of Jerusalem, assert that a glorious transformed city of Jerusalem would soon be revealed (4 Ezra 7:26; 13:35-36; 2 Bar. 4:2-6; 6:9; cf. also Ezek 40-48; 4 Ezra 10:25-28; 13:36; 1 En. 90:28-29; 2 Bar. 4:2-6; Heb 12:22; 13:14; Rev 3:12; Rev 21).[47] Paul picks up on this "well-established" apocalyptic idea, shapes it in light of the apocalypse of God in Christ and his allegorical reading of the slave woman and the free woman, and universalizes the heavenly Jerusalem to include Jewish and Gentile Christians.[48]

The promise of YHWH's future deliverance in LXX Isa 54, a deliverance that would result in Israel's seed inheriting the nations (*ethnē*) (LXX Isa 54:3), would come because he is Israel's husband, her redeemer, and the God of the whole earth (LXX Isa 54:5). The Lord declares he has abandoned Israel for a brief moment and that he turned his face from her with a little wrath (LXX Isa 54:7-8). But the Lord promises to show compassion and mercy to her (LXX Isa 54:8-10). He also promises he would not forsake the covenant of peace (LXX Isa 54:8-10), just as he promised in the days of Noah (LXX Isa 54:9), because his mercy will not depart from his people (LXX Isa 54:10-17).

The barren woman in LXX Isa 54:1 (the verse Paul cites in Gal 4:27) recalls Sarah's barrenness from Gen 16:1. Isa 51:1-3 is "the only reference to Sarah in the OT outside of Genesis."[49] The barren woman, who does not give birth (cf. Lam 1:1, 5, 16), the desolate woman, and the woman with a husband likely refer to Israel in LXX Isa 54.[50] Israel was desolate in LXX Isa 54 because she sinned against her God and suffered his judgment (LXX Isa 1:1-31). As a result, her husband (YHWH) temporarily forsook her (LXX Isa 54:5-8). But, on the other hand, God promises to make Israel fruitful again because he is her husband (LXX Isa 54:5-6). The Lord summons Israel to rejoice because she, though desolate in exile, will have more children than the one who has a husband. The latter

---

46 Hays 2000: 304. Also, Das 2014: 499–500; De Boer 2011: 301; Keener 2018: 221–23; Witherington 1998: 334; Dunn 1993: 253; Longenecker 1990: 213–14.

47 Das 2014: 500. Additional texts also cited in Hays 2000: 304.

48 Hays 2000: 304 influenced this thought. So also Longenecker 1990: 215.

49 Noted by many commentators. For one example, see Hays 2000: 304.

50 So also Moo 2013: 306; Goldingay and Payne 2006: 337; Starling 2011: 44–46; Willitts 2005: 195–97. Contra Oswalt 1998: 413. Against also Das (2014: 505), who asserts the married woman "is likely Babylon" (cf. Isa 47:1-4).

is a promise of God's eschatological restoration of Israel, a restoration that will include the Gentiles (Isa 49:19–21; 51:1–3; 65:17–25; 66:1–9; cf. 4Q164's citation of Isa 54:11–12).[51]

Paul interprets LXX Isa 54:1 to be fulfilled in the ingathering of Jewish and non-Jewish Christ followers into the Israel of God (=the heavenly Jerusalem) (cf. Gal 4:26; 6:15–16). Paul uses LXX Isa 54:1 as scriptural proof for his allegorizing of the Sarah and Hagar story to refer to the new age in Christ that provides freedom from the law (=Sarah) and the Mosaic covenant that enslaves (=Hagar). Paul aligns Jews without faith in Christ under the law with the woman who has a husband and the Gentiles in Christ with the barren woman who, though without a husband, has many children, in order to emphasize Gentiles and Jews in Christ are children of the promise and Jews under the law without faith in Christ are not. This interpretation is sustained by Paul's remarks in 4:28 ("But you, brothers, are children of the promise corresponding to Isaac.") and 4:31 ("Therefore, brothers, we are not children of the slave-woman but of the free-woman."). The day of rejoicing for God's cosmological restoration of Jerusalem has dawned in Christ (cf. Gal 1:4; 3:13–14; 6:15). This cosmological renewal includes both Jewish and Gentile Christ-followers. Paul especially wants the Galatians to know that Gentile Christ-followers, along with Jewish Christ-followers, are the heirs of the promise that God gave to Abraham (cf. Gal 3:8, 16, 29). Gentiles ("you") and Jews ("we") in Christ are "children of the free woman" (4:28, 31).[52]

Paul aligns the opponents (and implicitly the Galatians who embrace the opponents' message) with the desolate ones and with the slave woman and accuses them as persecuting the Galatians, just as the slave woman and her son persecuted Isaac and Sarah in LXX Gen 21:9.[53] Paul interprets Ishmael's playful behavior with Isaac as a form of persecution. When Sarah saw this playful behavior, she urged Abraham to cast out

---

51 Cf. also Isa 2:4; 42:1; 6; 49:6; 51:4–5; 52:10; 54:2–3; 55:5. Das (2014: 506) and Moo (2013: 306) pointed me to these texts.

52 Many commentators have made similar observations. Although each makes his own nuances and disagrees on certain specifics of the text, see, for example, Moo 2013: 29, 305–8; deSilva 2018: 397–406.

53 For a similar point about Paul aligning the opponents with slavery and aligning Christians with freedom, see Witherington 1998: 334–40; deSilva 2018: 397–406. Witherington 1998: 336 specifically notes that Paul represents Sarah in the crisis at Galatia.

Hagar and her son, because he was not an heir to the promise (LXX Gen 21:10).

Paul, citing LXX Gen 21:10, aligns Jews and Gentiles without faith in Christ and the opponents with Ishmael. He implicitly pronounces judgment upon them by saying the slave woman and her child will not inherit with the free-woman and her child (Gal 4:30). He also seems to encourage the Galatians to pronounce judgment upon the opponents by citing LXX Gen 21:10, which commands the expulsion of the slave woman and her son from the midst of the free woman and her son since the former group would not inherit the promise with the latter group (4:30).

Paul's language of inheritance recalls his earlier remarks about those with faith in Christ. Namely, they are the seed of Abraham and heirs of his promise (3:29). His reiteration of the language of inheritance anticipates his warning in 5:16–21 that those who walk "according to the flesh" (as children not of the promise) instead of in the Spirit (as children of the promise) will not inherit the kingdom of God. His conclusion of 4:21–31 comes in 4:31: if the Galatians are children of the promise in Christ (4:28; cf. 3:28–29), therefore, they along with Jewish Christ-followers (hence, "we") are children of the free-woman (i.e., children of the promise) (cf. 3:28–29). Freedom from the law's bondage comes to Jews and Gentiles in Christ because Christ freed them to be free from the law's bondage and curse (1:4; 3:13, 22–23; 4:4–5; 5:1a). Consequently, Paul urges the Galatians "to stand firm" and "not to subject themselves again to a yoke of slavery" under the law (5:1b) and to a yoke of slavery to idols (4:8–9). Paul reminds the Galatians that to put on the yoke of Torah is to subvert to a yoke of slavery to sin (cf. 3:22), slavery to the *ta stoicheia tou kosmou* (4:3), and slavery to the old age (i.e., the flesh) (4:29).

Galatians 5

*A Warning, an Anathema, and Exhortations to Walk in the Spirit
(5:2–26)*

In Gal 5:2–26, Paul offers a sharp warning to the Galatians of the judgment that awaits them if they embrace circumcision (5:2–5). He argues if they receive circumcision, Christ will not profit them in the judgment (5:2–4), unless they obey the entire law (5:3). He then asks a rhetorical question about the identity of those who mislead the Galatians (5:7). He reminds them their confusion about the gospel did not come from the God who calls (5:8). He warns that the one who troubles them will suffer judgment because of this evil and that this evil might permeate the entire lump of Galatians (5:9–10). He states he no longer preaches circumcision (5:11), and he anathematizes the opponents, praying they would cut off their penises (5:12). In 5:13–26, he urges the Galatians to walk in Spirit-empowered love for one another instead of walking in step with the flesh. Otherwise, they would not inherit God's kingdom.

Avoid Circumcision or Perish and Await the Hope of Righteousness by Faith and Live (5:2–6)!

Now that Paul comes to the end of his letter, he wants to shock the Galatians. In chapters 5–6, he forthrightly addresses circumcision. He accents "Look! I Paul myself say to you: if you are circumcised, Christ will not profit you!" Modern readers distant from the *sitz im leben* in Galatia explicitly see here for the first time that circumcision was the primary issue in the churches of Galatia. The Galatians were in danger of receiving the mark of circumcision and subscribing to other elements of the Mosaic law to become part of Abraham's family. Paul has already warned to embrace law is to reject Christ and to place oneself under the law's bondage and guardianship (3:22—4:7), under the law's curse (3:13), under sin (3:22), and to reject the Spirit-empowered promise (3:14). Now, he links circumcision with his previous negative remarks about the law. As a result, Christ will not profit those who embrace the law in God's eschatological judgment.

That Paul refers to eschatological profit seems right because he has argued from 1:1–5:1 for the superiority of his gospel over the opponent's false message; he has explained important elements of his gospel, in 5:21 he refers to inheriting the kingdom of God, and in 6:8 he refers to eternal life. But the kingdom of God/eternal life will come to those whom Christ delivered from the present evil age (1:4), redeemed from the curse of the law (3:10, 13; 4:5), to whom he distributed the blessing of Abraham, namely the Spirit (3:14; 4:6), to those adopted as sons (4:2–7), and to those liberated from slavery to the law (4:21—5:1). If they rejected Christ, they would forfeit the promise/blessing of the Spirit that universally comes to Jews and Gentiles by faith in Christ because of Christ's death (3:13–14).

In 5:3, Paul reiterates the above point by explaining the degree to which the Galatians had to keep the law before circumcision would profit them in the judgment. He asserts: "Now, I testify again to everyone who is circumcised: he is obligated to do the entire law" (5:3). The opponents' message seems to have simply emphasized the importance of circumcision and certain Jewish calendrical laws instead of emphasizing the necessity of obeying the "whole law" as a way of life (4:10).[1] Based on Paul's remarks in 5:3, the opponents did not emphasize perfect obedience to the law. Paul, on the other hand, does (5:3; cf. also Lev 18:5; Deut 22–30; Sir 7:8; 1QS I.13–14; Jas 2:10).[2] His remarks in 5:3 recall his comments in 3:10 ("as many are from works of law are under a curse"), the possible implicit premise to 3:10 ("because no one obeys the law to the fullest"), and his words in 3:10b ("everyone who does not abide by all things written in the book of the law to do them is accursed").

In 5:4, Paul continues his warning. He tells the Galatians those who seek justification (cf. 2:16; 3:1–8) in the law are "severed from Christ," namely, "they have fallen from grace" (5:4). Jewish literature speaks of justification in the law in the affirmative (cf. 2 Bar 4:1; 2 Bar 51:3–4; Sir 44:20–21; 4QMMT). But Paul says those seeking justification in the law

---

1 Against Hays 2000: 312–13.

2 Against Hays 2000: 312. Rightly Das 2014: 524–25; Schreiner 2010: 314; Betz 1979: 259–60; Moo 2013: 324. For the law as a comprehensive way of life without emphasizing the necessity of perfect obedience to the law, see comments in deSilva 2018: 417; Keener 2018: 230–33; Witherington 1998: 368; Longenecker 1990: 226–27; De Boer 2011: 313–14; Dunn 1993: 266–67.

rather than in Christ are severed from Christ and have fallen from grace (Gal 5:4).

Paul's remarks here are a sharp warning to the Galatians. To be severed from Christ and to fall from grace refer to failure to inherit the kingdom of God since Paul associates these warnings with justification (a forensic declaration in God's law-court—see comments on 2:16) and since he refers to the judgment that comes to those who reject his gospel about the cross of the Christ (1:4, 8–9; 2:11; 3:14; 5:12, 21; 6:8). The verbs "severed" and "fallen" support an eschatological context since Paul uses these words in context of justification (5:4) and awaiting the hope of righteousness by faith by the Spirit (5:5).

Elsewhere Paul uses the verb *katergeō* ("to abolish") to refer to putting something to an end (cf. Gal 3:17). In 1 Cor 15:26, Paul refers to Jesus abolishing death (cf. 2 Cor 3:14—refers to the putting away of the old covenant). To be severed from Christ is to be cut off from the justifying grace of the gospel, resulting in condemnation in the judgment instead of justification (6:8). To state it another way, the Galatians' fall from grace is a circumlocution for stating they are in danger of being cut off from the people of God. With these remarks, Paul recalls his warning in 1:8–9, his rebuke of Peter in 2:11–21, and anticipates his anathema of the opponents in 5:12.

In 5:5, Paul explains (*gar*, "for") his warning in 5:2–4: "For by the Spirit, we are awaiting by faith the hope of righteousness." In 5:5, Paul contrasts those who have been severed from Christ and fallen from grace because they were seeking justification in the law via circumcision (5:2–4) with those who await "righteousness" by faith, in hope, and in the Spirit. He recalls the theme of the Spirit from earlier in the letter. The Spirit came to the Galatians by faith (3:2). They began in the faith in the Spirit (3:3). God supplied the Galatians with the Spirit by faith (3:3). Jesus died to give to Jews and Gentiles the promise of the Spirit by faith (3:14). God sent the Spirit of his Son into the hearts of those with faith (4:6), and the Spirit enables them to cry out to God as Father (4:6). Isaac, the promised child, was born according to the Spirit (4:29). Those with faith should walk in the Spirit in order to inherit the kingdom of God (5:16–26; 6:8). Those who walk in the Spirit should restore those who have fallen into sin (6:1). Since Paul associates the Spirit with those who have faith and with those who receive the promise of Abraham (3:1—5:26), the "we" who wait in the Spirit by faith the hope of righteousness are those who have faith in Christ and have received the promised Holy Spirit (cf. 3:1–14; Rom 8:18–30).[3]

The most striking element of 5:5 is Paul speaks of justification as a future hope for which those from faith await by the Spirit. "Righteousness" (*dikaiosynē*) recalls the theme of justification. In 2:16–17, Paul discusses for the first time justification by faith apart from works of law with various forms of the verb *dikaioō*. In 2:21, he mentions righteousness (*dikaiosynē*) does not come "through the law." If it did, then Christ died in vain. "Righteousness" (*dikaiosynē*) is another way of talking about being justified (*dikaioō*).[4]

Justification comes to Jews and Gentiles by faith because God counts them as righteous by faith in Christ (2:16–17; 3:6). This interpretation is sustained by Paul's appeal to Abraham in 3:6 as an example of the means by which Gentiles receive the promise: "Abraham believed God and it was reckoned to him as righteousness [*dikaiosynē*]" (brackets mine). Then, in 3:8, Paul refers to scripture's announcement to Abraham that God would "justify [*dikaioō*] the Gentiles by faith" (brackets mine). In 5:4, he affirms those seeking to be justified (*dikaioō*) by/in the law have been "severed from Christ" and "have fallen from grace." Thus, in 5:5, righteousness refers to justification, and the combination of "hope" and "we await" communicates that justification is a future certainty. But Paul's remarks in Gal 2:16 and 3:10–14 suggest that this future hope has become a present reality for those who have faith in Christ because of Jesus' death for our sins and the distribution of the Spirit to us now in the present evil age as a result of his death for our sins (cf. 1:4; 3:13–14; 4:4–6). "Righteousness" (i.e., justification) is the "hope" for which we wait by the Spirit by faith and which we have already begun to experience because of the cross and the Spirit (1:4; 3:13–14).[5]

Waiting in the Spirit for future justification and walking in the Spirit will result in those whom Jesus delivered receiving the future kingdom of God. Righteousness/justification is already here by faith (2:16), but not

3 Rightly Betz 1979: 261–62; Das 2014: 527; Moo 2013: 327–28; Schreiner 2010: 315–16. Witherington (1998: 369–70) rightly sees an eschatological reference in Gal 5:5, but he thinks the pronoun "we" only refers to Jewish Christians.

4 Similarly Moo 2013: 328; Schreiner 2010: 316. For the view that justification is the object of hope, see De Boer 2011: 316. De Boer defines justification as God's future verdict on behalf of his people in the judgment and as God's deliverance of the cosmos from its "oppressive powers."

5 Rightly Betz 1979: 261–62; Das 2014: 527; Moo 2013: 327–28; Schreiner 2010: 315–16.

yet fully realized (5:5). The kingdom of God is already here and not yet fully realized (cf. 5:21). Both justification and the kingdom of God are certain because of the new age of the Spirit inaugurated by Jesus' death and resurrection (1:1; 3:5, 14). In 2:16, Paul describes justification by faith with a present tense verb, a future tense verb, and a subjunctive verb. Those from faith wait by the Spirit the future certainty of justification by faith, but the certainty of future justification has invaded this present evil age now through the invasion of God in Christ into this world and through the life-giving power of the Spirit (cf. 3:1—5:21).

In 5:6, Paul adds another explanatory statement (*gar*, "for") to 5:5: "for in Christ Jesus, neither circumcision nor un-circumcision prevails anything but faith working through love [prevails everything]" (brackets mine). In "Christ Jesus," the mark of circumcision will neither make the Galatians part of the family of Abraham nor will function as a sufficient act to justify them. The law requires much more than circumcision (cf. 5:3). "In Christ Jesus," changes the course of history and begins the turn of a new age in Galatians. Jesus delivered us from the present evil age by his death (1:4); God revealed Jesus in Paul so that he would announce his Son amongst the Gentiles as good news (1:15–16); Paul rebuked Peter for turning the clock back to the present evil age against the Gentiles when he began to impose Jewish identity on the Gentile Christ-followers in Antioch (2:11–14); the temporary guardianship of the law is now over (3:19—4:7), and Gentiles in Christ who turn to the law become idolaters (4:9–10). God has overcome the old age in Christ (1:4) and has inaugurated a new age in Christ (3:28; 6:15). This new age is dominated by the Spirit, not by the flesh (5:16–26).

The phrase "in Christ Jesus" also recalls the concepts of union with Christ (1:22; 2:4, 17) and the unifying power of his gospel (3:14, 26–29). "In Christ Jesus," circumcision, Jewish identity markers, and human effort are no longer marks of division or exclusion because of faith with the guiding principle of love. Faith profits in Christ Jews and in Christ Gentiles because it aligns those formerly under Torah's curse with Christ, who died to deliver them from the present evil age and from the curse of the law. Faith applies the legal verdict of not guilty upon those whom Christ delivered from the curse of the law (1:4; 2:16; 3:13–14).

Prevailing faith is a justifying faith that works through acts of love (5:6). Love is expressed through sacrificial actions in Galatians (1:4; 3:14; 2:20; 5:13—6:10; cf. John 3:16; Rom 5:8). Love is a key expression to the presence of faith. Without love, there is no faith.[6] Where faith is absent, there is no life-giving power of the Spirit (Gal 3:14; 5:22). Faith and love flow from the indwelling presence of the Spirit (4:6; 5:16–26), who is also the proof that those in Christ are now living as members of a new age by the Spirit in the midst of the old age (5:13–26).[7] "Faith is not merely a subjective mental attitude or an inventory of doctrinal beliefs; it refers— as it did in the case of Abraham—to trust lived out in practice."[8]

Circumcision Leads to Anathema (5:7–12)

Gal 5:7–12 recalls 1:6–9. In 5:7–12, Paul with concern asks the Galatians who hindered them from running well in the faith (5:7; cf. 3:2)?[9] His question is rhetorical, for he stated earlier that "someone is troubling you and wishing to distort the gospel of Christ" (1:7). He avoids stating the identity of his opponents, but he identifies the nature of their proclamation: it leads the Galatians away from Christ to another gospel (1:6), and it leads them away from the truth (5:7).

In 5:7, Paul also recalls his remarks about persuasion from 1:10. He states he persuades God (i.e., obeys him in the truth) (cf. 1:6–9), not man. In 5:7, he asks who persuaded the Galatians to disobey the truth. "Truth" refers to the gospel (cf. 2:5; 2:14).[10] Paul answers in 5:7 by asserting their persuasion to leave the truth does not come from "the one who called them." In 1:6, Paul expresses shock the Galatians were so quickly deserting the one who called them. Although he does not explicitly affirm this in 1:6, the one who calls is likely a reference to God, for Paul has already referred to the one who called him and separated him from his mother's womb to preach the gospel (1:15–16). Given the context, and since he argues more than once that his apostleship and calling come from God instead of man (1:1—2:10), God is likely the one who effectually calls in 1:6; 1:15; and 5:8.

Paul attempts to put distance between his opponents' gospel, the Galatians, and his gospel by experientially linking himself and the

---

6 Similarly Longenecker 1990: 229; Dunn 1993: 271–72.

7 For a similar interpretation of faith and love in 5:6, see Das 2014: 530–32; Schreiner 2010: 317–18; Moo 2013: 329–31; Witherington 1998: 370.

8 Hays 2000: 314.

9 For the athletic metaphor, see also 1 Cor 9:24–27; Phil 3:12–14; 2 Tim 4:7. Texts cited in Hays 2000: 314.

10 So many commentators. For one example, see Keener 2018: 237.

Galatians together as recipients of effectual calls from God (1:6, 15; 5:8). Paul also wants to distance the opponents' teaching from God, suggesting instead that it is hindering the Galatians from obeying the truth of the gospel (5:7). This latter point is supported by Paul's remarks that "you were running well" toward the gospel (cf. 3:3). The imperfect verb (*et-rechete*) suggests the Galatians' progress in the gospel was right until the opponents showed up and began to turn them away from the one who called them by the grace of Christ to a distorted gospel (cf. 1:6–7).[11] He warns them false teaching spreads like leaven increases a lump of bread. Leaven represents evil elsewhere in scripture (5:9; cf. 1 Cor 5:6). Here it refers to false teaching (Gal 5:7). With the proverbial statement in 5:9, Paul might be subtly exhorting the Galatians to expel the false teachers from their midst (cf. Gal 4:30; 1 Cor 5:6).[12]

After his warning, Paul affirms the Galatians will obey his gospel and resist the opponents ("I am confident about you in the Lord that you will not consider another [gospel]) (5:10) (brackets mine). Yet, he again warns the troublemaking opponent will bear God's eschatological judgment (5:10; cf. 1:8–9; 2:11; 3:10). Possibly in response to a charge,[13] Paul attacks the opponents' gospel, stating he does not preach the gospel of circumcision (5:11; cf. 1:10–15). If he does, how can the Galatians explain Paul's experience of persecution (5:11). This persecution likely derives directly from Paul's proclamation of the cross of Christ, which the opponents did not preach because they were afraid they would be persecuted (6:12). If Paul preached circumcision, the message of the cross, which causes people to stumble, would be severed (5:11).

Paul's suffering for the gospel proves he still preached the cross instead of circumcision or works of law (cf. 3:1; 6:17). Paul concludes with a sharp anathema in 5:12: "Oh, I wish those who trouble you would go all of the way and cut off their penises." To be sure, Paul is furious! However, his remarks are not unrelated to his argument. Instead, he prays an anathema upon the opponents. They preached circumcision as the means by which the Gentiles could enter into God's covenant community in addition to their faith in Christ. Circumcision is literally the act of cutting

---

11 Similarly deSilva 2018: 432–33.

12 Williams 1997: 140–41. In agreement, so also Hays 2000: 315.

13 For a discussion of various interpretations of this statement, see Das 2014: 536–40.

off flesh from the male's penis. So, Paul declares he hopes his opponents would cut off their penises since they are so fixated on circumcision![14]

For obvious reasons, a male without a penis could not receive the mark of circumcision. And, thus, he would be excluded from the Lord's covenant community. This interpretation is supported by a litany of people whom LXX Deut 23 forbids from entering the assembly of the Lord. They are all groups who violated the Mosaic covenant in some way (LXX Deut 23:1–5). Furthermore, Paul says he wishes they would "cut off" (*apokopsontai*) their penises with the same verb (but different form) as LXX Deut 23:2 speaks of the eunuch as one who is "cut off" (*apokekommenos*) from the covenant community.

LXX Deut 23:2 says those with their male organs "cut off" would not be allowed to enter into the assembly (*ekklēsian*) of the Lord (cf. Lev 21:18–20; 22:24). The assembly of the Lord refers to the covenant community. The term assembly (*ekklēsiais*) occurs in Gal 1:2 in Paul's salutation. He identifies the recipients of this letter as *ekklēsiais* ("assemblies") of Galatia. The opponents were accursed troublemakers entering into the assemblies of Galatia perverting the gospel of Christ (1:7) and zealously seeking to lead them away from Paul's God-given and Spirit-endowed gospel that centers on the cross of Jesus Christ (1:4, 6; 2:20–21; 3:1, 13, 5:7–9, 11). Paul does not think the opponents are part of the people of God. So, he offers a harsh wish they would demonstrate their exclusion from the in-Christ community by cutting off their penises and testicles (a mark of those outside of the covenant-community in the Torah). If the opponents followed through with Paul's wish, they would literally bear in their bodies the mark of those outside of God's covenant-community in the OT. But ironically, when the mark of circumcision is prioritized by Jews or required for Gentiles instead of faith in Christ, this mark becomes the mark of those outside of the covenant-community in Galatians.[15]

Walk in Step with the Spirit by Loving One Another (5:13—6:10)

Gal 5:13—6:10 probably comprises one unit. The unit accentuates specific acts of communal love the Galatians should show toward one another. The unit further highlights love as a fruit of the Spirit that leads to eternal

14 Similarly Schreiner 2010: 327. For discussion of a pagan background, see Witherington 1998: 374–75; Das 2014: 542–43; Betz 1979: 270; Martyn 1997: 478. See especially Keener's (2018: 241–43) discussion and the primary texts he cites.

15 Similarly Keener 2018: 242–43. See also brief discussion in Moo 2013: 338.

life (5:21–22). Paul's exhortations in this section would have likely baffled the Galatians since autonomy and boasting were important virtues in certain aspects of Greek Philosophical life.[16] Epictetus, a Stoic Philosopher, asserts "He is free who lives as he wills, who is subject neither to compulsion, nor hindrance, nor force, whose choices are unhampered, whose desires attained their end, whose aversions do not fall into what he would avoid" (Epictetus *Diss.* 4.1.1).[17] Paul commands the Galatians to be enslaved to one another in love.

Love for Fellow Christians Fulfills the Whole Law (5:13–15)

In 5:13–15, Paul sustains his previous statements in 4:21—5:6 by recalling the concepts of freedom in Christ and love. The *gar* ("for") in 5:13 links 5:13–26 with 4:21–5:6. This link is supported by the parallel concepts of freedom (4:21–31; 5:1, 6, 13–14) and love (5:6, 13–14). The Galatians were called to live in freedom from the law provided by Christ's death (5:13). They (Gentile Christians) ought not to use their freedom from works of law as an occasion for them to gratify their flesh (5:13b). Flesh is a negative term in Gal 5:13–26. It refers to a power or realm and life lived under the present evil age before Christ's deliverance (1:4). Paul urges them to use their freedom from works of the law and their emancipation from its slavery to be slaves of one another through love (5:13b), "because" God's entire law is fulfilled by love (5:14).

Interestingly, Paul now speaks positively of the law, whereas he spoke negatively of the law from 2:16 onward. In 5:14, he cites LXX Lev 19:18. This citation suggests he refers to fulfilling the entire Mosaic law. Based on the available Jewish sources, scholars have observed the idea of fulfilling the law is a "Christian locution."[18]

Interpreters must remember Paul is not talking about doing works of law in 5:14 (cf. 2:16; 3:12), which his argument from 2:16 onward should make apparent.[19] The phrase "law of Christ" supports this point (6:2).[20] Rather, he speaks of in-Christ, Spirit-empowered love that fulfills the entire Mosaic law. Jesus himself taught his followers that the intent

16 Hays 2000: 321–22.

17 Paragraph influenced by and quote cited in Hays 2000: 322.

18 Barclay 1988: 138; Hays 2000: 322–23.

19 Cf. Longenecker 1990: 242–43. Contra Dunn 1993: 290, who thinks the ideas of "doing the law" and "'fulfilling the law" are closely related in Paul's thinking.

20 Moo 2013: 348.

of the law is loving God and neighbor (cf. Matt 22:34–40). Followers of Christ fulfill the entire law's intent by the power of the Spirit when we love one another, not by trying to perform individual elements of the law (cf. 2:16; 5:3–4), which is the very thing against which Paul has argued so fiercely throughout the letter (cf. 2:16—5:12). That is, Christ-following Gentiles fulfill (i.e., bring to its intended purpose) the law in Christ by the Spirit when they love one another (cf. 5:16–26) and become slaves of love toward one another in the freedom they now share in Christ (5:1).

Jesus' love for the Galatians via his sacrificial death (1:4; 2:20–21; 3:13) personifies how and why the Mosaic law of love (Lev 19:18) has been fulfilled by love: namely, by Christ's act of love through his death for the Galatians (2:20–21; 3:1, 13).[21] Now, because of Christ's act of fulfilling the whole law through his greatest act of love via the cross (2:20) and because his greatest act of love distributes the Spirit to Jews and Gentiles by faith (3:13–14; 4:4–6), Paul exhorts the Galatians to love one another.[22] By doing so, Christians will fulfill the entire law. In 6:2, he restates 5:13–14 by giving them a specific example of how to love one another: bear the burdens of one another. The result of their burden-bearing love for another will be fulfilling the "law of Christ" (6:2). However, if they bite, consume, devour, and irritate one another (5:15, 26), they are in danger of falling short of the kingdom of God (5:21). This law-fulfilling love is a fruit of the Spirit. All followers of Jesus possess this love since they have the Spirit and since this love is distributed by faith by the Spirit to all whom Christ, Abraham's seed, redeemed from the curse of the law and to all who receive the inheritance of their new Spirit-empowered reality in Christ, which they inherit as the seed of Abraham (cf. 3:14, 16, 22, 29; see also Rom 8:3–4).[23]

WALK IN THE SPIRIT (5:16–26)!

In 5:16–26, Paul reiterates his exhortation in 5:13: Do not use your freedom as an occasion for the flesh (5:13). That is, walk in the Spirit, not in the lust of the flesh (5:16–26). He warns the Galatians they will not inherit the kingdom of God if they fail to heed to his exhortation to walk in the Spirit (5:21).

---

21 Similarly Hays 2000: 323–24; Das 2014: 553–54.
22 Similarly Moo 2013: 348.
23 Similarly Hays 2000: 323–24.

Paul begins 5:16–26 with the command: "Now, I say walk in the Spirit" (5:16a). Here he recalls the theme of the Spirit from 3:2—5:4. Since the verb "walk" communicates a perpetual activity, the present tense imperative should be pressed here: "keep walking." The Spirit is the proof that the blessing of Abraham has been distributed to Jews and Gentiles and that the new age has dawned in Christ (1:4; 3:13–14). The Spirit is the one who provided the Galatians with Spiritual and supernatural experiences (3:2–5). Those who have the Spirit are sons of God, heirs of the promise, and children of Abraham (4:5–31), just like Isaac, because Christ set them free from the law (5:1). Those in Christ await final redemption as they walk in the Spirit (5:5).

Now, Paul urges the Galatians to keep walking in the realm of the Spirit instead of the realm of the flesh (5:13). The Galatians must live in light of their deliverance from the present evil age (1:4) and in light of the freedom for which Christ redeemed them (5:1). To state the point in the words of 5:13: "do not use freedom as an occasion for the flesh" (5:13). Gal 5:16 tells the Galatians how to avoid using freedom as an occasion for the flesh: "Now, I say: walk in the Spirit, and you shall by no means fulfill the lust of the flesh."

Many English translations give the second clause in 5:16 the gloss "and you shall by no means fulfill the lust of the flesh." This interpretation suggests that if one walks in the Spirit, then one will by no means fulfill the flesh's desire. This is certainly true. Those who walk in the Spirit will not fulfill the flesh's lust. The NRSV interprets the second clause in 5:16b to define what walking in the Spirit entails ("Now, I say walk in the Spirit. That is, by no means fulfill the lust of the flesh."). Upon this reading, Paul emphatically explains to the Galatians that walking in the Spirit means they should not under any circumstances fulfill the flesh's desire (5:16). This use of a doubly negated subjunctive (*ou mē telesēte*) is not uncommon in Greek. In John 13:8, Peter forbids Jesus from washing his feet with a doubly negated subjunctive (*ou mē nipsēs*, "you shall by no means wash").

However, Gal 5:16 seems to be explaining to the Galatians how they can carry out the exhortation in 5:13–14. Gal 5:13 begins with a reminder that the Galatians were called by God to be free (cf. Gal 4:31; 5:1). This freedom entails that they become slaves of one another in love (5:13; cf. 5:6). Paul immediately urges them not to use their freedom as an occasion for the flesh (5:13). Instead, they should enslave themselves to love one another (5:13), for the entire law is fulfilled by loving their neighbor as themselves (5:14). He offers an example of love by stating its opposite: back-biting one another, devouring one another, and consuming one another (5:15).

After commanding the Galatians to walk in the Spirit and promising victory over the flesh in 5:16, Paul provides reasons in 5:17–26. In 5:17, he states flesh and Spirit have opposing desires as they are hostile toward one another, for they represent two contrasting ages and two different realms (1:4; 6:15).[24] The Galatians should not use their freedom as an occasion to gratify the fleshly desires when they desire them. That is, they do not have the freedom to do whatever they want (5:17).[25] Human agency is either dominated by the Spirit or by the flesh.[26] As a result, the Galatians "are not free to do whatever they want when they want."[27] God's divine action in Christ (1:1, 4), his distribution of the Spirit by faith to Jews and Gentiles via the cross and resurrection of Jesus (3:13–14; 4:5–7), and the Galatians' participation in this new age of the Spirit (3:2—5:26; 6:15) restrict them from doing whatever they want if they desire contrary to the Spirit (5:17).

In 5:17, Paul offers the reason for the command in 5:16: "because the flesh has desires contrary to the Spirit and the Spirit has desires contrary to the flesh, because these things are opposed to one another." Flesh represents the present evil age (1:4). Spirit represents the new age (6:15). Thus, these two ages (powers) have nothing in common. The new age of the Spirit leads to life (2:16–5:1, 5; cf. 4:3), and the old age of the flesh leads to a curse (1:8–9; 3:10–14): i.e., failure to inherit the kingdom of God (5:21). The old age of the flesh and the new age of the Spirit are opposed to one another. Since these things are opposed to one another, the intended result should be that those who walk in the Spirit will avoid doing the things of the flesh when they desire them (5:16–17). That is, since flesh and Spirit are opposed to one another, the Galatians cannot do what they want (5:17).[28]

The flesh in Galatians represents an existence in the present evil age (1:4), an existence under the curse of the law (3:10), an existence imprisoned under sin (3:22–24), an existence under the *ta stoicheia tou kosmou*

---

24 Similarly Das 2014: 563; De Boer 2011: 335–39; 352–53.

25 Barclay 1988: 112.

26 See Barclay 1988: 112.

27 Barclay 1988: 112.

28 For a helpful discussion of 5:17, see Barclay 1988: 115–16.

(4:3), an existence under slavery (4:1–8), and an existence under idolatry (4:9). The Spirit represents the new age in Christ, an age that personifies the fulfillment of God's promise to Abraham—realized through the universal outpouring of the Spirit upon Jews and Gentiles who have faith in Christ (Gal 3:14). The flesh and the Spirit have nothing in common! Consequently, those in Christ should not fulfill the flesh's desire. If the Galatians are led by the Spirit, they would not be under the law (5:18).[29]

In Gal 5:18, Paul shifts metaphors. He moves from commanding the Galatians to "walk" in the Spirit to stating the positive result of "being led" by the Spirit. Being led by the Spirit is another way of talking about walking in the Spirit and not fulfilling the lust of the flesh (cf. 5:16). To be led by the Spirit removes one from the domination of the law (5:18).[30] The Spirit's leadership in this verse is clearly discernible by avoiding the vices (and the things like these) mentioned in 5:19–21 and producing the virtues in 5:22–23.

However, the Spirit has already created these virtues in the lives of those who are in Christ. These virtues are fruit coming from the Spirit, who comes to Jews and Gentiles because of God's action for them and in them through Christ (1:4; 3:13–14; 4:4–6). Those who are led by the Spirit (i.e., "those who walk in the Spirit and who do not fulfill the lust of the flesh") are not "under the law" (=under the present evil age and the slavery that goes along with it [1:4; 3:10–14; 4:5–6]).[31] The idea of being led by the Spirit equals "living according to the Spirit rather than according to the flesh" (cf. Rom 8:1–14).[32]

In 5:18, Paul identifies the lust of the flesh in 5:16 as "works of the flesh." In 5:19–21, Paul gives explicit examples of the works/lust of the flesh. He asserts: "the works of the flesh are evident" (5:19). Earlier in the letter, Paul polemicized against "works of law" or "Torah-works" as a badge of covenant-membership within the people of God (2:16; 3:2–5, 10–14). Now he polemicizes against "works of the flesh" as an acceptable badge of those who are justified by faith in Christ apart from works of law (5:19; cf. 2:16; 5:4). His anti-Torah polemic does not in any way promote or encourage a fleshly life. To the contrary, the new age of the Spirit creates opposition between the old age, represented by the law and the

29 Similarly Das 2014: 565–67.

30 So Moo 2013: 357.

31 Examples where Paul talks about being "under the law," see 3:23; 4:4–5, 21.

32 Hays 2000: 327.

vices in 5:19–21, and the new age, represented by the Spirit and Spirit-empowered fruit (5:22–23).

The Gentile Christ-followers in Galatia would have in all likelihood practiced many of the vices mentioned in 5:19–21. Often a Gentile manner of life was contrary to the law from a Jewish perspective (cf. Jub. 22:16–22). Of course, there are exceptions. Certain groups of Gentiles were virtuous (cf. Seneca, *Lucil.* 68). Yet, some Jews would have generally associated Gentiles with a sinful pattern of life (cf. Wis 11–15; Gal 2:15).

Paul does not provide an exhaustive list of "works of the flesh." He selectively outlines in 5:19–21 the pattern of life that represents the works of the flesh (=the old age) and the grave consequence of fulfilling them (=failure to inherit the kingdom of God). Paul's catalogue of vices includes three sexual vices ("sexual immorality," "impurity," "indecency") (5:19), continues with two words for false worship ("idolatry," "sorcery") (5:20), continues with eight concepts related to the fracturing of social/communal relationships ("enmities," "dissension," "jealousy," "fits of angers," "selfish ambitions," "divisions," "factions," "envies") (5:20–21), and concludes with two concepts related to pagan feasts ("given over to drunken ways," "orgies").[33]

Paul could have gone further, which he demonstrates by concluding the vice list with the words "and things similar to these" (5:21). Each of these vices would fracture social relations within the community of faith and within the society at large. The law condemns each of these vices since each reveals a lack of love for God and neighbor (cf. Gal 5:13–14; LXX Lev 19:18). The result of giving into the flesh is failure to inherit the kingdom of God (5:21). Only those who walk in the Spirit inherit the kingdom. Those who walk in the Spirit are those who have been redeemed from this present evil age by the death and resurrection of the Christ and who have received the gift of the Spirit by faith (1:1, 4; 2:20–21; 3:1–14).

Readers must remember a walk in the Spirit is a pattern of life. This is one reason Paul says "walk" in the Spirit and refers to being "led" by the Spirit (5:16–17). The opposite of walking in the Spirit is to walk in the flesh. The latter means to stop walking in the Spirit. The opposite of being led by the Spirit is being led by the flesh (cf. Rom 8:4–5, 14). Those who have been justified by faith could (and unfortunately will) commit any one of the above vices in their lives. Paul does say, after all, that those who walk in the Spirit should restore the one within the community who has

---

33 Hays 2000: 327; deSilva 2018: 458–63; Das 2014: 567–75.

been overtaken by a certain transgression with the kind of gentleness that the Spirit gives (6:1). However, the spiritual ones (i.e., those who walk in the Spirit) must consider their own fragility lest they too be tempted to fall into that same temptation as the brother or sister who has been overtaken by it and whom they are trying to restore (6:1).

But the promise remains: those who walk in the Spirit and who are led by the Spirit will not gratify the flesh. Otherwise, they will not inherit the kingdom of God (5:21). Failure to inherit the kingdom of God refers to being excluded from the eschatological blessing of the inheritance that God promises to distribute to those who are united to Christ, the seed of Abraham (3:13–18; 3:29—4:7). This inheritance would at least include justification by faith (2:16; 5:6), the Spirit and his fruit (3:2—5:26), and new creation (6:15). Jews and Gentiles can receive the inheritance only because of Jesus' death (1:4; 3:13), resurrection (1:1), and faith in Christ (2:16; 3:6–8).

Paul contrasts the way of the flesh versus the way of the Spirit with a sample list of fruit in 5:22. The Spirit produces the fruit of "love," "joy," "peace," "patience," "kindness," "goodness," "faithfulness," "humility," "self-control," and the law does not condemn these vices ("against such things there is no law").[34] This fruit characterizes the community. This fruit is both individual and communal. But, as Hays says, "we should not interpret this fruit as referring only to character qualities of the individual; Paul is primarily concerned with the way in which the Spirit's work is made manifest in community."[35] This fruit is not something the Galatians produce on their own initiative. Rather, God created this fruit within the Galatians when he endowed them with the Spirit (5:16, 22): hence, the phrase "fruit [coming from] the Spirit" (emphasis mine).[36] This list of fruit represents the fruit that the Spirit produces in the community. This fruit is connected to God's action in Christ since the fruit flows from the Spirit. God's action in Christ distributes the Spirit and his

---

34 Das points out that Greco-Roman citizens shunned vices and valued virtues (Plato, *Resp.* 4.427E; 7.536A; *Leg.* 12.963C; Aristotle, *Rhet.* 1.6.6–16), as well as Second Temple Jews (1QS III.25—IV.25; esp. 1QS IV.3, 9, 21, 23). Das 2014: 559–60. 1QS IV refers to six of the nine virtues mentioned in Gal 5:22: "gentleness," "patience," "goodness," "kindness," "faith," and "peace." For this observation, see Das 2014: 560; Matera 1992: 208–9.

35 Hays 2000: 327.

36 Similarly Das 2014: 578; Moo 2013: 363; Schreiner 2010: 348–49.

fruit to the Galatian assemblies upon their identification with Jesus by faith (3:1–5, 13–14).

Paul describes a cosmological and eschatological war between the two ages: the age of the Spirit versus the present evil age. In Christ Jesus, the Spirit produces fruit that identifies the members with the eschatological communities of Christ-followers in Galatia. Those under the law are under sin, bondage, a curse, and a temporary guardian (3:10—4:7). But those in Christ have crucified the flesh along with its sinful passions and lusts (5:24; cf. 2:19–20; 6:14; Rom 8:12–14). This crucifixion of the flesh happened when the Galatians believed in Jesus Christ by faith, received the Spirit (cf. 2:19–20; 3:2–5; 5:16; 6:14), and put on Christ at their baptism (3:27).[37]

Those in Christ must walk in the Spirit in the ways Paul outlines in 5:13–26 or else they will not inherit God's kingdom (5:21). God's kingdom in Galatians is another way of talking about new creation (6:15) or eternal life (cf. 6:8). The kingdom of God in Galatians is the universal distribution of the eschatological inheritance upon Jews and Gentiles in Christ, who is the seed of Abraham, just as God promised to Abraham. Jesus, the crucified Christ, is the king of the kingdom (cf. 1:4; 3:13); Jewish and Gentile Christians are the residents of the kingdom (cf. 3:1—4:21); and the entire transformed/new creation is the location of the kingdom (cf. 6:15).[38] In this kingdom, Spirit-empowered Jewish and Gentile Christ-followers will inherit a new creation and reign with their Christ in eternal life.

Fusing the Horizons: The Christian and Sin

Paul's letter to various churches should make it plain that Christians and Christian churches are filled with imperfect and sinful people. This should not surprise us because Jesus died to atone for our sins and to make a diverse group of people from every tribe, tongue, people, and nation into a spotless and clean bride. Yet, Christians are engaged in a war against the power of the flesh. Flesh and Spirit have nothing in common. However, a

37 For the latter point, so Hays 2000: 328. See also discussion in De Boer 2011: 351–68.

38 For a short and accessible work on the kingdom of God, see Schreiner 2018. My comments about the kingdom as "person, people, and place" come from Schreiner's work.

practical point we can infer from Paul's comments in Gal 5:16–26 is that God's divine action in Christ has overcome the power of the flesh. The Spirit who dwells in us enables us to be co-participants in crucifixion with Christ and to the world. Our freedom in Christ and power over the bondage of the law and the flesh is not freedom to live in disobedience to God or to justify a sinful pattern of life. Rather, in Christ Jesus (not in the law), God has given Christians his Spirit, who provides us with every spiritual resource we need to live a life pleasing to God. Certainly, Christians throughout history have struggled and will continue to struggle with sin to different degrees throughout their Christian life. But they have the power in the Spirit to overcome the flesh because God's divine action in Christ has already overcome the flesh for them and in them via the cross, resurrection, and his divine enablement of the Spirit. Thus, Christians must lean into walking in step with the pattern of life in which God has freed them to live.

Walking in the Spirit is not optional! Obedience to our Lord is not optional! Christians must walk in the Spirit and avoid the lust of the flesh or else we will not inherit God's kingdom (5:21). Christ died to deliver us from the present evil age (1:4). Christ died to redeem Jews and Gentiles from the curse of the law and to endow them with the Spirit by faith (3:13–14; 3:2–5). Christ died to free Jews and Gentiles from bondage to the law (4:21—5:1). Paul encourages Christians by letting us know that we should walk in the Spirit, and we can walk in the Spirit since Jesus died for our sins "to deliver us from the present evil age'" and to "redeem us from the curse of the law'" (1:4; 3:13) and since God through Christ's death redeemed us from slavery to the law so that we would become his sons and daughters by faith in Christ, sons and daughters in whom his Spirit dwells and who enables us to cry out to God our father (4:4-6).

Galatians 6

A Final Shocking Appeal to the Galatians, a Final Attack of the Opponents, and a Final Defense of Paul's Gospel (6:1–18)

In 6:1–18, Paul concludes his most rhetorically charged letter. In 6:1–5, he further exhorts the Galatians to love one another by urging them to walk in the Spirit. He gives them examples as to how they should fulfill this exhortation. He says if a brother (or sister) should fall into transgression, those who are walking in the Spirit should restore that fallen brother or sister with Spirit-empowered humility (6:1). They should also examine their own hearts lest they too should be tempted (and fall) into the same transgression because of their spiritual arrogance (6:1b).

Paul commands the Galatians to bear the burdens of each other, because this sort of love for one another fulfills the law of Christ (6:2). He warns that if anyone arrogantly thinks he is anything although he is nothing he deceives himself (6:3). He, then, calls the Galatians to examine their own works as they seek to restore the fallen brother and sister with humility, and then he says that person would have a reason to boast in himself—but not with respect to the other (i.e., with respect to the one who sinned). Each person must examine his own work, because each person will bear his own load in judgment before God. In 6:6–10, Paul elaborates on the metaphor of walking in the Spirit with the metaphor of sowing in the Spirit.

In 6:11–16, he offers one final assault against the opponents' message about circumcision. He attacks their character, suggesting they preach circumcision only to avoid being persecuted because of the cross of Christ (6:12). He states they do not keep the law themselves (6:13), but they only want to boast in the Galatians' circumcised flesh in order to make a good showing in their own flesh (6:12–13). Paul presents himself as boasting only in the cross of Christ, not in circumcision (6:14). Circumcision no longer identifies the people of God but rather new creation (6:15). In 6:17–18, he appeals to his suffering for Jesus as the fundamental reason why no one should trouble him by troubling those who believed his gospel (6:17), and he wishes grace and peace upon the Galatians (6:18).

Bear the Burdens of One Another with Humility (6:1–5)

The address "brothers" (and "sisters!") is optimistic. Paul has just finished discussing the importance of walking in the Spirit to inherit the kingdom of God (5:16–26). Now, he identifies the Galatians as brothers and sisters. As a result, he gives them an example as to how they can walk in the Spirit and pursue love: namely, restore a person overtaken by any transgression (cf. Matt 18:15–18; Luke 17:3–4; Jas 5:19–20; 2 Cor 2:5–11).[1]

The verb "overtaken" might speak to a brother or sister who is surprisingly overtaken by a transgression. The verb occurs in the passive voice in Wis 17:17.[2] There the author discusses the fate of the lawless ones who were bound for judgment (cf. Wis 17:16–17). Paul's point here, however, is simply that when transgression overtakes a fallen brother or sister, the Christian community (i.e., those who walk in the Spirit) should seek their restoration.

"Any transgression" in Gal 6:1 recalls Paul's "works of the flesh" versus "fruit of the Spirit" theme in 5:16–26. Paul's exhortation that the "spiritual ones" should restore the one overtaken by a transgression supports this (Gal 6:1b). The "transgression" Paul has in mind includes, but should not be limited to, the vices mentioned in 5:17–21 and 5:26. The "spiritual ones" are those who walk in the Spirit since this statement follows Paul's exhortation to walk in the Spirit and not fulfill the lust of the flesh (5:16–26). He wants the ones walking in the Spirit to restore the one who is not walking in the Spirit. This interpretation is further supported in 6:1b when he tells the Galatians the appropriate posture with which the spiritual ones should restore the brother overtaken by the transgression: "by means of the Spirit with humility" (Gal 6:1c).

Most major translations interpret 6:1c to mean the spiritual ones should have a "spirit" of gentleness when they restore the fallen brother or sister instead of meaning that the spiritual ones should restore the fallen brother or sister with Spirit-empowered humility.[3] In my view, how-

1 A similar exhortation occurs in 1QS V.24—VI.1. Cited in Das 2014: 605.

2 See discussion in Das 2014: 601.

3 For a few major English translations that disagree with my translation of the verse, see ASV, ESV, NASB, NRSV, and the RSV.

ever, Paul urges those walking in the Spirit in Galatia ("spiritual ones") to restore the fallen brother or sister (the one who is not walking in the Spirit) with the kind of humility that the Spirit produces. This restoration is a communal act. That is, Paul commands the spiritual ones within the Christian assemblies in Galatia (i.e., those who walk in the Spirit) to restore the fallen brother or sister to the community with the humility that the Spirit gives to the community.

The following exhortation supports this reading: "bear the burdens of one another and so fulfill the law of Christ" (6:2). These "burdens" could be the burden of restoring a falling brother or sister (6:1) or the other emotional, physical, financial, or social burdens that arise in the community life of Christ-followers (6:6, 9–10). To bear the burdens as a community of Christ-followers is what it means in part to become one another's slaves in love and not to use our freedom as an occasion for the flesh (5:6, 13–14). This kind of self-less, sacrificial, and communal love imitates the Christ (2:20) and fulfills the law of Christ as the community of faith perpetually acts out Christ's sacrificial love for them via their love for one another.[4]

The law of Christ is the law of love mentioned in 5:13–14,[5] a law that Spirit-empowered Christians fulfill when they love one another (5:13–14). Christ takes hold of the law, and Christians who walk in the Spirit fulfill (bring to its intended purpose) the intent of the law when they love one another (cf. Lev 19:18; Matt 19:19; 22:39).[6] Love is a fruit of the Spirit (5:22). Spirit-empowered love reveals itself in a variety of ways. One way is by members of the in-Christ communities of faith helping fellow Christ-followers carry their burdens with the kind of humility given to the community by the Spirit, including the burden that arises in Christian assemblies when one is overtaken by a certain transgression.

Multiple translations render *praütēs* as "gentleness" instead of "humility" in Gal 6:1.[7] Paul has just stated a fruit of the Spirit is *praütēs* (the same word, but different form in Gal 5:23). "Gentleness" is a possible translation of this term, but "humility" or "compassion" better

4 Similarly Barclay 1988: 132–35; Martyn 1997: 554–58; Hays 2000: 333; Schreiner 2010: 359–60, esp. 360.

5 Against Murphy-O'Connor's provocative but improbable argument (2012: 123–43) that "the law of Christ" is Christ. That is, Christ is the law the Galatians fulfill when they bear the burdens of one another.

6 Similarly Das 2014: 602, 611.

7 For examples, see translations in note above.

communicates Paul's point since he refers to boasting (6:4) and since he warns the Galatians that everyone should examine himself or herself when seeking to restore someone overtaken by any transgression and that everyone will bear his own load in judgment (Gal 6:4–5). It is absolutely imperative that the spiritual ones restore the ones not walking in the Spirit with humility, because they too might fall into the same transgression and because both the spiritual ones and those who walk in the flesh will bear their own load in judgment (Gal 6:5). If Paul's remarks go unheeded, both groups could risk failing to inherit the kingdom of God (5:21). Those who love the fallen one in this way fulfill the law of Christ (6:2; cf. 5:13–14).

Paul makes the above point in the latter half of 6:1 ("and you consider yourselves so that you would not also be tempted"). By consider yourselves, Paul means "examine yourselves." He exhorts the Galatians not to think too highly of themselves (6:3) and to examine themselves (6:4). He states if they examine themselves, then they would have a reason to boast (in themselves) but not with respect to the "other." If the spiritual ones examine themselves, they will actually see that they have a reason to boast in themselves only because of the cross (cf. 1:4; 2:19–21; 3:1, 13–14; 6:14; Rom 15:17; 1 Cor 9:16; 2 Cor 1:12–14; Phil 2:16).[8] Boasting in one's co-crucifixion with Christ and in the transformation that co-crucifixion produces is perfectly fine since Paul asserts his crucified self boasts in nothing except the cross of Jesus Christ (cf. 2:20; 6:14). Those who walk in the Spirit should boast in the Spirit's work in them as a result of faith in the crucified Christ (3:1–6; 6:14), whereas those who walk in the flesh (like the opponents) boast in the flesh (cf. 6:12–13). A crucified boast attests to a walk in the Spirit, but a fleshly boast attests to a walk in the flesh because it lacks love for the other (cf. 5:13—6:2).[9]

The "other" in 6:5 is likely a reference to the one who is overtaken by a transgression mentioned in 6:1, because Paul explains the kind of humble posture the "spiritual ones" should have toward the one not walking in the Spirit in 6:1–4. In 6:5, he provides the reason: "For each one will bear his own load." Eschatological judgment is the burden to which Paul refers here (cf. 1:8–9; 2:11; 3:10).[10] 4 Ezra 7:104–5 provides a helpful parallel to Paul's remarks.

---

8 See discussion of boasting in antiquity in Das 2014: 613–17.

9 For alternative ways of understanding the text, see Das 2014: 614–16.

10 See the discussion in Kuck 1994: 289–97. See also De Boer 2011: 383–84; Hays 2000: 335.

The day of judgment is decisive and displays to all the seal of truth. Just as now a father does not send his son, or a son his father, or a master his servant, or a friend his dearest friend, to be ill or sleep or eat or be healed in his place, so no one shall ever pray for another on that day, neither shall anyone lay a burden on another; for all then shall bear their own righteousness and unrighteousness.[11]

In Gal 5:10, Paul uses the same verb (*bastazō*), as in 6:5, to refer to the future judgment of the trouble-maker who preaches another gospel to the Galatians (cf. 1:6–9). Sin is seductive and crafty. Those walking in the Spirit should restore those walking in the flesh with the utmost humility and careful self-examination because they too might fall into the same transgression as those walking in the flesh. As a result, they will give an account of their transgression in God's eschatological judgment, which might result in their failure to inherit the kingdom of God if they fail to pass their self-examination (5:21).

Do Good by Sowing in the Spirit and Reap Eternal Life (6:6–10)

In 6:6–10, Paul continues to discuss walking in the Spirit. But he does so by urging the Galatians to share (*koinōneō*) their material possessions ("all good things") with those who teach them the word (6:6). The idea of partnership (*koinōneō*) in the NT is often financial (cf. with the cognate *koinōnia* [Phil 1:5]). Sometimes partnership refers to participation in the sufferings of Christ (cf. 1 Pet 4:13) or a partnership with sins (2 John 1:11). In Gal 6:6, the partnership is likely financial since Paul modifies the imperative with the phrase "all good things." He urges the Galatians to share their financial/material possessions with those who teach them the word. This sharing of "all good things" gives evidence that the community possesses the fruit of "goodness" that comes from the Spirit (5:22).[12]

Those who teach are those gifted by the Spirit to build up the church for the work of service (cf. 1 Cor 12–14; Eph 4), not necessarily those with institutional credentials from the best universities, divinity schools, and seminaries. Paul gives these communal instructions regarding the appropriate way to treat teachers of the word in a section where he has emphasized walking in the Spirit as the community of faith (5:13—6:6). The Galatians, and all Christian communities, walk in the Spirit, and

11 Cited in Hays 2000: 335.
12 So Das 2014: 618.

become one another's slaves through sacrificial love as they learn in community together from those whom the Spirit gifts to teach the word. Jesus' self-sacrificial love serves as the model for all Christian communities how they ought to love one another (cf. 2:19–20). Sharing our resources with those who teach us the word is the appropriate communal response to teachers gifted by the Spirit to teach the word to the community (5:13–14, 22).

Given Paul's emphasis on the authority of his gospel over the opponents' gospel and given that Paul highlights his gospel comes from God (1:1—2:10), "word" is a metonym for gospel in 6:6. In Gal 4:12–20, Paul nicely illustrates exactly how the Galatians ought to share with those who teach them. When he suffered, they received him into their homes and did not despise his temptation in their flesh. Instead, they received him as an angel from God, as they would have received Christ Jesus himself.

In 6:7, Paul commands the Galatians not to be deceived. He follows this by saying "God is not mocked." The mocking of God in Gal 6:7 should be understood as despising God by making him a laughing stock (cf. LXX Prov 11:12; 12:8; 15:5, 20; Jer 20:7). In LXX 2 Chr 36:16, the terms for mocking (*muktērizō*) and despising occur in the same text as the chronicler reports Israel's mistreatment of God's messengers ("but they kept mocking the messengers of God, despising his words, and scoffing at his prophets, until the wrath of the LORD against his people became so great that there was no remedy" [NRSV]) (brackets mine). When those who identify with the Christian community begin to live a fleshly life of disobedience void of the Spirit, they mock God. But God will have the last laugh at the end of the age on the Day of judgment! He will make all of the injustices just and all of the wrongs right. Those who walk in the flesh will indeed bear their own load in judgment!

God must not be mocked, because "each one will bear his own load" in judgment (cf. 6:5). As Paul puts it, "whatever a man sows, this also he will reap." Jesus too used the sowing and reaping metaphor when teaching about the kingdom of God and eternal life (Matt 6:26; 25:26–46). Here Paul uses this imagery to emphasize the importance of walking in the Spirit. He connects walking in the Spirit with the kingdom of God in Gal 5:21 and with eternal life in 6:8. His remarks in 6:8 demonstrate that he moves beyond discussing the importance of sharing material blessings with those who teach the word to the Galatians to now emphasizing that walking in the Spirit includes more than financial partnership.

The words "sowing in the flesh" versus "sowing in the Spirit" recall Paul's remarks in 5:16–26 that walking in the Spirit is a prerequisite to inheriting the kingdom of God. To sow in the flesh is to sow to the power of the flesh. Sowing to the flesh refers to living in accordance with the power of the flesh and the present evil age. Paul says sowing in the flesh results in corruption (=condemnation), but sowing in the Spirit results in eternal life (6:8). Since Paul contrasts sowing in the Spirit with sowing in the flesh, Spirit and flesh here represent two ages. The Spirit represents the new age in Christ. The flesh represents a power within the old age antithetical to the Spirit and dominated by slavery, sin, a curse, and the *ta stoicheia tou kosmou* (cf. 4:3, 8–11; 5:16–26). As Das states "the flesh stands on the wrong side of the apocalyptic divide between this world and the next (5:13, 16–21, 24; but also 2:16; 3:3; 4:23, 29; 6:12–13; Rom 8:12–13; 1 Cor 15:42–50)."[13] "Flesh" here might also refer to circumcision since the Galatians were in danger of receiving this mark of entry within the family of Abraham (cf. 5:2–3, 11; 6:12–13, 15).[14]

In 6:9, Paul urges the Galatians not to grow weary in doing the good. This sentence has eschatological urgency. Each person will bear his own load (6:5); God will not be mocked (6:7); we must sow in the Spirit and not in the flesh in order to inherit eternal life (6:8); let us not grow weary to do the good, for we will reap the reward of eternal life if we do not grow weary in doing the good (6:9; cf. Rom 8:18–39; 1 Cor 15:58; Phil 3:10–14, 20–4:1; 2 Thess 3:13). The "good" should be understood as sowing in the Spirit and walking in the Spirit. That is, by the "good," Paul at least means walking in the Spirit and not fulfilling the lust of the flesh (5:16–26). He promises those who walk in the Spirit will reap (=inherit eternal life) if "we do not grow weary" in doing the good. He uses the sowing and reaping imagery from 6:8 in 6:9. Those who do not grow weary in doing good are those who persevere in walking in the Spirit, which will result in their inheriting eternal life. Those who grow weary in walking in the Spirit will not inherit eternal life (cf. 5:16—6:9). "Christians are not saved by good works, but they certainly are not saved without them."[15]

"Therefore," Paul urges the Galatians to work the good (i.e., to walk in the Spirit) with respect to their dealings with all people (those outside of the Christian community), but especially with those within "the

---

13 Das 2014: 620.

14 Entire paragraph influenced by Das 2014: 619–20.

15 Das 2014: 622.

households of the faith" (6:10; cf. 1:2). Christ-followers should walk in
the Spirit in their dealings with all people in so far as harmony and peace
are possible. Yet, we should especially seek the good of those within the
in-Christ communities.

An Appeal, An Attack, and a Final Defense of the Gospel (6:11–18)

In 6:11–18, Paul gives the Galatians his final remarks. These verses reinforce the superiority of Paul's gospel. He emphasizes one final time that
his gospel is centered on the cross of Jesus Christ.[16] He again verbally
assaults the opponents. He accentuates the importance of his words in
this letter ("see with what large letters I wrote to you with my own hand").
Paul likely takes up the pen himself and writes in order to emphasize
the points he dictated to his amanuensis throughout the letter (cf. 1 Cor
16:21; Col 4:18; 2 Thess 3:17; Phlm 19).[17]

In 6:12, Paul uses a rhetorical pun with the phrase "in the flesh." He
accuses the opponents of wishing to make a "good showing in the flesh."
They wanted to attain social honor.[18] Their good showing in the flesh was
predicated on the Galatians' circumcised flesh (Gal 6:12b; cf. 2:20; 4:13,
14, 23, 29). Paul appears to use crude humor here to emphasize the opponents' motives for preaching circumcision in Galatia. As Martyn states,
the Teachers in Galatia emphasized neither the Spirit nor focused on the
law but on the Galatians' "penis, and specifically on their own reputation
as its cultic surgeons (5:12)."[19]

Paul calls the opponents cowards who are afraid to be persecuted
for the cross of Christ ("only that they would not be persecuted for the
cross of Christ"). Galatians 6:13 provides the reason: "for these who are
circumcised are not keeping the law. But they desire to circumcise you,
so that they would boast in your [circumcised] flesh" (brackets mine).
Certain interpretations suggest this statement could refer to Gentiles in
Galatia who received circumcision, but did not follow the law.[20] Most
likely, though, those who think Paul's remarks refer to the opponents,
who are circumcised while not following other elements of the law, are

16 Martyn 1997: 561.
17 Das 2014: 632.
18 On the honor and shame point, similarly Witherington 1998: 446.
19 Martyn 1997: 561. Martyn's quote also cited in Das 2014: 634–35.
20 For a discussion of options, see deSilva 2018: 507.

correct.[21] The opponents, Paul criticizes, desire to win circumcised converts to what appears to be a form of Christian Judaism,[22] but they do not follow zealously that to which they attempt to recruit the Galatians. Rather, Paul criticizes they want to circumcise the Galatians so that they can boast in their circumcised flesh (i.e., in their circumcised penises).[23]

Paul again attacks the opponents' gospel and dissuades the Galatians from turning away from his gospel with his claim that he only boasts in the cross of Jesus Christ (6:14). Paul states the opponents do not boast in the cross of Christ, because they are afraid to be persecuted for the cross, the very thing that provides deliverance from the present evil age and redemption from the curse of the law (1:4; 3:13). The opponents are severing/cutting themselves off from the soteriological and eschatological benefit of the cross (5:2–4) and are falling from grace (5:4) as they seek to cut off/sever the Galatians' flesh from their penises. As a result, they preach circumcision, asserts Paul, so that they would have a reason to boast in the Galatians' circumcised flesh.

However, Paul avoids preaching the marks of circumcision to the Gentiles and rather boasts in the cross of Christ. He receives in his body marks of suffering for the cross as the symbol of the curse and suffering (3:13) and a source of persecution (5:11; 6:12). Paul's exultation is not in his Jewish identity (cf. 1:13–16), but in his new in-Christ identity (3:28–29; 6:14). He remains a Jew in Christ (cf. Rom 11:2), but his Jewish identity is transformed. Through Jesus' cross, Paul has died to the present evil age and now participates in Christ in Spirit-empowered new creation (2:17–20). Even the world has been crucified through the cross to Paul and Paul to the world (6:14–15). Consequently, "neither circumcision nor un-circumcision is anything, but new creation" (6:15).

The crucifixion of the world to the cross ushers in the new age inaugurated by Jesus' cross and resurrection (1:4; 6:14–17). Paul calls this new age "new creation" (6:15), and Jesus' cross creates this new creation.[24] New creation recalls Isa 65:17–25 (cf. Isa 66:22). Isaiah anticipates the new age in which God acts to redeem his people Israel, to bring salvation to the nations, and to provide cosmological renewal (see Isa 40–66; Rev 21–22). As Christians walk in step with the Spirit and love one another by

21 deSilva 2018: 507–8.

22 For an argument that Paul worked as an apostle within Judaism, see essays in Nanos and Zetterholm 2015.

23 Similarly deSilva 2018: 508.

24 For a recent work on crucifixion and new creation, see Hubing 2015.

bearing one another's burdens in the households of the faith (5:13—6:5), they attest to, live in anticipation of, and in continuity with the already-not-yet reality of new creation. They also demonstrate in the communities of faith that new creation is more important than social status or social privilege (cf. Gal 3:28).

Some Second Temple Jews often speak of new creation in the context of anticipating a new age to come.[25] Paul asserts in 6:15, and has argued throughout the letter what Isaiah and his contemporary Jews anticipated, that new creation is realized in the cross of Jesus Christ. Paul promises all who live by the rule of the cross, which has delivered us from the present evil age and from the curse of the law to distribute the blessing of Abraham to all in-Christ people (1:4; 3:13–14), peace and mercy will be upon them and upon the Israel of God (6:16), as they participate in new creation. Isa 54:10 ascribes mercy and peace to Israel, but Paul extends this blessing to "as many" live by the rule of new creation (6:15–16).[26]

In new creation, neither circumcision nor un-circumcision matters (6:15–17), but the transformed "Israel of God" will reside in this "new creation" (6:15–17). Christ inaugurated this new creation when he died to deliver "us" from the present evil age (1:4). Christ redeemed "us" from bondage to the law that is under the present evil age. (3:13; 4:5). The new age in Christ, inaugurated by the cross and resurrection, blows up the boundary markers between Jews and Gentiles in order to create something new: namely, a transformed creation filled with transformed Jews and Gentiles in Christ,[27] marked by the cross, marked by those who worship Jesus as the Jewish Messiah, and marked by the Spirit instead of circumcision.

The "Israel of God" in 6:16 might refer to ethnic Israel (cf. Rom 11:26). However, it seems unlikely in light of the context of the entire letter. Paul redefines the boundaries of Israel in Galatians. He argues arduously that Jews and Gentiles in Christ are descendants of Abraham and heirs of the promise (Gal 3:1–29). He identifies the Israel from below as enslaved and the Israel from above as free, concluding that the Israel from above consists of Jewish and Gentile Christ-followers who are likewise children of the promise (just as Isaac) (4:21–31). These children of the promise are

---

25 Cf. Paul's remarks about new creation with Jub. 4:26; 1 En. 72:1; 91:15–16; LAB 3:10; 4 Ezra 7:75; 2 Bar. 32:6; 44:12; 57:2; LAB 32:17; 1QS IV.25. So Das 2014: 643n85. See also White 2008: 90–106.

26 Also Keener 2018: 285–87.

27 Similarly Das 2014: 644.

also children of the Spirit (in accordance with Isaac) (4:29–31; cf. 3:2–3, 13–14; 4:5–6), who are free from the curse of the law (5:1).

"Israel of God" in 6:16 likely, therefore, refers to the family of Abraham, a family that includes both Jews and Gentiles in Christ. This is supported by Paul's earlier remarks. First, Jews and Gentiles in Christ are heirs and the seed of Abraham because of their faith in Jesus (the seed of Abraham [2:16—3:29]). Second, Jews and Gentiles in Christ are part of the heavenly Jerusalem (4:21–31). Third, neither circumcision is anything nor un-circumcision but "new creation" (6:15; cf. 5:6). The new creation promised in Isa 65:17–25 is realized in the current transformation of Jews and Gentiles in Christ by means of the indwelling power of the Spirit (cf. Gal 3:13–14; 4:5–7). The phrase "Israel of God" puts a final exclamation point on an already shocking letter: Jews and Gentiles are the Israel of God because they are Abraham's offspring since they belong to Christ, Abraham's promised seed (cf. 3:16, 29).[28]

In 6:17–18, Paul concludes the letter by urging the trouble-makers in Galatia to leave him alone since he suffered for the gospel of Jesus Christ ("I bear in my body the marks of Jesus"). The final jab against the opponents' gospel is Paul's remarks about suffering in his physical body for the gospel (cf. 4:12–20; 5:11), just as Jesus suffered (cf. 2 Cor 4; 11). The opponents avoided preaching the cross because they were afraid to suffer for the cross (6:12), but Paul celebrates his suffering as the emblem of his authentic gospel that he received from God (1:1; 1:13—2:10; 5:11; 6:17). His suffering for the gospel that he preached distinguishes his message from the opponents and aligns him with the cross of Jesus Christ, who suffered, died, and was cursed on the cross for Jews and Gentiles to deliver them from the law's curse (1:4; 3:13–14). Paul offers a final appeal to the Galatians to reject the opponents' gospel. Paul's marks of suffering on his flesh, marks that he received from preaching the cross, are superior to his mark of circumcision and to the mark of circumcision preached by the opponents, who are afraid to preach the cross.[29]

In 6:18, Paul prays grace upon the Galatians. In 1:3, Paul states grace and peace come from God, the Father, and the Lord Jesus Christ. In 6:18, he prays the grace of the Lord Jesus Christ would come upon them. Grace frames the letter (1:3; 6:18). The picture within the frame of grace is grace (cf. 1:6, 15; 2:9, 21; 3:18; 5:4). He concludes with a word of hope when he

---

28 Among many scholars, rightly deSilva 2018: 513.

29 Similarly Das 2014: 654.

calls the Galatians brothers and prays they would experience Jesus' grace: "May the grace of our Lord Jesus Christ be with your spirit, brothers. Amen." Amen, brother Paul! Amen!

Select Bibliography

"Agorazō." 2014. *New International Dictionary of New Testament Theology and Exegesis*, edited by Moisés Silva, 1:139–40. Grand Rapids: Zondervan.

Bachmann, Michael. 1999. *Anti-Judaism in Galatians? Exegetical Studies on a Polemical Letter and on Paul's Theology*. Translated by Robert L. Brawley. Grand Rapids: Eerdmans.

Bailey, Richard A. 2011. *Race and Redemption in Puritan New England*. New York: Oxford University Press.

Barclay, John M. G. 1987. "Mirror-Reading a Polemical Letter: Galatians as a Test Case." *Journal for the Study of the New Testament* 31: 73–93

————. 1988. *Obeying the Truth: Paul's Ethics in Galatians*. Edinburgh: T. & T. Clark.

————. 1996. *Jews in the Mediterranean Diaspora: From Alexander the Great to Trajan (323 BCE 117 CE)*. Berkley: University of California Press.

————. 2002. "Mirror-Reading a Polemical Letter: Galatians as a Test Case." In *The Galatians Debate: Contemporary Issues Rhetorical and Historical Interpretation*, edited by Mark D. Nanos, 366–82. Peabody, MA: Hendrickson.

————. 2008. "Grace and Transformation of Agency in Christ." In *Redefining First-Century Jewish and Christina Identities: Essays in Honor Ed Parish Sanders*, edited by Fabian E. Udoh, with Susannah Heschel, Mark Chancey, and Gregory Tatum, 372–89. Christianity and Judaism in Antiquity 16. Notre Dame, IN: University of Notre Dame.

————. 2015. *Paul and the Gift*. Grand Rapids: Eerdmans.

Bauckham, Richard. 1998. *God Crucified: Monotheism and Christology in the New Testament*. Grand Rapids: Eerdmans.

————. 2008. *Jesus and the God of Israel: God Crucified and Other Studies on the New Testament's Christology of Divine Identity*. Grand Rapids: Eerdmans.

Bernat, David A. 2010. "Circumcision." In *The Eerdmans Dictionary of Early Judaism*, edited by John J. Collins and Daniel C. Harlow, 471–74. Grand Rapids: Eerdmans.

Betz, Hans D. 1979. *Galatians: A Commentary*. Minneapolis: Fortress.

Bird, Michael F. 2006. *The Saving Righteousness of God*. Milton Keynes, UK: Paternoster.

————. 2010. *Crossing Land and Sea*. Grand Rapids: Baker.

————. 2016. *An Anomalous Jew: Paul among Jews, Greeks, and Romans*. Grand Rapids: Eerdmans.

Bird, Michael F., and Preston M. Sprinkle, eds. 2009. *The Faith of Jesus Christ*. Milton Keynes, UK: Paternoster.

Blount, Brian K., Cain Hope Felder, Clarice J. Martin, and Emerson B. Powery, eds. 2007. *True to Our Native Land: An African American New Testament Commentary*. Minneapolis: Fortress.

Bowley, James. 2010. "Abraham." In *The Eerdmans Dictionary of Early Judaism*, edited by John J. Collins and Daniel C. Harlow, 294–95. Grand Rapids: Eerdmans.

Braxton, Brad. 2002. *No Longer Slaves: Galatians and African American Experience.* Minneapolis: Liturgical.

Bruno, Chris. 2010. *God Is One: The Function of Eis ho Theos as a Ground for Gentile Inclusion in Paul's Letters.* Library of New Testament Studies Series 497. New York: T. & T. Clark.

Burns, J. Patout, Jr., and Robin M. Jensen. 2014. *Christianity in Roman Africa.* Grand Rapids: Eerdmans.

Burton, Ernest De Witt. 1921. *A Critical and Exegetical Commentary on the Epistle to the Galatians.* International Critical Commentary. Edinburgh: T. & T. Clark.

Byron, Gay. 2002. *Symbolic Blackness and Ethnic Difference in Early Christian Literature.* London: Routledge.

Caneday, Ardel. 1989. "Redeemed from the Curse of the Law: The Use of Deut 21:22–23 in Gal 3:13." *Trinity Journal* 10: 185–209.

Chapman, David W. 2008. *Ancient Jewish and Christian Perceptions of Crucifixion.* Grand Rapids: Baker.

Charlesworth, James H. 1983. *The Old Testament Pseudepigrapha.* Vol. 1: *Apocalyptic Literature and Testaments.* New York: Double Day, , 1989.

———. 1985. *The Old Testament Pseudepigrapha.* Vol. 2: *Expansions of the "Old Testament" and Legends, Wisdom and Philosophical Literature, Prayers, Psalms, and Odes, Fragments of Lost Judeo-Hellenistic Works.* New York: Double Day.

Chester, Stephen J. 2017. *Reading Paul with the Reformers: Reconciling Old and New Perspectives.* Grand Rapids: Eerdmans.

Ciampa, Roy E. 1998. *The Presence and Function of Scripture in Galatians 1 and 2.* Wissenschaftliche Untersuchungen zum Neuen Testament 2. Reihe 102. Tübingen: Mohr Siebeck.

Cohen, Shaye J. D. 1999. *The Beginnings of Jewishness: Boundaries, Varieties, and Uncertainties.* Berkeley: University of California Press.

Cook, John Granger. 2014. *Crucifixion in the Mediterranean World.* Wissenschaftliche Untersuchungen zum Neuen Testament 327. Tübingen: Mohr Siebeck.

Crosgrove, Charles H. 1988. *The Cross and the Spirit: A Study in the Argument of Galatians.* Macon: Mercer University Press.

Crownfield, Frederic R. 1945. "The Singular Problem of the Dual Galatians." *Journal of Biblical Literature* 64: 491–500.

Das, Andrew A. 2014. *Galatians: A Theological Exposition of Sacred Scripture.* Concordia Commentary. St. Louis: Concordia.

Davies, W. D. 1962. *Paul and Rabbinic Judaism: Some Rabbinic Elements in Pauline Theology.* London: SPCK.

Davis, Basil S. 2002. *Christ as Devotio: The Argument of Gal 3:1–14.* Lanham: University Press of America.

De Boer. Martinius C. 2011. *Galatians: A Commentary.* New Testament Library. Louisville: Westminster John Knox.

Deenick, Karl. 2018. *Righteous by Promise: A Biblical Theology of Circumcision.* Downers Grove, IL: InterVarsity.

deSilva, David A. 2000. *Honor, Patronage, Kinship, & Purity: Unlocking New Testament Culture.* Downers Grove, IL: InterVarsity.

———. 2014. *Galatians: A Handbook on the Greek Text.* Waco: Baylor University Press.

———. 2018. *The Letter to the Galatians.* The International Commentary of the New Testament. Grand Rapids: Eerdmans

Donaldson, Terence L. 1986. "The 'Curse of the Law' and the Inclusion of the Gentiles: Galatians 3.13–14." *New Testament Studies* 32: 94–112.

———. 2007. *Judaism and the Gentiles: Jewish Patters of Universalism (to 135 CE)*. Waco: Baylor University Press.

Dunn, James D. G. 1993. *The Epistle to the Galatians*. Black's New Testament Commentary. Grand Rapids: Baker.

———. 1998. *The Theology of Paul the Apostle*. Grand Rapids: Eerdmans.

———. 2007. *The New Perspective*. Rev. ed. Grand Rapids: Eerdmans.

Dunne, John Anthony. 2017. *Persecution and Participation in Galatians*. Wissenschaftliche Untersuchungen zum Neuen Testament 2. Reihe 454. Tübingen: Mohr Siebeck.

Dupont, Carolyn Renée. 2013. *Mississippi Praying: Southern White Evangelicals and the Civil Rights Movement: 1945–1975*. New York: New York University Press.

Eastman, Susan Grove. 2001. "The Evil Eye and the Curse of the Law: Galatians 3:1 Revisited." *Journal for the Study of the New Testament* 83: 69–87.

———. 2007. *Recovering Paul's Mother Tongue: Language and Theology in Galatians*. Grand Rapids: Eerdmans.

Eliav, Yaron Z. 2010. "Baths." In *The Eerdmans Dictionary of Early Judaism*, edited by John J. Collins and Daniel C. Harlow, 432–34. Grand Rapids: Eerdmans.

Elliott, Susan. 2003. *Cutting Too Close for Comfort: Paul's Letter to the Galatians in Its Anatolian Cultic Context*. New York: T. & T. Clark.

Emerson, Michael O., and Christian Smith. 2000. *Divided By Faith: Evangelical Religion and the Problem of Race in America*. New York: Oxford University Press.

Esler, Philip. 1998. *Galatians*. London: Routledge.

Fee, Gordon D. 2007. *Galatians*. Pentecostal Commentary Series. Dorsett, UK: Deo Publishing.

Ferguson, Everett. 2003. *Backgrounds of Early Christianity*. 3rd ed. Grand Rapids: Eerdmans.

Garlington, Don. 2008. "Paul's Partisan ek and the Question of Justification in Galatian." *Journal of Biblical Literature* 127: 567–89.

Gathercole, Simon J. 2002. *Where Is Boasting? Early Jewish Soteriology and Paul's Response in Romans 1–5*. Grand Rapids: Eerdmans.

———. 2015. *Defending Substitution*. Grand Rapids: Baker.

Goddard, A. J., and S. A. Cummins. 1993. "Ill or Ill-Treated? Conflict and Persecution as the Context of Paul's Original Ministry in Galatia (Galatians 4.12–20)." *Journal for the Study of the New Testament* 52: 93–126.

Goetz, Rebecca Anne. 2012. *The Baptism of Early Virginia: How Christianity Created Race*. Baltimore: Johns Hopkins University Press.

Goldingay, A. J., and D. F. Payne. 2006. *A Critical and Exegetical Commentary on Isaiah 40–55*. 2 vols. International Critical Commentary. London: T. & T. Clark.

Gurtner, Daniel M., ed. 2011. *This World and the World to Come: Soteriology in Early Judaism*. Library of Second Temple Studies. New York: Bloomsbury.

Guess, Teresa J. 2006. "The Social Construction of Whiteness: Racism by Intent, Racism by Consequence." *Critical Sociology* 32: 650–73.

Hansen,Walter G. 1989. *Abraham in Galatians: Epistolary and Rhetorical Contexts*. Journal for the Study of the New Testament: Supplement Series 29. Sheffield: Sheffield Academic.

Harmon, Matthew. 2010. *She Must and Shall Go Free: Paul's Isaianic Gospel in Galatians.* Beihefte zur für die neutestamentliche Wissenschaft 168. Berlin: De Gruyter.

Hays, Richard B. 1989. *Echoes of Scripture in the Letters of Paul.* New Haven: Yale University Press.

———. 2000. "The Letter to the Galatians." In vol. 11 of *The New Interpreter's Bible: A Commentary in Twelve Volumes,* 183–348. Nashville: Abingdon.

———. 2002. *The Faith of Jesus Christ: An Investigation of the Narrative Substructure of Galatians 3:1—4:11.* 2nd ed. Grand Rapids: Eerdmans.

Hengel, Martin. 1974. *Judaism and Hellenism.* Philadelphia: Fortress.

———. 1997. *The Zealots: Investigations into the Jewish Freedom Movement in the Period from Herod I until 70 A.D.* New York: Bloomsbury.

Hengel, Martin, and Anna Maria Schwemer. 1997. *Paul between Damascus and Antioch: The Unknown Years.* Louisville: Westminster John Knox.

Hodge, Caroline Johnson. 2007. *If Sons, Then Heirs: A Study of Kinship and Ethnicity in the Letters of Paul.* Oxford: Oxford University Press.

Howard, George. 1990. *Paul: Crisis in Galatia: A Study in Early Christian Theology.* 2nd ed. SNTSMS 35. Cambridge: Cambridge University Press.

Hubing, Jeff. 2015. *Crucifixion and New Creation: The Strategic Purpose of Galatians 6.11–17.* Library of New Testament Studies Series 508. New York: Bloomsbury.

Hübner, Hans. 1984. *Law in Paul's Thought.* Translated by James C. G. Greig. Edinburgh: T. & T. Clark.

Hunn, Debbie. 2007. "Ean mē in Galatians 2:16: A Look at the Greek Literature." *Novum Testamentum* 49: 281–90.

Isaac, Benjamin. 2004. *The Invention of Racism in Classical Antiquity.* Princeton, NJ: Princeton University Press.

Jervis, Ann L. 1999. *Galatians.* New International Biblical Commentary 9. Peabody, MA: Hendrickson.

Jewett, Robert. 1971. "The Agitators and the Galatian Congregation." *New Testament Studies* 17.2: 198–212.

———. 2002. "The Agitators and the Galatians." In the *Galatians Debate: Contemporary Issues in Rhetorical and Historical Interpretation,* edited by Mark D. Nanos, 334–47. Peabody, MA: Hendrickson.

Josephus. 1926–1965. Translated by H. St. J. Thackeray et al. 13 vols. Loeb Classical Library. Cambridge: Harvard University Press.

Kahl, Brigitte. 2000. "No Longer Male: Masculinity Struggles behind Galatians 3.28?" *Journal for the Study of the New Testament* 79: 37–49.

Keener, Craig S. 2012. *Acts: An Exegetical Commentary.* Vol. 1. Grand Rapids: Baker.

———. 2018. *Galatians.* New Cambridge Bible Commentary. Cambridge: Cambridge University Press.

Kennedy, George. 1984. *New Testament Interpretation through Rhetorical Criticism.* Chapel Hill: University of North Carolina Press.

Kepple, Robert J. 1977. "An Analysis of Antiochene Exegesis of Galatians 4:24–26." *Westminster Theological Journal* 39: 239–49.

Kerkeslager, Allen. 2010. "Athletics." In *The Eerdmans Dictionary of Early Judaism,* edited by John J. Collins and Daniel C. Harlow, 402–3. Grand Rapids: Eerdmans.

Kidd, Colin. 2006. *The Forging of Races: Race and Scripture in the Protestant Atlantic World, 1600–2000.* Cambridge: Cambridge University Press.

Kimber Buell, Denise. 2005. *Why This New Race? Ethnic Reasoning in Early Christianity.* New York: Columbia University Press.

Kuck, David W. 1994. "'Each Will Bear His Own Burden:' Paul's Creative Use of an Apocalyptic Motif." *New Testament Studies* 40: 289–97.

Lenski, R. C. H. 1961. *The Interpretation of St. Paul's Epistles to the Galatians, to the Ephesians, and to the Philippians.* Columbus, OH: Lutheran Book Concern, 1937. Reprinted Minneapolis: Augsburg.

Lightfoot, J. B. 1957. *The Epistle of St. Paul to the Galatians.* Grand Rapids: Zondervan.

Longenecker, Bruce W. 1998. *The Triumph of Abraham's God: The Transformation of Identity in Galatians.* Nashville: Abingdon.

Longenecker, Richard N. 1982. "The Pedagogical Nature of the Law in Galatians 3:19–4:7." *Journal of the Evangelical Theological Society* 25: 53–61.

———. 1990. *Galatians.* Word Biblical Commentary 41: Dallas: Word.

Lütgert, Wilhelm. 1919. *Gesetz und Geist: Eine Untersuchung zur Vorgeschichte des Galaterbriefs.* Gütersloh: Bertelsmann.

Martin, Troy W. 1999. "Whose Flesh? What Temptation? Galatians 4.13–14." *Journal for the Study of the New Testament* 74: 65–91.

Martyn, J. Louis. 1997. *Galatians: A New Translation with Introduction and Commentary.* Anchor Bible 33A. New York: Doubleday.

Matera, Frank. 1992. *Galatians.* Sacra Pagina 9. Collegeville, MN: Liturgical.

Mathews, Donald G. 2017. *At the Altar of Lynching: Burning Same Hose in the American South.* Cambridge: Cambridge University Press.

Mathews Swetnam, Mary Beth. 2017. *Doctrine and Race: African American Evangelicals and Fundamentalism Between the Wars.* Tuscaloosa: University of Alabama Press.

McLean, Bradley H. 1996. *The Cursed Christ: Mediterranean Expulsion Rituals and Pauline Soteriology.* Sheffield: Sheffield Academic Press.

Mitchell, Stephen. 1993. *Anatolia: Land, Men, and Gods in Asia Minor.* 2 vols. Oxford: Clarendon.

Moo, Douglas J. 1983. "Law, Works of Law, and Legalism in Paul." *Westminster Theological Journal* 45: 73–100.

———. 2013. *Galatians.* Baker Exegetical Commentary. Grand Rapids: Baker.

Morland, Kjell Arne. 1995. *The Rhetoric of Curse in Galatians.* Emory Studies in Early Christianity. Atlanta: Scholars.

Murphy-O'Connor, Jerome. 2012. *Keys to Galatians: Collected Essays.* Minneapolis: Liturgical.

Nanos, Mark D., ed. 2002a. *The Galatians Debate: Contemporary Issues in Rhetorical and Historical Interpretation.* Peabody, MA: Hendrickson.

———. 2002b. *The Irony of Galatians: Paul's Letter in Its First-Century Context.* Minneapolis: Fortress.

Nanos, Mark D., and Magnus Zetterholm, eds. 2015. *Paul within Judaism: Restoring the First-Century Context to the Apostle.* Minneapolis: Fortress.

Nock, Arthur Darby. 1938. *St. Paul.* London: Butterworth.

Oakes, Peter. 2015. *Galatians.* PAIDEIA Commentaries on the New Testament. Grand Rapids: Baker.

O'Brien, Kelli. 2006. "The Curse of the Law (Galatians 3.13): Crucifixion, Persecution, and Deuteronomy 21.22–23," *Journal for the Study of the New Testament* 29.1: 55–76.

Oswalt, John H. 1998. *Isaiah 40–66.* New International Commentary on the Old Testament. Grand Rapids: Eerdmans.

Philo. 1929–1962. Translated by F. H. Colson, G. H. Whitaker, and Ralph Marcus. 10 vols. and 2 supplement vols. Loeb Classical Library. Cambridge: Harvard University Press.

Rahlfs-Hanhart. 2006. *Septuaginta.* Editio altera. Stuttgart: Deutsche Bibelgesellschaft.

Richards, E. Randolph. 2004. *Paul and First Century Letter Writing: Secretaries, Composition, and Collection.* Downers Grove, IL: InterVarsity.

Riches, John. 2013. *Galatians through the Centuries.* Wiley-Blackwell Bible Commentaries. Malden, MA: Blackwell.

Riesner, Rainer. 1997. *Paul's Early Period: Chronology, Mission Strategy, Theology.* Grand Rapids: Eerdmans.

Robertson, A. T. 1937. *A Grammar of the Greek New Testament in the Light of Historical Research.* Nashville: Broadman & Holman.

Robinson, D. W. B. 1964. "The Circumcision of Titus, and Paul's Liberty," *ABR* 12: 24–42.

Ropes, James Hardy. 1929. *The Singular Problem of the Epistle to the Galatians.* Cambridge: Harvard University Press.

Sanders, E. P. 1977. *Paul and Palestinian Judaism.* Minneapolis: Fortress.

Sandnes, Karl Olav. 1991. *Paul—One of the Prophets?* Wissenschaftliche Untersuchungen zum Neuen Testament 2.43. Tübingen: Mohr Siebeck.

Schlier, Heinrich. 1989. *Der Brief an die Galater.* 15th ed. KEKNTMK 7. Göttingen: Vandenhoeck & Ruprecht.

Schmithals, Walter. 1972. *Paul and the Gnostics.* Translated by John E. Steely. Nashville: Abingdon.

Schreiner, Patrick. 2018. *The Kingdom of God and the Glory of the Cross.* Wheaton, IL: Crossway.

Schreiner, Thomas R. 1984. "Is Perfect Obedience to the Law Possible? A Re-examination of Galatians 3:10." *Journal of the Evangelical Theological Society* 27: 151–60.

———. 1985. "Paul and Perfect Obedience to the Law: An Evaluation of the View of E. P. Sanders." *Westminster Theological Journal* 47: 245–78.

———. 1993. "Did Paul Believe in Justification by Works? Another Look at Romans 2." *Bulletin for Biblical Research* 3: 131–58.

———. 2010. *Galatians.* Zondervan Exegetical Commentary on the New Testament. Grand Rapids: Zondervan.

———. 2015. *The Doctrine of Justification.* Grand Rapids: Zondervan.

Schröter, Jens. 2006. *From Jesus to the New Testament: Early Christian Theology and the Origin of the New Testament Canon.* Edited by Wayne Coppins and Simon Gathercole. Translated by Wayne Coppins. Waco: Baylor University Press.

Scott, James. 1995. *Paul and the Nations: The Old Testament and Jewish Background of Paul's Mission to the Nations with Special Reference to the Destination of Galatians.* WUNT 84. Tubingen: Mohr Siebeck.

———. 2010. "Covenant." In *The Eerdmans Dictionary of Early Judaism,* edited by John J. Collins and Daniel C. Harlow, 491–94. Grand Rapids: Eerdmans.

Sechrest, Love L. 2009. *A Former Jew: Paul and the Dialectics of Race.* Library of New Testament Studies Series. New York: Bloomsbury.

Seifrid, Mark A. 2003. "Paul, Luther, and Justification in Galatians 2:15–21." *Westminster Theological Journal* 65: 215–30.

Silva, Moisés. 1996. *Explorations in Exegetical Method: Galatians as a Test Case*. Grand Rapids: Baker.

———. 2014. *New International Dictionary of the New Testament Theology and Exegesis*. 5 vols. Grand Rapids: Zondervan.

Snowden, Frank, Jr. 1991. *Before There was Color Prejudice: The Ancient View of Blacks*. Cambridge: Harvard University Press.

Sprinkle, Preston M. 2008. *Law and Life: The Interpretation of Leviticus 18:5 in Early Judaism and in Paul*. Wissenschaftliche Untersuchungen zum Neuen Testament 241. Tübingen: Mohr Siebeck.

Starling, Daniel I. 2011. *Not My People: Gentiles as Exiles in Pauline Hermeneutics*. Beihefte zur für die neutestamentliche Wissenschaft 205. Berlin: De Gruyter.

Stendahl, Krister. 1963. "Paul and the Introspective Conscience of the West." *Harvard Theological* Review 56 (July) 199–215.

Thiessen, Matthew. 2016. *Paul and the Gentile Problem*. Oxford: Oxford University Press.

VanLandingham, Chris. 2006. *Judgment and Justification in Early Judaism and the Apostle Paul*. Peabody, MA: Hendrickson.

Wakefield, Andrew. 2003. *Where to Live: The Hermeneutical Significance of Paul's Citations from Scripture in Galatians 3:1–14*. Atlanta: SBL.

Watson, Francis. 2015. *Paul and the Hermeneutics of Faith*. 2nd ed. New York: T. & T. Clark.

Westerholm, Stephen. 2004. *Perspectives Old and New on Paul: The "Lutheran" Paul and His Critics*. Grand Rapids: Eerdmans.

White, Joel. 2008. "Paul's Cosmology: The Witness of Romans, 1 and 2 Corinthians, and Galatians." In *Cosmology and New Testament Theology*, edited by Jonathan Pennington and Sean McDonough, 90–106. Library of New Testament Studies 355. London: T. & T. Clark.

Williams, Jarvis J. 2012. *For Whom Did Christ Die? The Extent of the Atonement in Paul's Theology*. Paternoster Biblical Monograph Series. Milton Keynes, UK: Paternoster.

Williams, Sam K. 1997. *Galatians*. Abingdon New Testament Commentaries. Nashville: Abingdon.

Willits, Joel. 2005. "Isa 54,1 in Gal 4,24b–27: Reading Genesis in Light of Isaiah." *Zeitschrift für die neutestamentliche Wissenschaft und die Kunde der* älteren *Kirche* 96: 188–210.

Windsor, Lionel. 2014. *Paul and the Vocation of Israel*. Beihefte zur für die neutestamentliche Wissenschaft 205. Berlin: De Gruyter.

Witherington, Ben, III. 1998. *Grace in Galatia: A Commentary on Paul's Letter to the Galatians*. Grand Rapids: Eerdmans.

Wright, Nicholas Thomas. 1991. *The Climax of the Covenant: Christ and the Law in Pauline Theology*. Minneapolis: Fortress.

———. 2013. *Paul and the Faithfulness of God*. 2 vols. Minneapolis: Fortress.

———. 2015. *Paul and His Recent Interpreters*. Minneapolis: Fortress.

Young, Norman H. 1998. "Who's Cursed and Why (Galatians 3.10–14)." *Journal of Biblical Literature* 117.1: 79–92.

Ziesler, J. A. 1972. *The Meaning of Righteousness in Paul: A Linguistic and Theological Enquiry*. Society for New Testament Studies Monograph Series 20. Cambridge: Cambridge University Press.

Ancient Document Index

OLD TESTAMENT

Genesis

3:14	22
6:18	113
12–50	87, 90
12:1—23:20	119
12	106
12:1–13	116
12:1–3	33, 82, 88, 104, 110, 115, 119, 123, 131
12:3	22, 67, 82, 95–96, 110, 115
13:15	96, 114
15	106
15:1–6	88
15:1–5	104, 116, 119
15:5–6	115
15:6	67, 82, 87–88, 95–96, 119
15:13	116
15:16	131
15:18	113–14
16–21	143–44
16	142
16:1–16	141, 143
16:1–4	144
16:1	148
16:15	96
17	6, 41–42, 106, 115
17:1–27	114, 119
17:1–14	116, 118–19
17:1–9	114
17:2–23	131
17:2–21	113
17:2	113
17:4–14	88
17:4–6	113
17:7	119
17:9–14	130
17:9	141
17:13	119
17:15–16	130
17:23–26	141
18:8	116
18:18	89, 96, 115, 131
18:19	104
19:21	46
21	142, 144
21:1–12	143
21:1–2	144
21:1	144
21:2	96
21:4	141
21:9–10	96
21:9	148
21:10	149
22:1–18	115–16
22:10	119
22:17	115, 119
22:18	89, 116
24:7	96, 114
25:1–5	144
25:5	144
25:6	144
26:3–5	118
26:3–4	116
26:3	116
26:4	89, 119
26:5	118–19
28:14	89
32:21	46
41:57	105
42:5	105
48:20	116

Exodus

2:44	113
4:22	129
6:4–5	113

Exodus (continued)

12:40–41	117
12:44	105
13:3–10	136
16:34	113
19	100
20	135–36
20:1	123, 124
20:2	51
20:19	22
20:21	22
20:22	22
21:30	105
31:15–17	136
32:16	126
34:29	123

Leviticus

2:13	113
8:35	73
11:1–47	50, 65
12:3	41, 88
16:13	113
18:1–30	100
18:25–30	100
18:5	73, 76, 79–80, 91–92, 95–96, 100–103, 106, 125, 151
19:15	46
19:18	158–59, 163, 169
20:22	73
21:18–20	157
22:24	157
23	136
24:3	113
25	136
25:18–32	105
25:18	73
25:24	105
26:46	22, 123–24

Numbers

1:50	113
1:53	113
4:5	113
3:46	105
5:27	22
7:89	113
15:23	123
25	28, 59
25:1–13	28
25:1–11	29
26:46	124
36:13	123

Deuteronomy

1:17	46
4:1	80, 104
4:10	80
4:13	113
4:23	113
4:31	113
4:37	81, 123
5:2–3	113
5:4	22
5:5	22
5:12–15	
5:22	22
5:23	22
5:27	22
5:31	22
6:4	124
6:13	36
6:24	125
7	65
7:1–6	51
7:2	113
7:8	81
7:9	113
7:12	113
7:26	22
8:1	104
10:4	126
10:17	46
10:20	36
12:2–4	52
13:1–8	23
13:14	77
14:1–2	129
19:15	49
21–30	108
21:21–23	107
21:21	107

21:22	108
21:23	82, 107
22–30	151
23	157
23:1–5	157
23:2	157
25:1	49, 67, 102
27–32	92, 108
27–30	92, 101
27–28	94
27:1—28:68	92
27:1—29:20	94
27:3	92
27:8	92
27:15—28:19	22
27:17	17
27:26	91–92, 94–96, 106
28	93
28:1	92
28:15	92
28:54	83
28:56	83
28:58–59	91
28:58	91–92, 94–96
30:10	91
30:12–14	104
30:19	82
31:29	93, 101
32	93, 124
32:5–6	134
32:31	82
33:2	22, 123
33:29	51, 123, 136

Judges

1:17	22

1 Samuel

3:7	135
4:3–5	113
15:18–19	64
18:3	113
20:8	113
20:16	113
20:23	113

2 Samuel

3:12–13	113
3:21	113
5:3	113
7:12–14	104, 117
7:14	32
7:27	26
15:4	67
15:24	113
23:5	113

1 Kings

3:15	113
6:19	113
8:1	113
8:6	113
8:9	113
8:21	113
8:23–24	113
8:31–32	67, 102
11:2	139
11:11	113
19:10	113
19:14	113

2 Kings

11:4	113
11:12	113
11:17	113
13:23	113
17:15	113
17:35	113
17:38	113
18:12	113
23:2	113
23:3	113

1 Chronicles

2:7	23
11:3	113
15:25–26	113
15:29	113
16:6	113
16:15–17	113

1 Chronicles (continued)

16:37	113
17:1	113
22:19	113
28:2	113
28:18	113
29:24	47

2 Chronicles

5:2	113
5:7	113
5:10	113
6:11	113
6:14	113
7:18	113
13:5	113
13:7	77
15:12	113
21:7	113
23:3	113
23:11	113
23:16	113
24:6	113
29:10	113
30:8	47
34:30–32	113
36:16	113

Ezra

9:1–2	52
10:3	113

Nehemiah

1:5	113
9:8	113
9:32	113
13:29	113

Job

9:33	124
31:1	113
41:4	113

Psalms

1	100
1:1	64
1:5–6	64
9:10	135
14:1	83
22:27–28	119
25:10	113
47:4	81
50:6	102
54:4	64
58:10	64
86:5	147
89:3–4	117
91:18	64
100:3	121
105:31	87–88
110:8	64
124:3	64
128:3	64
118:53	64
143:1	70
143:2	66, 70

Proverbs

1:7	83
2:17	113

Isaiah

5:23	67
40–66	21
42:6	31
43:26	102
49:1	31
50:7–8	66
53:1	86
54:1	96

Jeremiah

1:5	31
3:16	113
6:4	86
11:2–3	113
11:6	113

11:8	113
11:10	113
13:8	140
20:7	172
21:3	140
14:21	113
30:8	86, 11
31:31–33	34, 85
45:10	140

Lamentations

1:1	147
1:5	147
1:6	147
5:6	47

Ezekiel

8:2–3	22
11:14–21	111
11:19–20	86
16:8	113
16:59–62	113
17:13–16	113
17:18–19	113
17:18	47
20:11	104
20:13	104
20:37	113
34:25	113
36–37	34, 85–86
36:22–27	111
37:1–14	111
37:26	113
44:7	113
40–48	147

Daniel

1:3–20	50
2:8	105
2:22	34
2:23	26
2:28–30	26
2:45	26
5:7–8	26

5:15	26
5:17	26
9:4	113
10:5–6	22
12:2	100

Hosea

2:18	113
3:1	81
6:7	113
8:1	113
11:1	129

Joel

2:27–28	115
2:28–29	86
2:28	111

Amos

1:9	113

Habakkuk

2:4	91, 96, 98–101, 103

Zechariah

2:7	22
9:11	113
11:10	113
14:9	124
14:11	22

Malachi

2:4–5	135
2:2–7	76
2:8	135
2:10	135
2:14	135
3:1	135

APOCRYPHA

Additions to Esther

14:17   50

Baruch

2:35   113
3–4   76, 92, 100
3:1—4:2   79
3:14—4:37   96
3:9   125
3:13–14   125
4   73
4:1   88, 104, 118

Bel and the Dragon

1:28   64

1 Esdras

3:20   20
8:16   85

Judith

9:13   113
10–12   50

1 Maccabees

1–2   43, 59
1   100
1:11–15   41
1:11   64, 77, 79, 113
1:15   41, 113
1:34   64, 77, 79
1:48   43
1:57   113
1:60–63   43
1:63   113
2   27
2:15–28   29
2:20   113
2:23–28   29

2:26   29
2:27   113
2:44   64
2:45   29
2:46   44
2:50   113
2:52   87, 118
2:54   28, 113
3:5   29
4:10   113
7:5   102
11:9   113
11:21   64
13:49   105
14:29   96

2 Maccabees

1:2   113
2:17–18   119
2:21   28
2:44   64, 77
4:2—8:36   28
4:7–15   41
4:2   29
4:13   28
6:1   46, 54
6:10   43
6:18–31   54
6:21   56
7:1–38   79
7:1   46
7:9   100
7:14   80
7:18   86
7:24   17
7:32   86
7:36   80, 113
9:1–17   64
14   80
14:20   113
14:26–27   113

3 Maccabees

1:3   64
2:17–19   79
2:17–18   64, 77

3:4–7	50
6:4	87

4 Maccabees

4:25	42
4:26	28
5:2	46, 50, 54
5:27	46
6:15	56
6:17	56, 87
6:22	87
7:19	80, 87
8:17	82
9:8	86
10:10	86
13:17	87
14:20	87
15:3	100
15:11	20
15:28	87
16:20	87
16:25	80
17:6	87
17:12	100, 104
18:1	64, 87, 116
18:12	28–29
18:20	87
18:23	87

Prayer of Azariah

1:11	113

Prayer of Manasseh

1–8	102
8	87

Sirach

1:12–28	79
3:6	79
3:30	70
4:14	81

7:8	151
7:16	64
9:11	64
12:3–7	70
14:2	49
14:6	83
14:8	83
17:11–13	114
17:11–12	114
17:11	79, 125
17:12	113
17:22	70
19:5	49
24:9	123
24:23	113–14
28:7	113–14
29:11–13	70
32:15	56
33:2	56
33:3	96
35:12–14	46
36:2	65
39:8	113–14
40:24	70
41:5–11	65
42:2	113
44—50	87
44:17	78
44:20	113
44:19–21	87
44:19–20	114, 118
44:21	119
44:22	113
45:5	79, 113, 129
45:7	113
45:15	113
45:23–24	28
45:24–25	113
47:11	113

Tobit

4	70
4:17	64
10	70
13:6	64
14:4–7	107

Wisdom of Solomon

1:16	113
2:13	135
2:22	100
4:1—6:5	102
6:1—12:27	102
6:17–21	102
7:17	127
11–15	163
13:18–19	136
14:1–29	135
17:16–17	168
17:17	168
18:4	118, 123
19:13	64

PSEUDEPIGRAPHA

Assumption of Moses

1:11	123

2 Baruch (Syriac Apocalypse)

2:2	70
4:1	151
4:6–9	147
6:9	147
14:7	70
14:12–13	119
14:12	70
32:6	176
41–51	92
44:12	176
48:22	70
51:3–4	151
51:3	70
51:7	70
56:6	140
57:1–3	87
57:2	71, 176
63:3	70
63:5	70
67:6	70
77:15	118
85:2	70

1 Enoch

1:2	22
5:4–7	64
62:4	140
72:1	176
81:5	70
90:28–29	147
91:15–16	176
99:2	118, 123

4 Ezra

2:5	113
2:7	113
2:44–45	22
3:15	113
3:32–33	114
3:28–36	64
4:1–4	22
4:2	140
4:23	64
6:9	15
6:27	96
6:28	96
7:24	114
7:26	147
7:28–29	32–33
7:28	117
7:29	33
7:46	113–14
7:75	176
7:88–101	97
7:104–5	170
8:27	114
9:7–13	96
9:37	118, 123
9:38—10:59	145, 147
10:22	113
10:25–28	147
13:32	32–33
13:35–36	147
13:36	147
13:37	33
13:52	33
14:9	32–33
14:30	125

Joseph and Aseneth

8:5	50
21:14–15	50
7:1	57

Jubilees

1:7—2:1	123
1:23–25	129
1:23–24	86
2:9	135
2:23	96
3:30–31	41
3:31	118
4:26	176
5:16	46
5:19	93
6—44	114
6:17	118
11:16–17	87
12:1–5	118
12:2–8	87
12:12–14	118
12:16–24	87
12:19–20	118
12:22–24	118
15:3	87
15:23–33	119
15:25–34	42
15:27	42
15:28	119
16:16–18	143
22:14	119
22:16–22	50, 64, 77–78, 135, 163
22:16–19	52
22:16–18	65
22:16	50–51
23:10	87, 93, 119
23:23–24	64
24:11	87
27:17	93
30:5–20	28
36:23	93
40:8	93

Liber antiquitatum biblicarum (Pseudo-Philo)

3:10	176
9:13–15	42
11:1–5	97
32:17	176

Letter of Aristeas

127	96, 100, 104
139–42	78
139	52, 65, 77
142	50, 52, 65, 77
149	87
219	56
267	56

Odes of Solomon

11:2	42

Psalms of Solomon

1:6	145
2:1–2	64
2:2	65
2:34–35	67
3:11–12	72
4	25
4:8	64
4:20	56
4:22	56
6:6	85
9:2	102
9:9	64, 87
12:6	119
13:6–12	64
14:1–10	92, 100–101
14:2–5	101
14:2–3	72
14:5	119
14:6–9	101
14:9–10	119
14:10	72
15:5	72
15:10–11	119

Psalms of Solomon (continued)

17:23	119
18:3	64, 87

Sibylline Oracles

2:246	87

Testament of Abraham

10:13	87

Testament of Asher

6:3	96
7:7	87

Testament of Benjamin

1:2	87
10:4	87
10:7	87

Testament of Dan

5:1	96
7:2	87

Testament of Joseph

6:7	87

Testament of Judah

17:5	87
17:25	87
25:1	87
26:1	96–97

Testament of Levi

9:1–14	87
13:1	96
13:2–3	97
13:5	97
15:4	64

Testament of Moses

8:1–3	41–42
6:9	108
8:1	108

Testament of Naphtali

1:10	87

JOSEPHUS

Against Apion

2.13	98
2.38	123
2.210	92

Jewish Antiquities

1.18	28
1.24	143
1.214	41
2.651	59
3.312	86
4.65	25
4.16–579	59
8.262	41
9.1	117
9.204	117
12.253–56	43
12.255–56	107–8
13.380–83	107–8
13.717	28
18.64	108
20.33–45	40
20.33–42	40, 44
20.41	40
20.44	40
20.45	40
20.46	41
20.97–117	59
20.102	107
20.129	109
20.186	59

Jewish War

1.34	43
1.97–98	107
2.75	107
2.241	107
2.253	107
5.159	35
7.43	48
7.44	64
7.45	48
9.4	117

The Life

113	41

PHILO

On the Life of Abraham

107–14	50
82	143

On the Preliminary Studies

86–87	100

Against Flaccus

36–40	41
72	107
83–85	107

On the Life of Joseph

96	107
98	107
156	107

Allegorical Interpretation

2:5	143

On the Life of Moses

1.28	93

2.3	136
2.14	123
1.162	93

On the Migration of Abraham

82	143

On Rewards and Punishments

1:158	143

On Dreams

2.213	107

On the Special Laws

1.1	42
1.51	64
2.253	29
3.151	107

Questions and Answers on Genesis

3.48	41
1.55	123

NEW TESTAMENT

Matthew

1:20	139
1:24	139
2:13	139
2:19	139
3:17	31, 129
4:3	129
4:6	129
4:24	86
5:21	27
5:27	27
5:33	27
5:28	27
5:43	27

Matthew (continued)

6:26	172
8:29	129
9:26	76
10:40	139
11:20–21	86
11:23	86
12:18	31
12:36–37	67
13:14	86
14:1	86
15:1	86
17:5	31
17:12	86
18:15–18	168
19:19	169
22:34–40	159
22:39	169
24:6	86
24:8	140
25:26–46	172
24:24	139
26:28	113
26:39	139
26:65	27
26:67	138
27:4	17
27:30	138

Mark

1:11	31
7:35	86
12:10	126
13:8	140
13:22	139
14:35	139
14:24	113
14:64	76
15:5	17
15:19	138

Luke

1:13	139
1:19	139
1:30	98
1:72	113
3:22	31
4:21	126
2:33	17
6:15	59
7:1	86
7:22	27
7:39	76
12:32	31
17:3–4	168
18:32	138
22:20	113
24:12	17
24:41	17

John

1:34	129
1:42	35
3:16	154
5:5	138
5:19	76
5:21	125
5:28	17
6:63	126
7:21	17
7:13	55
8:38	27
8:44	76
9:6	138
9:16	76
9:22	55
10:33	76
11:14	138
11:25	103
12:38	86
13:8	160
15:4	76
19:38	55
20:19	55

Acts

1:8	29
1:13	59
2	57
2:1–40	111
2:10	53

2:20	21
2:32	110
3:12	17
3:14	99
3:25	113
6	59
7–9	59
7:8	113
7:38	22, 124
7:52	99
7:53	123, 124
7:58—8:3	32, 36, 59
8–9	59
8:1–40	29
8:13	86
9	13, 27, 35
9:1–22	32
9:1–19	26
9:1–9	26
9:1–2	59
9:10–25	34
9:10–19	14
9:26–30	14
9:26–27	44
10–11	51, 53, 56
10	57
10:3	139
10:11–20	53
10:28–29	53
10:28	50
10:45	59
11:19–26	48
11:21	48
11:26	48, 57
11:27–30	45
11:27	48
13–14	8, 23, 27, 84, 138
13:1—14:28	44
13:1	48
13:5	57
13:36–37	31
14:1–2	53
15	7, 47, 58, 76
15:1–2	45
15:1–35	8
15:1–11	43
16:13–33	57
17:17	57
17:20	86
18:6–8	57
18:9–10	45
21:25	43
22:3	27–28
22:6–11	26
22:14	99
22:21	45
23:6	28
26:5	28
26:12–18	26
28:26	86

Romans

1:1–2	34
1:1	13
1:3	104
1:8–17	4
1:8	1
1:14	39
1:16	29
1:17	103
1:18—3:20	46
1:18–32	135
2:1—4:25	43
2:9–10	39
2:11	98
2:13—3:20	75
2:13	94, 98, 102
2:15	73
2:23	121
2:25—5:5	43
2:25	78
2:27	64
3:1–2	64
3:9	39
3:20–24	67
3:20–22	67
3:20	71, 73
3:21—4:25	67
3:22	74
3:23	77
3:28	73
4:1–25	130
4:1	139
4:6	139
4:8	139

Romans *(continued)*

4:9	139
4:12	59
4:15	121
4:17	19, 125
4:25	121
5:1	67
5:8–9	15
5:8	155
5:9–10	67
5:14	121
5:15–16	121
5:20	121
6:2–11	129
6:13	81
6:18–20	81
6:19	138
7:1—8:11	78
7:7	128
8:1–14	162
8:3–4	159
8:4–5	163
8:11	125
8:12–14	165
8:12–13	173
8:14	163
8:18–39	183
8:18–30	153
8:26	138
8:30	19, 64
9:1	81
9:3	23
9:24	19
10:12	39
10:14–16	86
10:16–17	86
10:15	76
11:1–2	81
11:1	28
11:2	175
11:13	13
11:12	121
11:23	76
11:26	176
11:27	113
14:1—15:12	4
15:4	85
15:17	170
15:18–20	34
15:22–28	4

1 Corinthians

1:1	14
1:9	19
1:12	35
1:21	31
1:22	39
1:24	39
1:30	81
2:3	138
2:4	24
5:6	156
7	131
7:15	19
7:18	19
7:17–20	43
8:8	76
9:1–7	34
9:16	76
9:24–27	155
10:5	31
10:32	39
11	131
11:23	23
11:25	113
12–14	171
12:10	19
12:13	39
12:17	86
12:26	86
13:1	76
14	131
14:6	76
14:7	76
14:9	76
14:11	76
14:28	76
15:1–8	26, 49
15:1–2	137
15:1	23
15:3	15
15:5	34, 35
15:7	34, 36
15:8–9	13
15:9	34

15:22	125
15:26	152
15:36	76, 125
15:39–41	19
15:42–50	173
15:43	138
15:57	173
16:21	174
16:22	23

2 Corinthians

1:1	14
1:12–14	170
2:5–11	168
2:13	39
3:6	113, 126
3:14	113, 152
4	177
4:6	33
4:10–11	85
4:10	138
6:1	45
6:4–5	138
7:6	39
7:13–14	39
8:1–15	47
8:6	39, 85
8:16	39
8:23	39
11	85, 177
11:4	19
11:23–26	29
11:23–25	138
11:32	35
12:3	45
12:9	138
12:7–10	138

Galatians

1:1—2:10	12–13, 155
1:1–9	82
1:1–5	12, 16
1:1	1, 6–7, 12–13, 15–16, 20–21, 23–24, 34, 37, 56, 68, 80, 82–83, 102–3, 117, 125, 129, 154, 161, 162, 164, 177

1:2	12, 22, 32, 54, 70, 174
1:3	1, 12, 15, 19, 27, 117, 177
1:4	1, 4–7, 12, 15–16, 19, 32, 37, 43, 49, 55–57, 60, 68–69, 75, 77, 79–81, 83–84, 86, 88, 94–95, 99, 102–3, 106, 108, 115, 120, 127–29, 136, 148–49, 151–54, 157–62, 164–66, 170, 175
1:5	17
1:6–16	26
1:6–11	84
1:6–10	12
1:6–9	6, 17, 19, 24–26, 60, 83, 141, 155, 171
1:6–7	1, 2, 6–7, 20, 24, 39, 78–79, 102, 155
1:6	1, 17–19, 21, 31–32, 37, 136, 155–57, 177
1:7–9	55
1:7	13, 18–21, 34, 37–38, 56, 76, 78
1:8–9	1, 2, 17, 19, 21–24, 43, 49, 56–57, 82, 106, 152, 156, 170
1:8	22, 138–39
1:9	17, 22–23, 27
1:10–24	24
1:10—2:10	7, 21, 43
1:10–15	156
1:10	18, 24–25
1:11—2:10	57–58
1:11–24	12, 25–26
1:11–14	33
1:11–12	13, 20–21, 24, 56, 125
1:11	6, 18, 21, 24–25
1:12	23–26, 33–34, 45, 104
1:13—2:10	27, 35, 55, 177
1:13–22	38
1:13–17	24
1:13–16	88, 175
1:13–15	59
1:13–14	27–29, 30, 32, 36, 43, 55, 59, 73, 105
1:13	24, 27, 29
1:14—2:21	138
1:14–16	97
1:14	26, 29
1:15–24	28, 30
1:15–21	37

Galatians *(continued)*

1:15–16	13–14, 19, 21, 23, 27, 30–31, 34, 56, 58, 80, 83–84, 102–3, 115, 127–28, 136, 154–56
1:15	31–32, 177
1:16–17	25, 30
1:16	6, 21, 26, 33–34, 40, 45
1:17–18	40
1:17	30, 34–35, 56
1:18—2:10	60
1:18	35–36, 56
1:19–20	25
1:19	19, 35, 76
1:20	36
1:21	36, 56
1:22–24	36
1:22	32, 36, 104, 129, 154
1:23	36, 43
2:1—5:12	130
2:1–10	8, 12, 38–39, 56
2:1–7	37
2:1–6	46
2:1–4	38
2:1–3	39
2:2–7	20
2:2–4	58
2:2–3	56
2:2	6, 40, 45, 47, 49, 56
2:3–10	47
2:3	13, 38–39, 44–45, 47, 49, 55, 70
2:4	39, 47, 104, 129, 154
2:5–10	56
2:5–9	47
2:5	6, 39–40, 58, 60, 140, 155
2:6–9	58
2:6	9, 49
2:7–10	35
2:7–9	20, 46, 59
2:8–9	57
2:9	12, 14, 19, 43, 177
2:10	12, 45, 47, 58
2:11—5:1	4, 125
2:11—3:29	14
2:11–21	47, 63, 66, 83, 152
2:11–16	117
2:11–15	138
2:11–14	5, 7, 9, 47, 72–73, 78, 130, 137, 154
2:11–12	47
2:11	19, 23, 28, 48–49, 152, 156, 170
2:12	50, 54, 57–59, 70
2:13–14	48, 60
2:13	28, 49, 54
2:14–15	49
2:14	6, 21, 28, 40, 46, 53–54, 56, 60–61, 131, 140, 155
2:15–21	47, 63, 81
2:15–16	48, 60
2:15	27, 56, 63–65, 70, 76, 78, 131
2:16—5:12	159
2:16—5:1	16, 43, 161
2:16—4:31	142
2:16—3:29	103, 119
2:16—3:14	6
2:16—3:12	4
2:16–21	19, 88
2:16–17	67, 79, 81, 104, 117, 153
2:16	3, 6, 9, 32, 46, 56, 61, 64–72, 74–77, 80–81, 84, 90, 97–99, 102–4, 127, 142, 151, 153–54, 158, 162, 164, 173
2:17–21	81, 127
2:17–20	175
2:17–18	78, 80
2:17	68, 76–78, 129
2:18	55, 78–79
2:19–21	5, 80–81, 117, 138, 170
2:19–20	33, 84, 86, 104, 112, 127, 165, 172
2:19	4, 15, 33, 72, 78–79
2:20–21	4, 81, 104, 157, 159, 163
2:20	33, 80, 98, 116, 174
2:21	14, 19, 32, 56, 67–69, 69, 75, 79, 81, 84, 97–98, 103, 126, 142, 153–54, 177
3:1—5:26	152
3:1—5:24	68
3:1—5:21	154
3:1—5:1	7, 26, 60, 70, 74, 77, 82, 106, 134
3:1—4:31	145
3:1—4:11	139
3:1–29	5, 33, 68, 127, 140, 176
3:1–20	125
3:1–14	6, 69, 99, 109, 120, 153, 163
3:1–12	109

3:1–9   88, 90, 98
3:1–8   151
3:1–6   170
3:1–5   82, 85, 87, 88, 98, 141, 165
3:1–2   110
3:1   2, 4, 23, 63, 68–69, 81–84, 104, 117, 139, 156–57, 159, 170
3:2—5:26   161, 164
3:2—5:4   160
3:2—4:31   72
3:2–29   127
3:2–22   127
3:2–18   121
3:2–14   99
3:2–10   110
3:2–9   102
3:2–6   18
3:2–5   68–69, 86, 110, 126, 162, 165–66
3:2–3   86, 177
3:2   18, 71, 85, 152
3:3–4   18
3:3   85, 152, 155–56, 173
3:4   86
3:5–9   119, 125
3:5   18, 71, 85, 110, 154
3:6—4:31   88
3:6–18   119
3:6–14   81, 86
3:6–9   82, 86–88, 107, 110, 114
3:6–8   164
3:6–7   88
3:6   18, 67, 87–88, 96, 98, 100, 102, 115, 141, 153
3:7–9   96, 98
3:7   88, 98, 110–11
3:8–9   119
3:8   33, 57, 67, 74, 88–89, 98, 107, 110, 113, 115–16, 148
3:9   69–70, 82, 90, 98, 107, 111, 119
3:9–10   102
3:10—5:26   78
3:10—5:1   135
3:10—4:31   81, 93
3:10—4:8   19
3:10—4:7   75, 77, 79, 103, 112, 120, 165

3:10–14   84, 90, 100, 104, 111, 127, 142, 153, 162
3:10–13   5, 16, 55, 69, 108, 111
3:10–12   6, 57, 72–75, 77, 80, 90–91, 95, 99—100, 107–8, 123, 125
3:10–11   19, 92, 100
3:10   7, 15, 17, 23, 49–50, 71, 75–77, 81–82, 91, 94–95, 97—100, 103–6, 108, 110, 120, 126–27, 136, 142, 151, 156, 170
3:11–12   81
3:11   67, 80, 91–92, 96–99, 102–3
3:12   76, 91–92, 95–96, 100–102, 158
3:13—4:6   128
3:13–29   119
3:13–18   104, 121, 164
3:13–14   5, 7, 16, 18, 32, 43, 68–69, 79–80, 88, 90, 98, 104, 106–8, 117, 120, 127–29, 131, 135–36, 148, 151, 154, 159, 161–62, 165–66, 170, 176–77
3:13   1, 4, 6, 15, 32–33, 50, 55–56, 60, 69, 75, 77, 80, 84, 86, 94, 102–10, 115, 127, 149–51, 157, 159, 164–65, 175
3:14   7, 33, 57, 68, 69, 81, 88, 93–94, 103, 105, 107–8, 111, 114–15, 119–20, 122, 128–29, 131, 141, 150–52, 154–55, 159, 162
3:15—4:31   6, 95
3:15—4:11   94, 112
3:15—4:7   75, 81, 105, 108, 126
3:15–19   1, 123
3:15–18   112
3:15–17   113
3:15   18, 113, 119
3:16–29   89, 113
3:16–18   113
3:16–17   96, 117
3:16   33, 69, 82, 89–90, 104, 114, 116–17, 120–21, 123, 129–31, 141, 148, 159, 177
3:17–18   114, 118
3:17   119, 121, 152
3:18   118, 121, 141–42, 177
3:19—5:1   106
3:19—4:31   95
3:19—4:7   15, 105, 121–22, 128, 154

Galatians (continued)

3:19–29	105–6
3:19–25	121
3:19–23	79
3:19–22	112
3:19–20	1, 22, 124
3:19	22, 75, 78, 108, 117, 121–24, 138, 142
3:20—4:7	122
3:20	123–24
3:21—4:/	142, 145
3:21–22	75, 126
3:21	50, 67, 69, 76, 79–81, 88, 92, 98–99, 104, 118, 125–26, 142
3:22—4:7	150
3:22–24	161
3:22–23	104, 127, 142, 149
3:22	15, 74, 77, 89, 104, 114, 122–23, 126–27, 136, 149–50, 159
3:23—4:25	1
3:23—4:7	120, 128
3:23—4:3	136
3:23	7, 122–23, 126–27, 142
3:24—4:7	142
3:24–25	134
3:24	67, 104, 128, 159
3:25–27	129
3:25	122, 129
3:26–29	117, 129
3:26–28	104, 116
3:26–27	128–29
3:26	129
3:27	75, 89, 129, 165
3:28–29	33, 117, 131, 149, 175
3:28	5, 15, 44, 50, 69, 124, 130–32, 154, 176
3:29—4:7	127, 164
3:29	56, 68–69, 96, 104, 114, 116, 119, 124–25, 141, 149, 177
4:1–9	105
4:1–8	127, 162
4:1–7	105
4:1–4	105
4:1–2	134
4:1	68, 77, 105, 122
4:2–9	135
4:2–7	127
4:3–9	57
4:3–7	134
4:3–5	127, 136
4:3	1, 77, 105, 122, 127, 134, 136, 149, 161–62, 173
4:4–6	33, 55, 88, 99, 106, 159, 162, 166
4:4–5	105, 128, 149
4:4	122, 128, 138
4:5–11	15
4:5–7	161
4:5–6	5, 6, 69, 94, 135, 162, 177
4:5	4, 7, 105, 120, 127, 134, 151, 176
4:6	6, 33–44, 88, 105, 131, 134, 151–52, 155
4:7	68–69
4:8–11	6, 95, 134, 141–42, 173
4:8–9	135–36, 145–46, 149
4:8	127, 135
4:9–11	73, 135
4:9–10	154
4:9	1, 77, 105, 127, 135–36, 162
4:10–11	135
4:10	9, 72, 136, 151
4:11	2, 23, 136–37, 140
4:12–20	27, 137, 172, 177
4:12–19	23
4:12–16	138
4:12	18, 137–39
4:13–14	85, 137
4:13	138, 174
4:14	86, 104, 137–39, 174
4:15	137, 139
4:16	137, 140
4:17–18	137
4:17	78, 140
4:18	40, 140
4:19	104, 117, 135, 137, 140
4:20	2, 40, 137, 141
4:21—5:6	81, 158
4:21—5:1	19, 106, 120, 127, 141, 145, 151, 166
4:21–31	5, 55, 57, 105, 120, 141–42, 146, 158, 176–77
4:21–27	6
4:21–26	75
4:21–25	7, 77
4:21–24	96
4:21	127, 142

4:22–24	143
4:22–23	143–44
4:22	142–44
4:23	141, 144–45, 173–74
4:24–26	143
4:24	143–44, 146
4:25–27	146
4:25–26	143
4:25	144–46
4:26–27	146
4:26	145, 148
4:27	141
4:28—5:1	96
4:28–31	6
4:28–29	18
4:28	114, 120, 141, 148–49
4:29–31	177
4:29	70, 85–86, 144, 149, 152, 173–74
4:30	89, 149, 156
4:31—5:1	16
4:31	18, 141, 148–49, 160
5:1—6:10	7
5:1–15	43
5:1–5	5
5:1–2	104
5:1	7, 18, 105, 141–42, 145, 149, 158, 160, 177
5:2—6:18	5
5:2–26	150
5:2–6	6, 20, 56, 73, 96
5:2–5	9, 18, 55, 73, 83, 85
5:2–4	7, 78–79, 150, 152, 175
5:2–3	13, 72, 102, 173
5:2	72
5:3–4	72, 142, 159
5:3	73, 75, 94, 96, 106, 150–51, 154
5:4	19, 56, 69, 104, 110, 151–53, 162, 174
5:5	16, 23, 67–69, 99, 120, 152, 154, 160
5:6	5, 43–44, 104, 129, 154, 158, 160, 164, 177
5:7–12	155
5:7–9	83, 157
5:7–8	83
5:7	18, 40, 83, 140, 150, 155–56
5:8	96, 150, 155
5:9–10	150

5:9	156
5:10–11	106
5:10	18–19, 83, 156
5:11	4, 8, 13, 55, 72, 86, 96, 150, 156, 171, 173, 175, 177
5:12	1, 22, 141, 146, 152, 156, 174
5:13—6:10	155, 157
5:13—6:5	176
5:13—6:2	170–71
5:13–26	77, 150, 158, 165
5:13–21	94
5:13–15	158
5:13–14	5, 111, 158–60, 169, 172
5:13	18–19, 96, 158–60, 173
5:14	158, 161
5:15	96, 159, 161
5:16—6:9	120, 173
5:16–26	16, 68–69, 80, 85, 99, 122, 127, 152, 154, 159, 166, 168, 173
5:16–24	68–69
5:16–21	23, 68, 77, 85, 106, 149, 173
5:16–17	163
5:16	69, 99, 136, 160–62, 164–65
5:17–26	161
5:17–21	168
5:17	161
5:18	72, 162
5:19–21	162–63
5:19	162–63
5:20–21	112, 163
5:20	163
5:21–22	158
5:21	2, 16, 23, 68, 84, 88, 93, 106, 116, 120, 140, 151–52, 154, 159, 163–66, 171–72
5:22–24	69
5:22–23	112, 162
5:22	75, 155, 162, 164, 169, 171–72
5:23	169
5:24–26	84–85
5:24	4, 104, 165, 173
5:26	159, 168
6:1—18	167
6:1–10	112
6:1–5	167–68
6:1	18, 164, 167–70
6:2	94, 104, 111, 158, 167, 169–70
6:3	167, 170

Galatians (continued)

6:4–5	170
6:4	19, 170
6:5	170, 172–73
6:6–10	171
6:6	169, 171–72
6:7	172–73
6:8–9	2
6:8	77, 99, 152, 165, 172–73
6:9–10	169
6:9	173
6:10	174
6:11–18	6, 43, 174
6:11–17	84
6:11–16	7, 167
6:12–13	9, 13, 56, 78, 85, 102, 140, 167, 170, 173
6:12	1, 4, 32–33, 46, 55, 60, 72, 83–86, 104, 117, 127, 167, 174–75, 177
6:13	2, 167, 174
6:14–17	175
6:14–16	5
6:14–15	108, 175
6:14	4, 15, 104, 112, 117, 127, 165, 167, 170, 175
6:15–17	176
6:15–16	148, 176
6:15	1, 4–5, 15, 23, 43–44, 72, 77, 80, 88, 99, 106, 120, 128, 148, 154, 161, 164–65, 167, 175, 177
6:16	14, 82, 176–77
6:17–18	167, 177
6:17	86, 156, 168, 175, 177
6:18	14, 18–19, 104, 117, 168, 177

Ephesians

1:1	13
1:17	26
2:11–22	43
2:14–15	55
3:2	27
3:3	26, 84
4	171
4:21	27
5:16	105

Philippians

1:3	1
1:5	171
1:6	85
1:29	86
2:16	45–46, 170
2:26	27
3	43
3:4–10	79
3:4–6	28–29
3:5	64, 73
3:9	78
3:10–14	173
3:12–14	155
3:20—4:1	173
4:9	23, 27

Colossians

1:1	13
1:3	1
1:6	27
1:19	31
1:23	27
2:6	23
3:11	39
4:1	59
4:5	105
4:18	174

1 Thessalonians

2:12	19
2:13	23
3:5	45
4:1	23
4:2	23
4:7	19
4:5	135
5:24	19

2 Thessalonians

1:3	1
1:6	98
1:8–9	135
2:13	86

3:6	23
3:13	173
3:17	174

1 Timothy

1:1	13
2:5	124
2:7	13
5:18	126

2 Timothy

1:12	86
3:16	126
4:3–4	86
4:7	155
4:10	39

Titus

1:1	13

Philemon

19	174

Hebrews

2:2	22, 121, 124
7:22	113
8:6–10	113
8:6	124
8:13	113
9:1	113
9:4	113
9:15	22, 113, 121, 124
9:18	113
9:20	113
10:16	113
10:29	113
10:38	31, 103
12:22	147
12:24	113, 124
13:14	147
13:20	113

James

2:1–7	46
2:8	126
2:10	151
2:11	78
5:11	27
5:19–20	168

1 Peter

1:4	119
1:17	46
3:9	119
3:17	86
3:18	99, 125
4:13	171

2 Peter

1:17	31
2:8	86

1 John

2:1	99
2:7	27
2:18	27
2:24	27
3:11	27
3:13	17
3:20–21	49

2 John

1:6	27

Revelation

2:10	86
3:12	147
11:19	113
12:2	140
21—22	175
21	147
21:7	119

DEAD SEA SCROLLS

Damascus Document

II.15–16	93–94
III.2–3	87
III.14–25	72
III.14–20	100, 104
VI.10	15
XVI.6	42

Thanksgiving Hymns

III.7–10	140
IX.26	71
X.8–12	64
XII.27–28	26
XII.31	71
XIV.20	42

War Scroll

XII.8–9	89

Pesher Habakkuk

V.4–8	64
V.4	89
VII.4–5	26
VII.14—VIII.3	99
XII.13	89
XIII.3–4	89

Rule of the Community

VII.14–16	41
XI.2	71
XI.6	71
XI.13	71
XI.14–15	71
XI.17	71
X.13	71
X.18	71

Rule of Community Appendix

II.11–12	32

Florileguim, Midrash on Eschatologya

I.7	71
I.10–13	32, 117

Pesher Nahum

1.7–8	107

Pesher Psalmsa

2.13–14	72

Testament of Naphtali

A ii 2–7	72

papMMT^e

Frag. 2.II.7–8	87

MMT^f

Frag. 1.II.4–5	87

Some Precepts on the Law (4QMMT)

26–27	72
117–18	87

11QT

LXIV.6–13	107–8

RABBINIC WRITINGS

m.Qidd.

4:14	119

m. Tanh.

Exod 34   119

GRECO-ROMAN WRITINGS

Aristotle

Rhet.

1.6.6–16   164
3.17.22   27

Cicero

Inv.

1.17.25   17

Epictetus

Diss

2.920   49
4.1.1.   158

Horace

Sat.

1.9.68–74   41

Juvenal

Sat.

14.96   136
14.99   41

Lucian

Tox.

40–41   139

Quintilian

Inst.

3.8.36   27
3.8.66   27
5.6.1.–2   36
6.2.20   137
9.2.28   36

Plato

Resp.

4.427E   164
7.536A   164
9.592A–B   145

Leg.

12.963   164

Plutarch

Quast. Conv.

681 A–D   83

Seneca

Ot. Sap.

4.1   145
6.4   145
8.1–3   145

Lucil.

68   163

Strabo

Geogr.

16.2.28   145
16.2.37   41

Suetonius

Dom.

12.2   41

Tacitus

Hist.

5.2   42

**EARLY CHRISTIANS
WRITINGS**

Justin Martyr

Dial

9.5.1   94

Chrysostom

Hom. Gal.

13:26–27   94

Author Index

Bachman, Michael, 71
Barclay, John M. G., 2, 9, 14, 35, 41, 48, 53, 81, 101, 118, 158, 161, 169
Bauckham, Richard, 15, 124
Bernat, David A., 41–44
Betz, Hans D., 11, 15–16, 28, 49, 55–56, 60, 64–65, 86, 91, 104, 114–15, 123, 126, 136, 140, 151, 153, 157,
Bird, Michael F., 40, 51, 54, 65, 74, 85, 97
Blount, Brian, 48
Bowley, James, 118–19
Braxton, Brad, 53
Bruno, Chris, 124
Burns, J. Patout Jr., 48
Burton, Ernest, 71, 124, 136
Byron, Gay, 57

Caneday, Ardel, 69, 109
Chapman, David W., 108
Chester, Stephen J., 103
Ciampa, Roy E., 22
Cohen, Shayne J.D., 41
Cook, John Granger, 108
Cosgrove, Charles H., 3, 124
Crownfield, Frederic R., 10

Das, Andrew A., 8, 13, 15–20, 22–23, 25–36, 38–39, 41–43, 46, 48, 50–51, 53–54, 56, 58–59, 64–65, 67, 69–72, 75–76, 78–81, 83–94, 97–101, 104, 107–8, 111, 113–19, 121–22, 126, 128–30, 134–40, 143–48, 151, 153, 155–57, 158, 161–64, 168–71, 173–74, 176–77
Davies, W. D., 11
Davis, Basil S., 23

de Boer, Martinus C., 33, 35, 58, 83, 87, 98, 108–9, 115–16, 126, 139–40, 146–47, 151, 153, 161, 165, 170
Deenick, Karl, 44
deSilva, David A., 22, 32, 36, 49, 72, 75–76, 80, 83, 86, 94, 96, 110, 115–16, 129, 139–40, 144–45, 148, 151, 156, 163, 174–75, 177
Donaldson, Terrence L., 5, 40, 53, 55–56, 64, 107, 136
Dunn, James D. G., 22–23, 32–33, 66, 72–73, 75, 81, 102, 122, 129, 136, 140, 147, 151, 155, 158
Dunne, John, 86

Eastman, Susan Grove, 33, 83
Eliav, Yaron Z., 41
Elliott, Susan, 145–46
Esler, Philip, 49

Fee, Gordon, 2, 79, 130

Garlington, Don, 70
Gathercole, Simon J., 97, 102
Goddard, A. J., 138
Goldingay, A. J., 147
Gurtner, Daniel M., 73, 92, 97, 125

Hansen, Walter G., 11
Harmon, Matthew, 21
Hays, Richard B., 53, 59–61, 66–67, 75, 85, 89, 92–94, 99–100, 109, 111, 113, 116–17, 121–22, 124, 128, 134, 138, 144, 147, 151, 155, 156, 158–59, 162–65, 169–71
Hengel, Martin, 27, 48
Hodge, Caroline Johnson, 27, 57
Hubing, Jeff, 175
Hübner, Hans, 121

Hunn, Debbie, 75, 76, 129

Isaac, Benjamin, 27

Jervis, Ann L., 33
Jewett, Robert, 10, 58–59

Kahl, Brigitte, 140
Keener, Craig, 8, 22, 88, 97, 115, 135,
    138, 140, 145, 147, 151, 155, 157,
    176
Kennedy, George, 94, 137
Kepple, Robert J., 143
Kerkeslager, Allen, 41
Kimber Buell, Denise, 27, 57
Kuck, David W., 170

Lenski, R. C. H., 71
Lightfoot, J. B., 109, 124
Longenecker, Richard N., 8, 10, 12,
    32–33, 46, 76, 91, 109, 116, 122,
    128, 135–36, 140, 147, 151, 155,
    158
Lütgert, Wilhelm, 10

Martin, Troy, 42
Martyn, J. Louis, 25, 33, 60, 106, 110,
    121, 140, 143, 145, 146, 157, 169,
    174
Matera, Frank, 110, 122, 164
McLean, Bradley, 23, 107
Mitchell, Stephen, 7–8
Moo, Douglas J., 8, 18–19, 23, 25, 39,
    67, 79–80, 89, 91, 98–99, 109,
    116, 121, 124, 126, 139, 140, 143,
    147–48, 151, 153, 155, 157–59,
    162, 164
Murphey-O'Connor, Jerome, 169

Nanos, Mark D., 10–11, 27, 39, 175,
    179
Nock, Arthur Darby, 46

Oakes, Peter, 19, 97, 101–2, 127
O'Brien, Kelli, 108
Oswalt, John H, 147

Richards, E. Randolph, 13–14
Riches, John, 2

Riesner, Rainer, 38
Robertson, A. T., 19
Robinson, D. W., 46

Sanders, E. P., 71
Sandnes, Karl Olav, 31
Schlier, Heinrich, 56, 104
Schmithals, Walter, 10
Schreiner, Patrick, 165
Schreiner, Thomas R., 2, 7–8, 10–12,
    19, 23–24, 27, 30, 39, 58–59,
    73, 75–76, 78–80, 86, 97, 110,
    112–13, 115, 118–19, 123, 129,
    134–36, 140, 143–44, 151, 153,
    157, 164, 169
Schröter, Jens, 19
Scott, James, 57, 11–14
Sechrest, Love L., 27–28, 57
Seifrid, Mark A., 69
Silva, Moisés, 21, 105,
Snowden, Frank Jr., 27
Sprinkle, Preston M., 65, 74, 92, 97,
    100–101
Starling, Daniel I., 147
Stendahl, Krister, 71, 73

Thiessen, Matthew, 141, 142, 144

VanLandingham, Chris, 70

Wakefield, Andrew, 94
Watson, Francis, 89, 103
Westerholm, Stephen, 3, 71–72
White, Joel, 176
Williams, Jarvis J., 15, 51, 67, 71–72,
    89,
Williams, Sam K., 117, 156
Willits, Joel, 147
Windsor, Lionel, 31
Witherington, Ben III, 11, 49, 91, 107,
    109–10, 135, 138, 144, 147–48,
    151, 153, 155, 157, 174
Wright, Nicholas Thomas, 54, 66, 69,
    72–74, 93, 101, 103, 106–7, 124

Young, Norman H., 94

Ziesler, J. A., 65, 70, 81